Representing Children

Power, Policy and the Discourse on
Child Labour in the Football
Manufacturing Industry of Pakistan

Representing Children

Power, Policy and the Discourse on
Child Labour in the Football
Manufacturing Industry of Pakistan

ALI KHAN

OXFORD
UNIVERSITY PRESS

OXFORD
UNIVERSITY PRESS

Great Clarendon Street, Oxford OX2 6DP

Oxford University Press is a department of the University of Oxford.
It furthers the University's objective of excellence in research, scholarship,
and education by publishing worldwide in

Oxford   New York

Auckland Cape Town Dar es Salaam Hong Kong Karachi
Kuala Lumpur Madrid Melbourne Mexico City Nairobi
New Delhi Shanghai Taipei Toronto

with offices in

Argentina Austria Brazil Chile Czech Republic France Greece
Guatemala Hungary Italy Japan Poland Portugal Singapore
South Korea Switzerland Turkey Ukraine Vietnam

ISBN 978-0-19-547478-7

Typeset in Times
Printed in Pakistan by
Pixel Grafix, Karachi.
Published by
Ameena Saiyid, Oxford University Press
No. 38, Sector 15, Korangi Industrial Area, PO Box 8214
Karachi-74900, Pakistan.

CONTENTS

LIST OF ILLUSTRATIONS

Map of Sialkot

Villages Visited During Fieldwork

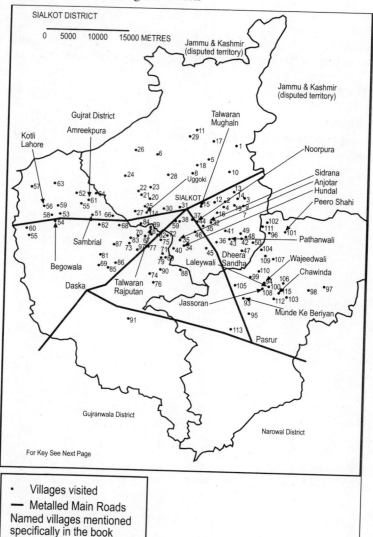

For Key See Next Page

KEY TO MAP OF SIALKOT—VILLAGES VISITED DURING FIELDWORK

No.	Village	No.	Village
1	Najwal	31	Paka Gara
2	Langray Wali	32	Sandrana
3	Mali Chak Purana	33	Dheera Sandha
4	Oura	34	Hundal
5	Sarfrazpur	35	Anjotar
6	Khana	36	Ghuna Khurd
7	Haripur	37	Nawan Pind
8	Kharota Syedan	38	Pakki Kotli
9	Wagran	39	Miani
10	Jalfanwali	40	Ladhar
11	Ghari Gondal	41	Kase
12	Kake Wali	42	Nidokey
13	Pataisar	43	Pathan Wali
14	Bramey Chak/Dalowali	44	Noorpura
15	Talwaran Mughlan	45	Sahuwali
16	Rakhana	46	Bhadhal
17	Zahoora	47	Garbalan Syedan
18	Marakiwal	48	Jaspal
19	Sahbo Sandhah	49	Kala Harwan
20	Bhagwal Awan	50	Ghogha
21	Ulakh Shanker Pur	51	Sambrial
22	Jourian/Sukhnian	52	Haddokey
23	Baho Bhati	53	Begowala Adah
24	Khambran Wala	54	Begowala Jahmat
25	Raheem Pur	55	Begowala Village
26	Abiyala	56	Kotli Loharan
27	Raipur	57	Randheer Bagherian
28	Machi Khokher	58	Randheer Morh
29	Rattowal	59	Jahrian Wala
30	Muzaffarpur	60	Fateh Garh

No.	Village	No.	Village
61	Amrikpura	89	Talwaran Rajputan
62	Allewali	90	Islamabad
63	Malian Wali	91	Dhale Key
64	Karn Wali	92	Kotli Bhago
65	Jathekey	93	Munde ke Beriyan
66	Bhalo Chak	94	Wajeedwali
67	Ismaeel Awan	95	Ramkey
68	Sahuwala	96	Jhar Mahia
69	Bahno Pindi	97	Thro Mandi
70	Kot Karam Bakhsh	98	Dogri Harian
71	Adam Daraz	99	Bheelo Key
72	Hapu Garah	100	Laleywali
73	Kharolian Khas	101	Peero Shahi
74	Behare Pur	102	Balar Wali
75	Bheer	103	Rajian
76	Seokey	104	Bhagowal Chowk
77	Gohinkey	105	Purab
78	Manpur	106	Kale Wali
79	Bhakhian Wala	107	Kakhan Wali
80	Lakra Khurd	108	Jassoran
81	Rehan Cheema	109	Sangrai Pur
82	Ada	110	Gulle Wali
83	Ladhar	111	Moqaber
84	Dogranwala	112	Hameed Pur
85	Bahnokey	113	Nool
86	Jamkey Cheema	114	Uggoke
87	Raliokey	115	Chawinda
88	Baphangi		

Tariq, extreme left and Waseem, second from right, stitching footballs at the Laleywali unit.

Inside the Laleywali stitching unit.

Afzal with his bag of footballs.

Completed footballs being transported from the Peero Shahi unit to Ali Trading headquarters in Sialkot city.

PREFACE

My aim when I wrote this book was to combine two relatively new research perspectives to provide a fresh point of view to readers. Part of this urge came from a frustration that the majority of research on child labour and child work in Pakistan had been quantitative studies undertaken in the field of economics and there was little if any sound qualitative academic work in the area. As a result the perspectives that guided my research were firstly, an anthropological and hence qualitative view of the lives of children who stitch footballs; and secondly, a viewpoint that placed children firmly at the centre of any analysis thereby recognising their decision making capabilities.

The first, I believe, allowed a more grassroots perspective of the motivations and reasons behind children's decisions to start stitching footballs. The second meant recognising and accepting that children have agency and can and do make decisions themselves. Neither of these perspectives is entirely new and both have been used in the study of child labour in other contexts. It would therefore be wrong for me to claim that this is a pioneering piece of research. However, what is novel is my application of these two tools to a Pakistani environment. Then we have a situation in which anthropological methods of research have been used to investigate the lives of children stitching footballs in a district of north-eastern Pakistan. Furthermore, in a society where age hierarchy is deeply entrenched the recognition that children do have agency brings a new dimension to the research.

I have also been fortunate with timing. I started my year long fieldwork in Sialkot in 1999 when a major restructuring of the football industry was taking place following allegation of widespread child labour in the industry. This provided fertile ground for research and if anything in the course of the year I was to find that from what I thought was a relatively self-contained topic had expanded to include the influence of geo-political power structures, issues of globalisation and local and global discourses of development. Then seven years later as I prepared this final version of my research, Sialkot's football industry is again in the doldrums.

In some ways the findings of the research are vindicated by the re-emergence of the child labour issue in Sialkot in late 2006. In November 2006 one of the world's major multi-nationals sourcing footballs from Sialkot cancelled its long standing relationship with its Sialkoti partner over allegations of the repeated use of children in football stitching. This is an issue that is flagged in the research.

But it is not feelings of smugness or pride that I associate with this development. What became increasingly apparent throughout my research was that no matter what setback Sialkot's football industry faced, it was always the already vulnerable groups of people that appeared to suffer the most—and invariably these were women and children. I fear that this will happen again even though it may well be in the name of development as it was in the past. The burden is always carried by those least able to carry it.

Today as talk of growing unemployment, poverty and even increasing resentment against outsiders grows, Sialkot's football industry faces an uncertain future. And yet the region that produced two of Pakistan's greatest poets—Faiz Ahmed Faiz and Allama Iqbal—has always shown innovation and resilience in the face of adversity. Sialkot's industrialists and the workers have similarly, in the past, highlighted these two qualities—first in establishing this district as a world leader in sports goods manufacturing—and then ensuring that it survived the adverse publicity it faced in the late 1990s as a result of the child labour issue. It is my sincere hope that some of the issues faced by the football stitching families in Sialkot do come through to the reader and provide a meaningful insight and understanding of their situation.

I would like to acknowledge, at the very outset, that this research was made possible through the cooperation of the football stitchers of Sialkot, many of whom went out of their way to volunteer sensitive information. I owe them the largest debt of gratitude for taking me into confidence and placing their trust in my judgement. I hope that I have been able to repay this through producing a balanced piece of research. I am also grateful to the representatives of the Sialkot Chamber of Commerce and Industry, government institutions, international agencies and NGOs who made time to see me and share their views.

I must also thank all those who assisted me during my fieldwork, particularly Shaheen Atiq-ur-Rehman whose expertise aside, ensured that I gained the maximum from my time in the field. My NGO 'research assistants' from Bunyad were instrumental in facilitating my

field relations with informants. Particular note must be made of Malik
Nazir, Abdul Razzaq, Mohammed Aslam, Danish Reza, Iftikhar Ahmed
and Tariq Javed all of whom agreed, without ever complaining, to ferry
me daily on the backs of their motor bikes from one part of Sialkot to
the other.

During writing I regularly turned for clarifications to Dr Faiz Shah
for his knowledge of the football industry in Sialkot. Dr Ranjit Nayak
provided early feedback on my field notes. Dr Robert Crawford kindly
shared his material on Sialkot with me and Dr Khalid Nadvi also
clarified key points. Dr Virginia Morrow took time out from her busy
schedule to give me detailed comments on a draft chapter.

My gratitude also to my colleagues at the Department of Social
Anthropology at the University of Cambridge for consistently providing
feedback during the writing up process. In particular, Dr Magnus
Marsden for rigorously going through and commenting on my draft and
Dr Annalise Moser and Dr Hayley McGregor for reading numerous
chapters. Dr Helen Watson, my first year supervisor, provided early
guidance; my main supervisor Dr David Sneath brought his
meticulousness and insight to the final draft; and my external examiners
Dr Sue Benson and Dr Jo Boyden provided the constructive criticism
that allowed me to further refine the thesis that was the basis for this
book.

I must also thank Ammara Maqsood my research assistant at the
Lahore University of Management Sciences (LUMS), and the editors
at Oxford University Press for editing the final version of the book.

Finally, I would like to thank my entire family for their support over
the time taken to complete this venture. In particular, my father
Shaharyar Khan for twice reading my final draft and my wife Mariyam
for painstakingly going through and providing comments on all the
drafts of my book.

ABBREVIATIONS

BLCC	Bunyad Literacy Community Council
BLLF	Bonded Labour Liberation Front
ILO	International Labour Organisation
NGO	Non Governmental Organisations
NWFP	North-West Frontier Province
SCCI	Sialkot Chamber of Commerce and Industry
SCF	Save the Children Fund
UNICEF	United Nations Children's Fund

GLOSSARY

Baithak	Guest room
Biraderi	Patrilineage
Burka	Loose garment covering the entire body used specifically for the purpose of *purdah*.
Charpai	Basic bed made of a wooden frame and strung with a rope meshing
Chowkidar	Guard
Desi	Lowest quality football
Dupatta	Headscarf
Eid	Muslim festival. There are three Eid festivals during the Muslim year celebrating respectively the end of the month of fasting (*Eid-ul-Fitr*), the Prophet Muhammad's (PBUH) birth anniversary (*Eid-i-Milad-un-Nabi*) and the commemoration of Abraham's sacrifice of his son (*Eid-ul-Azha*)
Hijab	Veil wrapped tightly round the face in order to conceal the hair
Izzat	Honour/Status
Khan	Traditional title of landowners in the North West Frontier Province
Khokha	Roadside restaurant
Kholru	Half a stitched football
Kutcha	Houses made of wood and bamboo and coated with baked mud
Lahori	Middle quality football usually used in the lower end of the sporting ball market by amateur clubs and for general sports retail
Lohar	Caste of blacksmiths
Maker	Football subcontractor
Muhajir	Muslim migrants who moved to Pakistan from parts of present day India
Pathan	Inhabitants originally of Afghanistan, Pakistan's Tribal Areas and the North-West Frontier Province
Peshgi	An advance of money

Pir	Custodians of Muslim holy shrines and representatives of 'popular' Islam
Pukka	House made of oven baked bricks
Purdah	Literally 'curtain', refers to the separation of the sexes in Islam
Sahab	Term of respect equating roughly to 'sir'
Sardar	Traditional title of landowners in Balochistan province
Shagird	Apprentice
Shalwaar Kameez	Traditional dress of tunic and baggy trousers
Sharam	Shame
Sufi	Early Muslim mystics responsible for converting large parts of the Indian subcontinent to Islam
Tehsil	Smallest administrative unit of a district. Two or more *tehsils* constitute a district. Three or more districts form a division
Ulema	Orthodox religious leaders and parties
Vilayati	Highest quality football. Used for professional matches
Wadera	Traditional title for landowners in Sindh province
Zaat	Caste
Zamindar	Term for landowners in general and used more specifically to refer to landowners in Punjab

1

CHILD LABOUR
REPRESENTATIONS AND REALITIES

In the town of Sialkot, scores of children, most of them aged five to ten, produce soccer balls by hand for forty rupees, or about $1.20 a day. The children work eighty hours a week in near total darkness and total silence. According to the foreman, the darkness is both an economy and a precautionary measure; child-rights activists have difficulty taking photographs and gathering evidence of wrongdoing if the light is poor. The silence is to ensure product quality. The children are permitted one thirty minute meal break each day; they are punished if they take longer. They are also punished if they fall asleep, if their workbenches are sloppy, if they waste material or mis-cut a pattern, if they complain of mistreatment to their parents or speak to strangers outside the family. Punishments are doled out in a storage closet at the rear of the factory. There, amid bales of wadding and leather, children are hung upside down by their knees, starved, caned or lashed. The punishment room is a standard feature of a Pakistani factory, as common as [the] lunch room at a Detroit assembly plant (J. Silvers, 1996).

Three years later, a transformation had taken place in the Sialkot football industry described above.

Today the work has been taken up by women in 80 poor villages in Pakistan, giving them new employment and their families new stabilities. Meanwhile, their children have started to go to school, so that when they come of age, they will be able to do better jobs raising the standards of living of their families, their villages and their nation (President Clinton's address to the ILO Conference, 18 June 1999).

The closed, grim environment of 1996 had been replaced by the buoyant, rehabilitated optimism of 1999. How these differing representations of Sialkot developed and how the 'reality' of Sialkot in development and wider public discourses moved from one extreme to the other in the space of three years is the focus of the first two chapters. What transpired in the three years during which the representation of Sialkot changed from the environment of the first quote to that of the second is the subject of the rest of the thesis.

DISCOURSES OF DEVELOPMENT AND CHILD LABOUR

Underlying an understanding of the change in representations is what Crush (1995, 2) points out as the 'power of development': 'The power to transform old worlds, the power to imagine new ones'. In this case it is the ability of the development process to both represent children, as exploited and abused in the first quotation, and also re-present them as rehabilitated in the second quotation.

This power to transform and imagine is made possible through the establishment of dominant discourses, which in turn work through setting agendas, influencing interests and securing 'support for a particular definition of reality' (Hajer 1995, 59). By discourse, I refer to a notion that draws inspiration from the works of Foucault and which anthropologists have used increasingly in their examination of the anthropology of development.[1] Thus, Hobart (1993, 12) defines discourse as what is said and done, including importantly the conditions of knowledge and power. Escobar (1995, 39) refers to discourse as being the articulation of knowledge. However, discourses, including that of development, are not created in a vacuum but reflect the existing social, cultural and political balance of power. Much of the power of development, as J. Crush points out, lies 'quite patently within the realm of the economic and political' (1995, 7). But the interaction is not one-way. While discourses may be influenced by the existing economic and political power structure, they also validate this structure, as well as define what kind of intervention by political and economic powers is legitimate. To understand the 'development discourse', it is essential to take into account these overarching influences. As Esther Goody (2002) stated at a recent keynote address:[2]

> The challenge for social anthropological research that is most relevant to the 21st Century lies in the politicisation of both policy and the practice of the problems we study. This politicisation occurs at all levels: international,

national, and local. Sometimes it is crystal clear and publicly proclaimed; sometimes it is hidden behind the closed portals of international agencies and ministerial offices. Very often the actual outcomes of politically framed policies are unintended consequences of implementing international-level blueprints in the real world of constrained resources, ethnic tensions and powerful entrenched interests. But as anthropologists we must study the whole process of making and implementing policy; the hidden as well as the public, the unintended as well as the blueprint. (forthcoming, *Cambridge Anthropology*, Vol. 23, 1).

The development discourse can be seen to encompass a number of 'sub-discourses'. These both influence and are influenced by the wider discourse. One such sub-discourse is constructed around the idea of child labour—the greater the incidence of child labour in a country, the more underdeveloped it is seen to be. The presence or absence of child labour then becomes an indicator of development, a yardstick by which countries are ranked. An examination of the particular case of the child labour discourse[3] is therefore necessarily framed by the emergence of the wider general discourse of development. In addition, few sub-discourses of development display the effects of the global socio-economic and political influences as clearly as child labour. As Ennew (1997) points out, 'Child labour is not just a topic for legislation, programming and research, it is also a public issue in which information is used and often generated by mass media, as well as being part of the folk history of industrialised nations'. This contributes to making child labour a public issue with the potential of being widely influenced by mass media and in turn influencing the wider perceptions of the public through its depiction in the media.

This chapter and the following one look at how the issue of child labour developed in Pakistan and in Sialkot, examining in particular the interests, values and norms of certain groups that have been responsible for directing the dialogue on child labour (Goody's politicisation of policy) and linking this emerging discourse with the more general discourse of development. It is through an examination of both, as well as the linkages between the two, that we are able to establish how a particular dominant discourse emerged and how this came to define the representation of 'reality' of child labour in Sialkot. As this representation has been globalised it has come into contact and conflict with more localised versions, leading to the emergence of two contrasting and divergent representations. The means by which one representation becomes a 'reality' in the wider public discourse not only has implications for remedial interventions that may be taken at a local level on the basis of that reality, but also reflects the wider power structures inherent in the current world order.

Moreover, the development discourse promotes and justifies concrete interventions and practices with very real consequences, some unintended, so that the dominant discourse of development is dynamically interrelated with development practice, affecting the actual design and implementation of projects. The fact that the effects of the development discourse are not simply confined to texts (J. Crush 1995, 6) makes it essential to incorporate Goody's advice on studying the whole process of making and implementing policy, while also considering the politicisation of policy and the problems we study.

The thesis therefore moves from 'theory' to 'practice'; from transnational and elite discourses and practices to local ones; from the establishment of a particular dominant discourse and representation of child labour to the use of this representation as the basis of a project to 'correct' competing representations. However, the gap between the neat rationality of development agencies' representations, and the actualities of situated social practices, leads not only to those represented as being at the heart of the entire process of 'development' being marginalized, but it also results in 'unintended consequences' to which the marginalized groups have to adjust. Ultimately, the question arises of why the discourse of development so often marginalizes the people it is meant to benefit. It is the aim of this research to examine this central question through the example and analysis of child labour in the football manufacturing industry of Sialkot. In conclusion, a theory on why children stitch footballs, revolving around the wider context of football stitching as a domestic based productive activity and the importance of local agency, is forwarded. Much of this contradicts the accepted wisdom of the determinants of child labour being based on broad, ahistorical causes such as poverty, tradition and underdevelopment.

My work draws upon anthropologically based qualitative research and seeks to shift the emphasis from solely economic based determinants of child labour to a more complex understanding of working children's lives. Therefore, this thesis places the daily lived experiences and understandings of children at its heart, while also recognising the influence of broad social and economic changes. This requires that children's own agency and decision-making capacity be recognised. In support of this hypothesis, I found my child informants open, extraordinarily articulate and imbued with social competencies. This emphasis on children as active objects rather than passive subjects is therefore identified in later chapters as one of the main determinants for children taking up stitching in the football industry and is crucial to understanding the reasons for their involvement in football stitching.

CHILD LABOUR AND THE INFLUENCE OF THE ECONOMICS DISCOURSE

Studies on working children in development literature have been dominated by perspectives derived largely from economics. South Asian work in particular has been marked by an absence of anthropological examination and a proliferation of research based around quantifying and classifying child labour. This has tended to produce a somewhat repetitive, static picture that has concentrated on questions such as socio-economic determinants and the magnitude of child employment (Tripathy, 1989, Basu, 1998, Gupta and Voll, 1987, Bhalotra, 2000). Furthermore, research by economists on children has frequently overlooked or even denied their social and economic role. As emphasized in the previous section, in the context of the current study this neglect of children's own agency would lead to a partial and unsatisfactory understanding of the reasons for children taking up work. As Boyden and Levison point out:

> In as much as children are considered at all, the mainstream economic view is of children as household dependants—neither decision-makers nor productive economic actors—who have value as potential economic resources, a status they attain with adulthood. In effect, economics represents children as dependents who thereby personify household and societal costs, there being no workable theory of children as economic agents. Investment in children is assessed in terms of its role in increasing their economic productivity as adults rather than its potential for furthering the interests and welfare of children themselves. This is extremely important because economic policies nevertheless have a major effect on all policies about children, and therefore on children (Boyden and Levison 2000, 10).

This tendency to systematically overlook the agency of children has meant that influential economic theories on education, human capital accumulation and child work have failed to take into account the complexity of children's realities or to incorporate empirical evidence on children into their research. This has prevented the development of a more child-centred, policy relevant economics.

For example, human capital theory, which developed in the late 1950s and is most closely associated with the work of Gary Becker, recognizes that increasing the skills and knowledge of humans leads to economic returns in the form of increased future earnings for workers and higher profits for their employers through the provision of a more skilled labour force. Drawing on this perspective, development economists have emphasized the large 'social returns' that could accrue in the form of economic growth and development by increasing human capital. For example, increasing literacy rates is seen as bringing gains in health and reduced fertility rates, and participation in schooling is seen as beneficial for children's economic roles.

Economists working in the human capital tradition have undertaken a considerable amount of research on calculating the individual rates of return accruing from different levels of schooling. A broad view of such individual 'returns' should, one might argue, include an assessment of the possibilities of, amongst other factors, increased income, social status, self-esteem, and happiness resulting from school education. Human capital economists have, however, taken a much narrower view of individual returns—that an additional year of schooling in many Third World countries results in adult wages that are substantially higher, 11 per cent on average, than they would otherwise have been (Boyden and Levison 2000, 11). Moreover, studies estimating rates of return to human capital rely on information about *adult* earners to estimate the value of those adults' past formal education, apprenticeships, or on-the-job training. *Children* are only of interest as the learners who will later be workers. Moreover, the reduction of the complexity of reality is apparent in 'education' being defined in highly institutional terms—years in school—rather than in terms of knowledge or skills. Knowledge and skills attained outside the environs of the school, for example in the context of the family and the household, are ignored, implying that human capital is developed primarily outside the family rather than within it. Thus what is overlooked almost entirely in these perspectives is the role of children's participation in work towards building human capital skills and attitudes. In contrast, positive estimates of the 'returns' from investment in schooling as human capital has provided a justifiable economic rationale for government spending on schooling, especially primary education in Third World countries.

It is therefore unsurprising to note that there is a substantial body of research where the focus is precisely on the schooling opportunities for Third World children—in particular the determinants of school enrollment and number of school years completed. This research, in turn, is increasingly combined with studies on child work.

A number of these studies try to determine the degree to which various characteristics affect children's school attendance and grade attainment, with the goal of identifying useful policy measures to encourage schooling while discouraging children's involvement in 'work' related activities. Such research, Boyden and Levison (2000, 12) argue, often has three limitations. First, studies rely upon data collected in censuses or large sample surveys. Standard household questionnaires usually include information on household structure and the age, sex, education and earnings of household members but relatively little about crucial health, intelligence or psychological factors relevant to children's schooling experiences. Nor do such data usually include details relating to the quality and costs of schooling for each child. Second, many studies of children's schooling do not consider any alternatives to schooling. The importance of play has yet to be taken into account by economists and any advantages of 'work' related activities are rarely acknowledged. Third, learning is associated with progress through school. Alternative forms of socialization or skill enhancement such as home-based work are neglected.

Where work activities are examined, economists have, as in the case of determinants for school enrolment, used data sources from large surveys and censuses to consider which basic child and family characteristics are associated with increased probabilities of child work. But while the focus is on sources such as labour force employment surveys, these do not generally provide adequate information on children's participation.

One exception to this pattern is provided by Richard Anker's (1998) series of studies of Indian industries. Anker and his collaborators do not focus primarily upon child workers and their families, but have studied industries and production processes in India in order to determine the prevalence and importance of children's work in these processes. From this research Anker argued that children did not play an important role in the workplace and could theoretically be replaced in a number of production processes; that in spite of the 'nimble fingers' argument, child workers were not particularly skilled and could be replaced by adults, but that employers benefited from the low wages and piece rates paid to children. Such findings reinforce the view that the place for children is not at work but in school, but it leaves many questions unanswered. How 'generalisable' are Anker's findings? What would happen if we attempted to consider homeworking as well as factory work? How would a consideration of the home circumstances of young workers affect the analysis? Nevertheless, Anker's approach is a timely one, stressing as it does the need to consider the complexity of child labour and the variety of different activities in which children are involved and his awareness that this cannot be adequately captured through relying on quantitative measures.

In general then, the existing biases within economics, particularly the neglect of children's agency, has led to research that is narrow in its focus and coverage, and lacking in holism. In particular, economic models do not attempt to consider the implications of maximizing children's well-being. Thus, the economist's approach has tended to look at what it would take to discourage child economic participation, but not at whether discouraging work is in fact in the best interests of the child, or even in the best interests of the rest of society. Reducing child work is simply assumed to be the goal. Similarly, economists have looked at whether or not children are in school and not whether this school attendance necessarily leads to human betterment.

The gap between children being in school and not working and whether these conditions imply that the child is better off is explained by de Vylder (1996, 30) as being the difference between the narrow human capital approach and the more holistic human development approach. De Vylder differentiates between human development as a means (human capital approach) and human development as an end (human development approach). Thus, in contrast to the human capital approach, which would consider outcomes such as the number of children in school and the number of classes completed, a human development approach to education would consider outcomes for children in terms of substantive material learned and understood, ability to apply and generalise from the material, the acquisition of social skills, and engagement in the process of learning. Therefore, economics' overlooking of the maximizing of children's well-being.

TOWARDS A UNIVERSAL CHILDHOOD

It can be argued that much existing research, including that from the economist's perspective, is informed by a shared basic concept of 'childhood', a particular view of childhood presented as a universally accepted and shared reality. If we recognize that there is a 'universal childhood', then children the world over should have similar experiences of the phenomenon. In fact, the images of children increasingly broadcast across the globe highlight very contrasting representations of childhood. But it was this apparently shared and universal experience that 'defined' what was and what was not childhood in other cultural contexts, and it was this definition that acted as a normative basis for remedial action elsewhere.

The history of childhood and its changing nature has been extensively researched. As early as 1909, Ellen Key wrote *The Century of the Child* (1909). Key drew her ideas mainly from literature and focussed on a framework of childhood that had been socially and psychologically conditioned. While Key's work had a decisive influence, directly and indirectly, on the study of childhood as a social and cultural construct, it was Phillipe Aries who, through his seminal work on childhood *Centuries of Childhood* (1962), is often credited with challenging the orthodox view of a universal childhood. Through the use of primarily historical sources, and paying particular attention to medieval icons, Aries claimed that the current notion of childhood emerged in Europe between the fifteenth and eighteenth centuries. Though Aries has been criticised for disputing that childhood was a human universal and that it did not exist in Western societies prior to the fifteenth century (L. De Mause 1976, Pollock 1983), the consensus that emerges from these debates, and which has subsequently been further refined by Boyden (1997), amongst others, is that the particular form of modern childhood which Aries refers to can indeed be treated as an historically and culturally specific construct.

This construct, Zelizer (1985) has argued, involved the 'sanctification of childhood' in Europe and America. It gave children a new role and identity, whereby their 'economic value' was replaced by their expressive value — 'children have become relatively worthless (economically) to their parents, but priceless in terms of their psychological worth' (Scheper-Hughes 1998, 12). This concept of childhood defined 'happy' children's primary concern to be the pursuit of emotional attachment and love for their parents. Economic activity was to be confined to the adult world. Children transgressing these parameters were represented as no longer having a childhood or having been robbed of it.

> The norms and values upon which this ideal of a safe, happy and protected childhood are built are culturally and historically bound to the social preoccupations and priorities of the capitalist countries of Europe and the U.S. It is a model of childhood—along with the legislative frameworks, policies and codes of welfare practice applied in its pursuit—which has resulted from the historical interplay of the Judeo-Christian belief system and changes in the productive and demographic base of society corresponding with capitalist development. It was during the 18th and 19th centuries that qualities of innocence and nobility were first associated with children and the desire to foster these qualities through conscious parenting emerged (J. Boyden 1997, 192).

The need to see ideas of childhood as historically and culturally specific is also supported by anthropological research. As early as 1928, Margaret Mead, through her ethnographic work in Samoa, challenged Stanley Hall's argument that adolescence was a period of 'natural' rebellion, through showing its absence in Samoan society. Some years later Benedict (1935) comparing childhood among the Zuni, Dobu and Kwakiutl, found marked differences in terms of responsibility that children are allowed to assume, their degree of subordination to adults and the way the characteristics of the genders are distributed (James and Prout 1997, 17). This argument is taken further by Jo Boyden (1997, 203) when she states that the different competencies and incapacities perceived to be associated with childhood in different societies are numerous and often imply contradictory conceptions of the child. Boyden gives the example of the numerous countries in which children are seen as dependant until well into their teens, contrasting with others where they are expected to be fully independent from an early age.

Similarly, recent work has taken a more critical look at Western ideas of childhood and argued for a more complex reality lying behind the simple Aries hypothesis of the emergence of a single 'modern' European understanding of childhood. Childhood, or more appropriately childhoods, vary not only across time and space but also across cultures, class and ethnic boundaries. There was no single Western childhood.

Firstly, there is no easy straightforward replacement of the 'economically useful' child by the emotionally priceless one.

Cunningham (1996, 43) for example, points out that the amount of child labour in England in the nineteenth century varied enormously from one part of the country to another and even within towns quite close to one another. He reports that in the 1840s while there was an outcry about the extent of child labour in the textile areas of Lancashire, the lord mayor of the port city of Liverpool, in the same country, was lamenting the lack of job opportunities open to children. Similarly, while child work was common throughout Europe in the 18th and 19th centuries, its nature and magnitude varied considerably across the various countries. Thus, while most of northern Europe had achieved high rates of literacy and low rates of child labour by the 18th century, the percentage of people who could read during the same period in the southern and eastern countries of Europe was less than 20 per cent (Weiner and Noman 1997, 152). Even today, in the southern European countries, particularly Greece, Portugal and Italy, children are still important contributors to the family economy, both in family businesses and in wage labour. Morrow, (unpublished paper), in fact, points out that there is evidence that some children in the aforementioned countries drop out of school early in order to enter the labour force on a full time basis. This is not the case in northern European countries, the USA, Canada, Australia and New Zealand, where children appear to undertake part-time work in combination with education.

Therefore, just as the social environment within the 'West' is so varied, so too was the context in which children's participation in the labour force declined. In the largely Protestant countries of northern Europe, Protestant leaders, believing that education was essential to salvation, successfully persuaded governments to make education compulsory. In contrast, in Britain, the Anglican Church initially opposed compulsory education fearing that it could reduce the influence of the Church itself. Instead, Cunningham (1996) states that compulsory schooling in Britain was initially introduced in order to cater to 'unemployed' children. Thus, work and school served the same function—to socialise children and prevent their much feared idleness. Idleness, it was believed, would lead to disorder, and to children growing up without being habituated to the labour that would be their lot in life.

In contrast, Ennew (1997) points out that in New York, child labour legislation in the nineteenth century was supported by several groups, including upper class industrialists who did not depend on cheap child labour for their manufacturing opportunities. She goes on to state that here the abolition of child labour could be viewed as a means of driving out marginal manufacturers and tenement operators, hence increasing the consolidation and efficiency of business. In the New York case the rise of compulsory education was closely tied to the changing forms of industrial production. In Britain it revolved more on the maintenance of social control. Elsewhere in northern Europe, the need to be able to read the Bible saw religious leaders push for compulsory education.

Those who subscribe to Zelizer's hypothesis and emphasize the influence of cultural values, would argue that it is possible to explain different levels of child labour in different societies by reference to their value systems with respect to children and the family. Cunningham (2000, 418) points out that a striking example of the cultural determination of child labour is the low level of child labour in Japan in the late nineteenth century, despite ongoing industrialisation and the absence of legal prohibition of child labour. Cunningham highlights the Japanese penchant for 'indulging their children' and contrasts this with the notoriously high level of child labour in Belgium 'where there seem to have been deep-rooted and almost universal expectations that children would work at an early age' (Cunningham 2000, 418).

But apart from childhood experiences varying across countries and cultures within the 'West', they also differed, and continue to differ, within countries across class and ethnic boundaries. The childhood experiences of upper and middle class Americans, Europeans or for that matter Pakistanis (as we shall see later in this chapter) differ substantially from the childhoods of their working class compatriots. In fact, as Boyden (1985 in Ennew 1997) points out, a paradox that highlights the importance of social class difference is that, within the labour force of developing nations, child domestic workers are frequently serving older, less capable children, whose childhood is more prolonged. Similarly ethnic minorities in comparison to the dominant population often have quite different notions of what constitutes a 'normal' childhood. Solberg (1997) examines the differences in childhood within a community living in Norway, as well as the wider differences between Norwegian and British childhoods.

Weiner and Noman (1997, 110) also emphasize that while Zelizer's sanctification of childhood may have been adopted by the upper and middle classes for their own children, these classes did not readily apply this concept to the children of the poor. Child labour, moreover, had its strongest and most persistent advocates within the working class where the 'economic usefulness of the child' was often a critical aspect of household survival. This again highlights the coexistence of different 'childhoods' in the 'West'.

What this points to is the need to move beyond naturalised ideas of childhood or any simple idea of traditional/modern or western/other childhoods and to investigate in detail both the particular structures in which children live and the cultural contexts that shape the understanding of the child. Some anthropological research has begun to redress this omission, even though it needs to be remembered that even anthropology as a discipline has only recently begun to address research on children in a more complex manner. However, the work of anthropologists such as Reynolds (1991), Boyden (1991, 1994, 1997), Ennew (1986, 1989, 1997) and Nieuwenhuys (1994, 1996) has been at the forefront of a significant shift which has seen children moved to the centre of their analyses. Reynolds (1991), for example, in her examination of child labour in rural Zimbabwe, showed that a study of children's work patterns was essential to understanding agriculture there. Nieuwenhuys' ethnography of children in Kerala, as well as Reynolds' work in Zimbabwe, both illustrate how education and work, far from being mutually exclusive, are often complementary activities. Importantly for this study, some work is seeking to go beyond the economic analysis of child labour. Ennew and Boyden's work has critically examined the sweeping generalisation that all child work is harmful. In contrast to this view, they have argued that child work can have positive benefits for the child alongside and occasionally over schooling. They also argue that it is important to treat children as agents in their own lives.

To sum up, the above discussion emphasises the fact that while the Western construct of childhood is often used as if it refers to a single concept there is in reality little uniformity in the experiences of Western childhoods. Even today, childhood in the west means many different things for the peoples in the diverse areas that constitute the 'West'.

Yet despite the tensions clearly inherent in a unified notion of 'Western' childhood, separate aspects of this diverse concept have been brought together to produce the universal Western construct. It is this composite, idealised concept of Western childhood that has been adopted by international agencies and that has been exported to the developing world.

But while this universal childhood is the sum of concepts and notions that developed historically and intrinsically in the West, it has been promoted as a context free, universal norm in societies that have a quite different social, economic and historical context.

FROM COLONIALISM TO DEVELOPMENT

The use of this specific Western construct of childhood as the *definitive* universal childhood became part of a wider process of diffusion of Western values and norms as part and parcel of 'development'. As an ideology, development can be seen to have emerged from colonialism; 'where colonialism left off, development took over' (Kothari, 1988, 143), with the linearity inherent in the process tracing its roots to the idea of the 'brave new world' so that 'by the nineteenth century the central thesis of developmentalism as a linear theory of progress rooted in Western capitalist hegemony was cast in stone' (M. Watts 1995, 47).

It has subsequently been widely[4] argued that development has come to constitute, in sum, 'an expression of modernity on a planetary scale' (Berthoud 1990, 23). The values and norms, taken from the West, were seen as the ideal that developing nations should strive to achieve. Modernisation was equated with Westernisation and development was the process by which countries moved towards that ideal. 'Historically, modernization is the process of change towards those types of social, economic and political systems that have developed in Western Europe and North America from the 17th century to the 19th century. In a word, development means Westernisation' (S.N. Eisenstadt 1966:1 in Marglin and Marglin (ed) 1990, 2). Therefore, although different cultural contexts were allowed in the development discourse, the way in which political and economic forms were evaluated, and the overall frame into which 'culture' was fitted, was essentially based on Western models. This meant that the different cultural contexts were placed at different points along the envisaged unilinear path towards modernization. Furthermore, while 'development' has increasingly forwarded itself as becoming more culturally flexible, it is surprising in the extent to which it has failed to break free of its linearity, from notions of growth and from the preoccupation of 'catching up with the West' (Escobar 1995, 216). This is an issue that is implicit throughout the thesis but is analysed in detail in Chapter 4, which examines the influence of linearity on the design and implementation of the project to remove children from the football stitching labour force.

Freeman (quoted in Boyden 1997, 203) and Ennew (1997) both point out that the dominant view of the child's role in society has been globalised through the wider process of 'development' and its agents, namely international agencies, the media, and even international human rights treaties such as the United Nations Convention on the Rights of the Child. But while a culture or society may have dominant ideas and values imposed on it, there is no reason to suppose that a concept born of a particular indigenous, historical, social process will be applicable or acceptable to a different social environment.

Tellingly for this thesis, Mamdani (1972), undertaking fieldwork in Punjab, emphasised that in Punjabi society there was no extended and protected period of childhood akin to that of the West—only a swift transition from dependent infant to young adult.[5] It is possible, then, that local ideas of human maturation and capacity were simply ignored by the development discourse.

In fact, as Boyden (1997, 254) points out, the Convention on the Rights of the Child (CRC) provided a prime example of the unease among certain welfare practitioners from the Third World about the global export of perceptions of childhood and family. According to Newman-Black (1989), during discussions on the draft of the Convention, several Third World delegates expressed dissatisfaction that the drafting group was predominantly Western in its orientation, and argued that greater account should have been taken of the cultural diversity and the economic realities of developing countries (J. Boyden 1997, 204). Fyfe (1989) goes on to point out that input to the drafting process from the majority of countries in the Third World was minimal, primarily because it was felt that the Convention embodied the values of a universalised 'normal' childhood—a concept that many felt was foreign to them and inapplicable to their societies. Nevertheless, the globalisation of this view of childhood has continued. The CRC, for example, was adopted unanimously and has been almost universally ratified.

Development discourse, as mentioned earlier, is constituted and reproduced within a set of material relationships, activities and powers—social, cultural and political. Therefore, the ability to export and propagate Western norms and values as universal is a reflection of the existing power structure between developed and 'developing' countries—an outcome of the political, economic and cultural dominance of the West, which started with the expansion of imperialism and that today allows the West to exercise a degree of control over other nations.

Glauser (1997, 151) points out that people do not form the concepts they use but rather apply those currently dominant within their society. Those with social power, which may in itself stem from political and economic power, can define the reality of others through setting up terms of reference, thereby disallowing or constraining others, often by concealing parts of the social reality. This allows them to control and manipulate societies in favour of dominant interests. Tracing how certain dominant values and norms were inculcated into specific sections of society in South Asia and how the larger mass of people were made subject to these by the actions of the state and commercial, bureaucratic and educated elites reveals much about the way issues such as child labour are locally construed.

HEGEMONIC UNIVERSALISM

The encoding of Western values in international conventions is a relatively recent process, proliferating after the formation of the United Nations in 1945. The cultural diffusion of Western norms however, began much earlier, through the period of the first globalisation—the colonial expansion. Nandy (1997) distinguishes between two types of colonialism—the first referring to military conquest and the second to 'the one which at least six generations of the Third World have learnt to view as a pre-requisite for their liberation' (Nandy 1997, 170). This 'cultural colonialism' alters the cultural priorities of colonised societies, colonising minds as well as bodies. 'In the process, it helps generalise the concept of the modern West from a geographical and temporal entity to a psychological category. The West is now everywhere, within the West and outside, in structures and in minds. This is the colonialism which survives the demise of empires' (Nandy 1997, 170). Immanuel Wallerstein (1983) refers to this process as *Hegemonic Universalism*. Examining how modern South Asian history was moulded by the capitalist world system, Wallerstein argues that the 'protonationalist' elites of India and Pakistan became impregnated with 'the ideology of Hegemonic Universalism'. This ideology emerged out of 'Western Enlightenment' and now stands as the dominant culture, or culture of dominance, worldwide (Wallerstein, 1983, Chapter 3).

The 'colonisation of the mind', to use Nandy's term (1997), targeted the South Asian elite and led to a point where the 'indigenous' rulers of the newly independent nations came to believe that the complexities of the modern world could only be overcome through a sustained programme of development, and the only way for their people to re-emerge as dignified human beings was to prepare them for the sacrifices necessary to 'catch up' with the West. Only the model of society incarnated by their colonial predecessors would allow these new nations to overcome the consequences of low economic and political power in global affairs.

But as Washbrook (1990) points out, it was not only South Asian society's perception of the future that was influenced by Western notions of modernity. It was also and more crucially, its perceptions of the past. Watts (1995) and Manzo (1995) both emphasise that the linear nature of theories of modernization and development work through 'dichotomous images' that contrast the developed West with the non-developed rest of society. 'In the case of South Asia, images of the enervated past tend to be reinforced by suppositions about the proclivities of Oriental social structures and/or minds—rigid, irrational, and incapable of generating change' (Washbrook 1990, 481). Thus, hegemonic universalism not only seeks to capture the future of society but also its past and the non-modern elements in its culture and to render them vacuous through its concept of tradition. In fact, while Washbrook questions hegemonic universalism's ability to transfer the notion of 'modernisation' beyond the narrow confines of South Asia's ruling elites, he is more certain of the process's capacity to imprison the past. Universalism, therefore, is able to pass on a distorted version of tradition to the wider population, thereby making it the basis of mass identity in South Asia.

Popular conceptions of the social meanings of caste, religion, community and gender today tend to take their references from charters derived from traditional versions of the past: a past comprising centralised ancient empires, the varna theory of caste, and localised village communities which many historians would insist, bears little relation to anything that actually existed two centuries and more ago. If not in its ability to imprison the past, from which they gain their identities, in rigid, irrational and changeless structures, the culture of Hegemonic Universalism has become unquestionably dominant over the society of contemporary South Asia (Washbrook 482, 1990).

The result, then, is a complex situation in which, as Washbrook argues, hegemonic universalism has become dominant in elite society, while ideas of 'tradition' became central to the representation and framing of the practices of the wider population. The perceptions of the South Asian elites were imbibed with notions emanating from Western Enlightenment (nation-states, individual autonomy, protected childhoods) which were not indigenous concepts. These same elites, in much the same way, were able to pass on a self-serving version of the past (tradition) to the wider population.

Hegemonic universalism exacerbated social, economic and psychological differences between rulers and ruled that were already inherent within South Asian society. One of the ways that this increasing differentiation among the elite and the masses manifested itself was in the distinction drawn by those with power and control of the state between their own children and the children of the 'traditional' poor. For while the values of Western childhood were adopted by the elite for their own children, the children of the poor—in a manner reminiscent of nineteenth century Europe—were seen as counting for very little. The following section examines how the elite emerged in Pakistan and how their background influenced the emerging national discourse on child labour. The result, I argue, was a national discourse which continued to adopt two separate approaches towards the children of the elite on the one hand, who were to be educated in high quality schools, and the children of the poor on the other, who were at most expected to receive some token education at substandard schools but were more often expected to start working from an early age. It is therefore not surprising that the issue of child labour only came to be seen as problematic when international organisations such as the ILO and UNICEF began pressing for reform in Pakistan. The pressure for change did not emerge from within.

THE SOCIO-POLITICAL ORDER—ROOTS OF THE NATIONAL CHILD LABOUR DISCOURSE

THE PAKISTAN STATE AND ITS COLONIAL LEGACY

The British ruled over the vast territory of colonial India through a complex hierarchy of indirect rule, using pre-existing political structures to maintain stability and extract the revenue that financed their rule. Nasr (2001, 42) states that the system of indirect rule also built on, and deepened, the existing bifurcation of society into the 'masses' and the 'elite', and it was the elite who served as the pillars of British rule. At the apex[6] of this political hierarchy were the Indian princes who ruled over their peasants under the watchful gaze of the resident British political agents. More common, particularly in the areas that came to constitute Pakistan, were tribal leaders and *zamindars* (landlords) who collected revenue from the peasantry on their land and repaid official recognition of their titles with loyalty.

Specifically, in the areas that came to constitute Pakistan, British rule emphasised the requirements of law and order rather than those of popular representation. Talbot (1998) attributes this as being the result of the Muslim dominated areas of north-west India (later Pakistan) constituting, in essence, a security state for colonial authorities. The tribal composition of these areas, the threat of Russian expansion from Central Asia and Afghanistan and the fact that the British saw Muslims as fierce invaders prone to waging holy wars, and therefore difficult to rule over, all contributed to the emphasis on autocratic rule in these regions. While force had been applied to acquire territory elsewhere in the subcontinent, it could be discarded more readily as commercial rather than strategic considerations gradually held sway. This was never the case in much of north-west India. The British, therefore, looked more narrowly to feudal and tribal affiliations in these regions in order to maintain stability. The preservation and strengthening of the existing social system came to be regarded as essential to the maintenance of 'order' in the 'security state'. Support for tribal affiliation was later extended to feudalism as the development of agriculture made *zamindars* more important to social control, particularly in western Punjab.

The collaboration of the rural elite, which included the tribal chiefs—the *sardars* of Baluchistan and the *khans* of the North West Frontier Province, as well as the *zamindars* of Punjab and Sindh (known locally as *waderas*) was secured through awards of cash and land and allowing them local administrative and judicial powers. They were also showered with honorary military ranks, colours of regiments and imperial titles.

Also included in the rural elite were religious leaders known as *pirs*. In Pakistan, *pirs* are seen as the descendents of *sufis*—early Muslim mystics responsible for converting large parts of the Indian sub-continent to Islam. *Pirs* are not only the custodians of the holy shrines of their *sufi* ancestors but through these ancestors they are thought to possess thaumaturgical powers or *barkat*. The political power and mass followings[7] of the *pirs* was based on their powers of divine intercession though they were also often large landowners.

> A pir equipped with these powers is viewed by his followers as superhuman, equal to the Prophets of God and a little less than Almighty God. All the followers' fortune is due to the pir's favours. He can protect followers from all afflictions, cure any disease both in men and animals, and can give a boost to bankrupt business. He can bestow offspring to barren women. He has a status which no other secular leader nor the most prominent and erudite of the ulema can achieve. (S.R. Sherani 1991, 223).

The *pir* therefore represents popular, syncretic Islam (Geertz 1968). In contrast, the *ulema* represent official, scripturalist Islam. In a largely rural society, it has been the rural based *pirs* rather than the urban *ulema* that have maintained influence since their *sufi* ancestors began converting large parts of the subcontinent to Islam in the early thirteenth century. During Mughal times, the most powerful *pirs* benefited from royal patronage, often receiving vast landed estates. As a result, the *pirs* of Sindh and southern Punjab were also amongst the largest landowners of the country. During the colonial period, *pirs*, with landed estates, along with *zamindars*, served their own interests by supporting the colonial power. In return, the British recognised these *pirs* as members of the landed gentry and some were appointed as provincial and vice-regal officials and honorary magistrates. This rural elite—the regional landlords, the tribal chiefs and the *pirs* were the intermediaries whose role and power the British helped articulate in return for their cooperation in maintaining social control and, as Alavi (1989) emphasizes, they played a far more important role in the policies of South Asia, before and after Independence, than is generally recognised.

Apart from the landed gentry, colonial rule led to the emergence of further small groups of elites that, along with the rural elite, had a crucial influence on the postcolonial state in Pakistan. The colonial government required a civil and military bureaucracy staffed by 'natives' to control their vast Indian Empire. This necessitated the recruitment and training of administrative and technical functionaries to man the lower-level positions in government departments. Thus, an educational system was established along the lines of British schools and universities where [some] vocational and professional instruction was imparted. Much emphasis was given to learning the English language, customs, manners, political and moral ideas, arts and literature. These institutions produced masses of clerical workers, minor administrators and some professionals such as lawyers, college teachers, medical doctors, and accountants. During a later stage of colonial rule, when some local functionaries were permitted to enter higher provincial and central government services, care was taken to instill in them a thoroughly British style of thinking and acting, thereby initiating the process of what Nandy (1987) calls the 'colonisation of the mind'.

> They were sent to exclusive academies in the subcontinent and in England, where instruction ranged from observance of British table manners and horse-riding techniques to maintaining law and order. A basic mechanism of maintaining law and order was to impress upon the people that the higher administrator was a superior being. He not only knew the routine of his office, but was initiated into the folkways of the ruling aliens and was thus entitled to the same deference and respect. His psychic and cultural distance from the people was maintained by providing him with retinues of attendants dressed in courtly costumes of the Mughal kings. While the landed gentry and the professional classes were relatively free to maintain contact with the people, the senior administrators had few such opportunities. They were inbred in exclusive 'civil lines' colonies that were removed from the fret and struggle of the common man's life. With rare exceptions the senior civil servants of Pakistan maintain this style of life to this day (H. Gardezi 1991, 26).

Through the new system of education, these classes were removed sufficiently from their indigenous culture to become socially and culturally marginal to their own society, becoming, in the words of Lord Macaulay 'a class of persons, Indian in blood and colour, but English in taste, in opinions, in morals, and in intellect' (quoted in Gardezi 1991, 26).[8] These elite Indians added their caste consciousness to the class consciousness of their rulers, to become 'more British than the British' thereby further differentiating themselves from the masses. Moreover, as both Gardezi (1991, 26) and Washbrook (1990, 480) point out, these groups were encouraged to view other groups in society as inferior and rightly subordinate to their supremacy. By the time the British were forced to grant the subcontinent independence it was felt that the success of the colonisation of the mind would mean that those inheriting the reins of power would be incapable of posing a threat to the essential continuity of 'colonial' policy in the post-independence period.

This power structure was in fact reinforced by conditions just before and immediately following independence. Ironically, the Muslim League, the party that was at the forefront of the struggle for securing Pakistan as a separate homeland for the Muslims of India, lacked support in the Muslim dominated provinces that later became Pakistan. This was primarily because they were unable to garner votes through the traditional channels of political mobilisation in the countryside—the patron-client ties between tribal chiefs and their followers, between landlords and tenants and through the networks of disciples of the leading *pirs*. It was only after Mohammed Ali Jinnah secured a deal with the landed elite and the *pirs* in the Muslim majority provinces, especially in the Punjab and Sindh, that the Muslim League was able to mount an effective campaign for the creation of Pakistan. But as Alavi (1991, 169) points out, the League's dependence on landlords for securing goals and its inability to mobilise the Muslim masses was to have far-reaching consequences for the state of Pakistan.[9]

Furthermore, the Indian army had been dominated by Punjabis and Pathans,[10] which meant that half the military officers and soldiers of the colonial army ended up in Pakistan, ensuring a powerful say for the military in the new state's politics. Moreover, the lack of industrial development in the areas that came to constitute Pakistan, and the low level of education amongst the Muslim community in general in the subcontinent, meant a correspondingly small bourgeoisie and intelligentsia element. Not only were these groups unable to absorb the functions of a strong colonial state but they were also unable to challenge the existing entrenched power structures.

The weakness of the post-colonial state meant an almost immediate reliance on foreign donors and the key classes and social groups that had in the past bolstered colonial authority. The state needed the landed elite, the military and the civil bureaucracy in much the same fashion as the British had. The tribal leaders and landed elite thus became intermediaries in establishing political order in rural areas. But in return for helping establish state authority, the oligarchy secured their social and economic position. The state gave them great discretion in local affairs, with the effect of confirming and strengthening their authority. As the local role of the new state became integrated into the organisational design of the new state, the seeds of future state policies were sown.

Thus, Pakistan was from the outset ruled by the same bureaucratic and military elite that had been in the service of the British Raj, in alliance with the intermediaries that had also supported British rule. This allowed the continuation of administrative and political structures and practices of the Raj to carry over into the post-colonial state, prompting critics to dub Pakistan a 'vice-regal state' (Talbot 1998, 54).

The result has been that throughout Pakistan's history, the rural elite have not only provided the bulk of parliamentarians but they are also heavily represented in political parties and other powerful decision making bodies, including the military and the bureaucracy. One-third of the cabinet in 1998 was made up of *zamindars*. In 1999, 126 out of 207 National Assembly seats were taken by individuals from the same influential families of *zamindars*, *waderas*, *khans*, *sardars* and *pirs* (Figures from Haq, 1999). As Jones emphasises:

> It is indisputable that successive Pakistani parliaments have been filled with landowners and tribal leaders who have not hesitated to use their power to protect their own interests. It is beyond doubt that some feudal landowners have held onto their authority by blocking the government's attempts to foster social and economic development in their areas. (O.B. Jones 2002, 244).

ELITE GOVERNMENT—ELITE POLICIES

The separation of the ruling elite, economically, socially and psychologically, from larger society and the appropriation of state power by this oligarchy has meant, as Alavi points out (1991, 164), the identification of the state and the nation with the elites' own particular purposes and interests. For example, land reforms and direct agricultural taxes focused on large landowners have been avoided, and even when half-heartedly implemented, there have been enough loopholes for the landowners to circumvent the measures.

The military, too, has guarded its privileged status, and with just over half of Pakistan's 55-year existence under military regimes, the army has gradually increased its influence.[11] Jalal (1995) goes as far as referring to Pakistan's political economy as being defence rather than development oriented, arguing that the military has been able to translate its dominance over the state structure to become deeply entrenched in the political economy. Military regimes in Pakistan have regularly rewarded senior officers in the defence establishment with top positions in the state structure as well as in semi-government and autonomous organisations. In addition, Pakistan's military dominated state has at each step awarded its principal constituents with land grants, defence contracts, permits, licenses and ambassadorial appointments (Jalal 1995, 142). Invariably, the military are catered to by schools and hospitals on par with similar facilities in the developed world. The army have even managed to extend their reach into the country's economy and presently own several major manufacturing units.

The examples of government policy highlighted in the previous section on elite government and elite policies indicate the priorities and motivations of the ruling classes. The divergence between government policies and the basic needs of the masses is reflected in the country's poor social indicators: 'Among 150 nations, Pakistan ranks 130 as far as proportion of school age children attending school, 120 in literacy rate and 118 in per capita expenditure on health. There is in brief, a wide gulf between Pakistan's economic growth and local development performance' (M. Weiner and Noman 1997, 209). While these figures are part of the 'development discourse' and must be seen in that light, they do provide an indication of where the government's priorities have been focussed.

Perhaps most relevantly for the issue of child labour is the government's attitude towards education. The approach to education is a prime example of the way norms and values inculcated in the South Asian ruling elite merged with existing traditions to produce two almost schizophrenic approaches towards 'us', the elite and 'them', the masses. It is also a key reflection of the separateness and insular nature that the elite developed.

Critics of educational theory point out that educational institutions generally function to 'reproduce structures of class dominance and their ideological justification, excluding subordinate classes and minorities from access to occupational and intellectual preparation, or providing them with a restricted education which reinforces their marginal position in society' (C. Seymour-Smith 1986, 90). At independence Pakistan inherited a bifurcated education system. The ruling elite had Western style, English language schools to meet their demand for a 'modern' Western-oriented education. For the rest of society there were government schools in which the medium of instruction was the local vernacular. Education, therefore, came to be used as a means for social reproduction. In this, education and schooling found fertile ground in a society with strong hierarchies, which had for generations limited social mobility between groups ranked according to hereditary occupations. The education system therefore reinforced divisions inherent in South Asian society thereby strengthening the existing process by which social classes reproduced themselves. The higher castes had, by virtue of their position in the caste system, been imbibed with a feeling of superiority. Education reinforced this feeling of superiority and otherness, distancing them evermore from the larger mass of people that did not have the benefits of the elite. 'Those who are educated dress and speak differently from those who are not educated. Those who are educated have power over those who are not. The educated can give commands to and shout at the uneducated and can expect deference and obedience' (M. Weiner and O. Noman 1997, 190).

Such ideas echo the divisions found in nineteenth and early twentieth century European attitudes to privileged and ordinary children. But they act as more than a marker of distinction. The concept that some people are born to rule and to 'work' with their minds while others, the vast majority, are born to work with their hands and be ruled over was widespread in Britain (M. Weiner and O. Noman 1997, 188). In South Asian society, moreover, the caste system had institutionalised a system whereby the artisan and service castes provided services to the landowning castes in exchange for grain and other products. As a result, the elite—who were born to rule—received the relevant education allowing them to monopolise top positions in the military, government and commerce. The children of the poor, it was believed, could best assume the same role as their parents by early entrance into the labour force. If they did receive some education it was to prepare them, at most, for employment in menial vocations, thereby producing a cheap, malleable labour force for jobs that needed to be undertaken in society and which in the past were undertaken by the lower castes. Thus, poor people with low quality government funded education were denied any opportunity for upward social mobility. In this way, traditional notions of social rank and hierarchy are subtly incorporated into the way educated people distinguish between education for the children of those who do manual work and those who are in services, while ideas of what is 'traditional'—i.e. appropriate for the masses—serves to legitimise this lack of concern for the fate of the children of the poor.

The 'fact' that children of the poor should work and not go to school, continues to be propagated through the attitudes of upper class families who want docile servants that accept their 'inferior' position in society, through middle and lower middle class families who employ them as cheap labour in their small enterprises and workshops and who frequently cite child labour as providing relief for the poor, and through the child's family who often not only need the extra income but who see it is as their lot in life that their children start work from an early age. Furthermore, many of those from poorer families who perhaps did believe in educating their children have been dissuaded through their experience with low-quality schools and the failure of education to improve their choices in life. On numerous occasions during my fieldwork, I came across workers who simply reiterated the comments made over 70 years ago by a landless peasant interviewed by Malcolm Darling during his travels through India: 'To run the world both rich and poor are needed. If all are rich like you, who will cut the grass for your horse?' (M. Darling 1934, 293).

The result of the propogation of these hierarchies was a continued concentration of state power in the hands of a small elite dominated by landlords, bureaucrats and army officers. The outcome has been the state's indifference to education, child labour and the social sector in general. If the children of the poor fail to enrol, or drop out of substandard schools, or end up working at an early age, this is likely to be seen as their lot in life.

The reluctance towards reform and the overwhelming importance of military expenditure, magnified even further when considering the limited sums set aside for the social sector, reflect the influence of a ruling elite divorced from the aspirations of the masses and supremely indifferent to the promotion of basic social services to the people. The elite are also the group with social power and are therefore able to define the social reality of others. In this way they are able to propagate a self-serving version of the social order and accordingly dictate future government strategy for their own benefit. It is with reference to the values and norms of those holding power within the existing economic and political structure that the state's attitude towards, and performance on, reform and social development must be seen.

RESISTANCE TO ELITE POLICIES

Ironically, one of the strands of opposition to the ruling elites' policies and particularly their social policies comes from within the 'elite' itself, but involves a group that has remained divorced from political power.[12] Take, for example, the career of Anees Jillani, one of Pakistan's leading lawyers and human rights activists. Jillani has undertaken extensive research on child labour in Pakistan and heads a non-profit organisation called the Society for the Protection of the Rights of the Child. He also represents the 'Westernised' intelligentsia within the 'elite' and is highly critical of government inaction on social issues.

> The biggest hurdles to implementing any sort of reform plan was the failure of the government and the bureaucracy to move with any kind of determination and speed. There is a complete lack of new or innovative ideas coming from the bureaucracy. There is constant opposition towards change.

The quotation above reflects the Western, liberal origins of Jillani's thinking—the stress on education for the masses, the opposition to child labour and a resistance to the 'traditional' views of the landed elite.

The specific nature of the Westernised intelligentsia sets them apart from both the masses and the ruling elite. They remain culturally and socially distant from the masses by virtue of their 'elite' educational backgrounds—often in universities outside Pakistan—and their high income and status in society. They also tend to be urban based which differentiates them from the landed elites. The intelligentsia are also characterised by their separation from political power and are often referred to in Pakistan as the 'silent majority' within the elite—a reference to their inability and lack of inclination towards challenging the existing political structure. It is the landed elite that retained political power and it is their views rather than those of this intelligentsia that shape state policy.

However, of all the government officials I met, the most frank and forthright was Najmuddin Najmi. Najmi has been in charge of the Directorate of Workers Education since it was established in 1982 to provide training and awareness on labour issues. Perhaps it was his background as a social worker, and not being one of the privileged ruling elite, which made him as perceptive as he was to the issue of child labour and allowed him the 'distance' to criticise government efforts:

> There is simply no political will on the part of the government to tackle social issues. No political party has ever come to power in Pakistan with a manifesto that has targeted education or social services. Policy-makers are not willing to pour funds into a sector that shows benefits much later. They think that a subsequent government will reap the harvest of the seeds they have sown. As it is, none of our last five governments have managed to complete their terms. So when someone comes to power they go for quick fix solutions. Also whoever comes to power is beholden to the zamindars. They are the ones who make people vote and in return the government cannot act against them. Now with the economy crumbling, child labour isn't one of the government's priorities.

Najmi's views point to the long-term effects of the colonial 'deal' on the shaping of the Pakistani post-colonial elite, and to the radical separation of the interests of the elite and the masses:

The moral character of the country has declined alarmingly so that there is no longer any pride in the country, no nationalism, no patriotism. There is no research being done on our traditions, values and past heritage. There is no desire to solve social problems. Life is cheap, there is no respect for human dignity or life—just apathy all round. We need to produce a love for humanity, a love for the nation and a desire to improve the welfare of the people. But we have no concept of collective action within communities. While people have food in Pakistan, things will be okay. The day people start starving, this country will be like Somalia or Rwanda.

Anees Jillani also pointed to the decline in 'moral character' and the absence of any collective action.

> All over the world you see people coming together to champion causes—saving tigers in India, preventing the dumping of nuclear waste, highlighting the plight of women in Afghanistan etc. This concern for collective issues is missing in Pakistan despite the stress on joint living. We subscribe to a culture where we clean our houses but throw the collected rubbish on the street outside. We may like to send our children to the best schools and universities in the West but couldn't care less if other children don't go to school at all. Pakistan is a poor country and miserably lags behind in social progress of its populace. Its classic excuse for this state of affairs is lack of resources although it has one of the largest defence forces in the world and

is able to make nuclear weapons. It is a question of priorities and the lack of political will to ameliorate the lot of the poor.

Both Jillani and Najmi seemed to be subscribing to the idea that the indifference of the ruling classes had filtered down to society in general, with the result that Pakistan remains a society that is dominated by the values and traditions of its ruling class.

However, since independence, the nature of the Pakistani oligarchy has changed. It is no longer neatly divided into the bureaucracy, the military and the landowning class as it was in the first decade of the country's history. Matrimonial alliances with the military and the bureaucracy have given the rural elite added influence. Today all these segments have come closer together through inter-marriages and a commonality of economic and political interests. Retired generals and bureaucrats are landowners and captains of industry. Former landowners are industrial barons. The old industrial houses have married into the old landed aristocracy. In Punjab family connections have created a '*zamindar*-business nexus'. By distributing land in return for favours, military rulers in the early 1960s and late 1970s also helped create a new set of landlords who are now as powerful as the older *zamindar* families. Industry has been gradually 'feudalised', with *zamindars* branching out into the industrial sector. The consolidation of power amongst these groups marginalized other elite groups such as the intelligentsia, divorcing them from the emerging political structure.

It is interesting to note that in Pakistan the term 'feudal' has come to refer to the entire ruling elite examined above. Yet apart from a small proportion of the largest landowners amongst that elite, it is difficult to see how, even if a loose definition is employed, the term 'feudal' could apply to the entire group. Instead 'feudal' has come to refer to more than simply owning land.[13] Today when people talk about 'feudals' in Pakistan they are referring to those individuals that are able to ignore state institutions and use religion, their landholdings and their local tribal political systems[14] to wield personal or family power and influence. Thus it is not only *zamindars*, but those who try and emulate them, that move between their family-owned village fortresses and sprawling residences in the country's major cities. Many participate in exclusive *shikar* (hunting expeditions)—once the favourite pastime of Indian princes and the British. Feudalism has become a state of mind. The feudal landlords are 'untouchable'—normal rules and laws do not apply to them and in an example of reference group behaviour, people in Pakistan try to emulate the feudal lifestyle because it is seen as successful. Therefore even those who are able to rise from the 'masses' tend to leave their old identities behind, preferring to differentiate themselves from their past, thereby maintaining the 'exclusivity' of the group. This inevitably means very little commonality of interests remains between the elite and the rest of society. This absence of a merging of state and society as common expressions of a set of shared values has in fact been identified by a number of theorists[15] of the 'Third World' state as being characteristic of weak post-colonial states. Pakistan clearly shows this trend. All this complicates the picture of 'Hegemonic Universalism' with which I began this analysis. For if there is one section of the elite where universalist values are part of the culture with which they distinguish themselves from the 'backward' and the 'traditional', for others—and these are more closely involved in the running of the state—it is the enactment or imitation of the 'traditional' and hierarchical that distinguishes them.

Having examined the worldview and values of those controlling the state, it becomes easier to understand the response of the government to the issue of 'child labour' when confronted with it. The growing external interest in child labour and the internal response to this unwanted exposure also lies at the heart of the formation of two contrasting representations of 'reality'. This forms the basis of the discussion in the next chapter.

NOTES

1. For example, Ferguson (1990), Escobar (1995), Gardner (1996), (1997), Hobart (1993).
2. Address to Pan-African Association of Anthropologists, biennial meeting on 'Challenges for Anthropological Research in the 21st Century', Legon, Ghana.
3. The use of the term 'discourse of child labour' here and subsequently refers to the sub-discourse of child labour within the wider discourse of development.
4. See Watts (1995), Cowen and Shenton (1991, 1996), Crush (1995), Marglin and Marglin (1990), Banuri (1990), Manzo (1995).
5. The fieldwork for the current thesis, like Mamdani's, is set in the Punjab. However, Mamdani's fieldwork was undertaken in the Hindu majority area of Eastern Punjab (India) whereas the fieldwork for this thesis was undertaken in the Muslim majority area of Western Punjab (Pakistan). Despite the religious differences there is a considerable cultural overlap between the two separate regions.
6. For a description of the political structure prior to colonial expansion see, for example, C. Fuller (1989) or H. Gardezi (1991).

7. Pir Pagara, one of the most famous *pirs* in Sindh, is rumoured to have in excess of one million followers.

8. M.K. Gandhi referred to the education system introduced by the British as a 'poisonous gift to the people of India'. In a speech in 1937 (reproduced in Rahnema and Bawtree 1997, 121) Gandhi stated that the British education system constituted a major colonial instrument for the enslavement and destruction of the cultural roots of the Indian people. He emphasised that the system was surreptitiously destabilising its consumers from the mainstream of life in India, making them strangers in their own land.

9. For details see Talbot (1998), Nasr (2001).

10. Inhabitants originally of the North-West Frontier Province.

11. Pakistan spends almost one third of government funds on military expenditure, has one of the largest standing armies in the world and continues to pour scarce funds into the purchase of advanced weaponry and the development of its nuclear programme. Defence expenditure as a percentage of expenditure on health and education stands at 181 per cent (Figures from Haq, 1997).

12. More general opposition to government policy involves a wider range of groups including the *ulema* (orthodox religious leaders and parties). However, Nasr (1995, 81) points out that these parties, the largest of which is the Jamaat-i-Islami, have tended to focus on ideological concerns with the objective of taking over the state from secular leaders, rather than giving a voice to the demands of the masses. As a result, their political manifesto has been indifferent to socio-political concerns such as child labour, which is why there has been little criticism from religious parties on many of the government's social policies.

13. See Akbar Zaidi (1999) for a discussion of whether Pakistan can be seen as a feudal society. For a general description on feudalism see Bloc (1962), E. Wolf (1966), M. Weber (1968), Alavi (1982).

14. For example in parts of rural Pakistan tribal councils or *jirgas* still impose their own punishments on individuals and are often more influential than the government judiciary. These *jirgas* generally comprise the village's influential 'feudals'.

15. See Talbot (1998) for a discussion of this.

2

CHILD LABOUR
EMERGING AND OPPOSING REPRESENTATIONS

The renewed interest in child rights when the United Nations adopted the Convention on the Rights of the Child in 1989 meant a new focus on the plight of children the world over. Prior to ratifying the Convention, the Pakistan government had not admitted to the existence of child labour. In the early 1990s, under increasing pressure from the international community, the government attempted to forestall punitive action by passing two child-labour related Acts.[1] Behind these largely cosmetic efforts little practical progress was made, even though the minister responsible insisted that as laws had been passed the problem had been effectively eradicated. Said Minister Sheikh Rashid, *'Things have changed a lot in Pakistan. After the 1991 Supreme Court verdict our government has, through a legal process, abolished the tradition of bonded labour in Pakistan. Therefore people can no longer keep slaves.'* (Sheikh Rashid, interview with a local newspaper). Unfortunately for the government, external attention on child labour continued to build and the government was far from prepared to deal with the fallout.

As Majyd Aziz notes:
When a worldwide campaign against child labour, spruced up by the introduction of the Child Labour Deterrence Act of 1993 in the U.S. Senate, picked up momentum, Pakistan was caught in a tornado of accusations and condemnations. As the campaign became more intense, the government became more adamant in trying to prove to the world that child labour was not present in the country. The ensuing result was counter productive for the nation and the focus of international eyes was squarely on Pakistan. (Majyd Aziz, 1998).

The Harkin Bill[2] sought to ban the import into America of goods produced by children less than 14 years of age. While the tabling of the Bill was hailed as a breakthrough in the United States, Crawford (1999, INSEAD) states that its ultimate effect was minimal as the agent of enforcement—the US customs service—was ill-equipped to carry out its mandate. However, the bill had a very different impact on the 'source' countries that it targeted. In Bangladesh, fearing that the vital US market would close, garment factory owners turned some 50,000 working children into the street virtually overnight. Unfortunately, rather than re-entering school, many children were forced to find work in more hazardous occupations such as prostitution, rag-picking and brick baking.[3] The threat of the Bill being passed had been enough to cause an enormous and unseen backlash on the 'target beneficiaries'. In Pakistan the reaction was less dramatic, but the tabling of the Bill succeeded in bringing child labour into public debate. However, it was an event within Pakistan that caught the attention of the international press. In 1994, human rights organisations the world over acclaimed a 12-year-old bonded-labourer-turned-child-labour-activist. For the international press and community, Iqbal Masih was an unlikely new crusader.

> Masih had been bonded at the age of 4 to a village carpet maker in Punjab. He spent his next six years knotting carpets, paying off an inter-generational debt that would never be repaid. At the age of 10, Masih escaped from his slavery and took shelter with a local NGO—the Bonded Labour Liberation Front. Masih was 'rescued' by the NGO and placed into primary school. But this extraordinary child possessed an intellectual maturity beyond his years and a precocious sense of justice. He applied these gifts to the anti-slavery movement, and achieved results that would be impressive for a Nobel Laureate, let alone a schoolboy. By his twelfth birthday he had helped to liberate 3000 children from bondage at textile and brick factories, tanneries, steelworks—industries at the heart of the Pakistan economy. (Silvers, 1996).

The International Labour Organisation held a ceremony in honour of Masih in Sweden. The sports manufacturer, Reebok, presented him with its prestigious Human Rights Youth in Action Award in Boston. Even the American television network ABC featured him as its 'Person of the Week' in their news programme.

In Pakistan, the new attention on child labour, and particularly on the carpet industry, was beginning to have adverse effects on exports. In 1992, carpet exports declined by 3-4 per cent for the first time in two decades. By 1993 and 1994, sales had fallen sharply in several of the largest markets for Pakistani exports. But if the government and carpet exporters thought that the child labour issue might subside through the passing of laws, and by dismissing reports of abuses as exaggerated and isolated, they were to receive a rude shock with an event that led to a snowballing of media interest. In April 1995, Iqbal Masih, the child labourer turned human rights activist, was shot dead in his village.

Iqbal's high profile abroad meant that the western press immediately picked up the story. Crucially, the NGO that had freed Masih played a catalytic role. Ehsanullah Khan, the head of the Bonded Labour Liberation Front (BLLF), misjudged the sensitivity of the situation and almost immediately issued a statement: 'I emphatically say that the carpet mafia is responsible for this brutal killing… I have no doubt that the police are also part of the conspiracy'. However, Khan did not support his accusations with evidence. 'I do not rely on evidence', he told his critics, 'I have my instinct'. Ehsanullah Khan left Pakistan to consult with child rights activists in Europe. There he repeated his accusations to great effect at conferences, on television and before lawmakers, calling on the United Nations Human Rights Commission to ban the import and sale of all products made by children, especially carpets. The child labour issue had well and truly blown up and was rapidly spiralling out of control for the government. The effects were devastating, as Pakistani carpet exports plummeted by 50 per cent compared to the same period of 1994.[4]

OPPOSITION TO THE EMERGING REPRESENTATION OF CHILD LABOUR

There was a sharp reaction within Pakistani society as well. The government and the press closed ranks against outside pressure, passing off the 'controversy' as propaganda against Pakistan's export industries.

> The countries inimical to Pakistan are trying to exploit the issue, blowing it out of all proportion to tarnish this country. India is already trying its utmost to tarnish our image in foreign countries. That the propaganda has worked is evident from the steep decline in carpet exports. (*The News International*, 20 July 1996).

Within the country, the government turned its ire on NGOs and individuals they dubbed 'so-called human rights activists'. The government's relationship with NGOs has at best been ambivalent and more often simply adversarial. The government, saw NGOs as being beyond their control. At the same time, non-governmental agencies increasingly began to impinge on areas long since seen as the preserve of the government—for example social sector delivery. Recently NGOs have increasingly competed with the government for donor funding. The government also felt that NGOs tended to pander to foreign agencies, passing on negative information that would show Pakistan, and therefore the government, in a poor light. The implication was that NGOs tend to exaggerate the extent of problems in Pakistan in order to drive home the seriousness of the situation, thereby facilitating donor funding for themselves. This further upset the government, which, particularly in the case of child labour, has attempted to downplay the issue.

In the case of the Bonded Labour Liberation Front, the government already had misgivings. The International Labour Organisation World Report 1993, had quoted the inordinately high figure of 20 million bonded labourers in Pakistan. In response, a body of industrialists based in Pakistan sent a query to the ILO Pakistan office regarding the source of the figure. On investigation it was found that the ILO had based these figures on information from a local NGO report from Pakistan that was presented at an international conference. The ILO admitted that the original report was not based on a scientific study by an organisation or the ILO. It was later revealed that the NGO was the Bonded Labour Liberation Front. As such the government saw the BLLF not only as an organisation that consistently highlighted abuses of child labour, thereby embarrassing the government, but also as an organisation that had fed inflated figures to international agencies, further embarrassing the government.

The head of the BLLF, Ehsanullah Khan had angered the government through his hasty remarks following the mysterious death of Iqbal Masih. The government responded with a barrage of equally unsubstantiated publicity against Khan. He was characterised as a philandering bigamist with indisputable ties to Jewish and Indian agencies hostile to Pakistan. Some newspapers even suggested that Khan had used children freed by BLLF as his own personal sex slaves, and that Iqbal was a 35-year old midget masquerading as a child. One report went as far as stating that Khan had murdered Masih himself to win sympathy for BLLF. The struggle within the child labour discourse had clearly intensified, with the different representations of reality looking to gain authority, legitimacy and dominance.

> Those who harboured no goodwill for the country prominently flashed child labour in Pakistan on the global scene. Those forces got considerable support from a plethora of NGOs and human rights organisations working in Pakistan. Pakistan was under direct attack not only from external sectors but also more ominously from organisations based inside the country. These NGOs come up with outlandish figures of child labour, and those illusionary statistics become the basis for international organisations and anti-Pakistan elements to continue their tirade against Pakistan. Child Labour in Pakistan got more prominence after the murder of a bonded labour activist, Iqbal Masih in 1994. Ehsanullah Khan, Chief of the BLLF exploited this senseless killing and took sinister advantage of the sympathy generated for Iqbal Masih in Sweden and other European countries. He milked NGOs in these countries out of millions of dollars, ostensibly to build schools in memory of Iqbal Masih and to release bonded children from the captivity of brick kiln owners. (Majyd Aziz, 1998).

Ehsanullah Khan, fearing for his safety, accepted asylum in Sweden. For the government and local press this was an admission of his guilt—according to them he was a traitor to Pakistan and showed his treachery by fleeing the country,

> Ehsanullah Khan, a so-called labour leader who is in self-exile and has taken refuge in Sweden to continue his nasty and immoral mission against the carpet industry in Pakistan. (*The News International*, 20 July 1996).

Neither Ehsanullah Khan's claims nor the government's counter claims could be verified but Masih's death marked the commencement of a high-profile and intensive focus on child labour in Pakistan. It also started a process that culminated in the creation of two conflicting and competing representations of child labour in Pakistan. Until this point, most international reporting on child labour in Pakistan had been based on second-hand accounts or situational analyses by international agencies and local NGOs. Following the death of Iqbal Masih, and with interest in child labour at an unprecedented high, more and more foreign journalists and media sought to provide 'first-hand accounts' of the situation. While it could have been expected that this qualitatively different method of reporting would provide a more accurate view of the situation on the ground, the result was quite the opposite. The divergence in the perspectives of 'outsiders' and 'insiders' increased, until ultimately any similarities between the views became so cursory that it became difficult to recognise that the same geographical area was being discussed. The following section examines the emerging dominance of one discourse through the development of a particular stereotype of child labour in Sialkot, and how this stereotype came to be seen in the development and the wider public discourse as the reality of Sialkot's working children.

FORMING THE REPRESENTATION OF CHILD LABOUR IN SIALKOT

The Iqbal Masih episode and the ensuing media coverage crippled the carpet industry. It also increased the anxiety of industrialists throughout Pakistan, including sports manufacturers situated in Sialkot. The foreign media searching for more stories was now constantly on the alert for opportunities. In 1995 an American news channel aired an expose attacking the American sports company, Reebok, for making footballs with child labour in Sialkot. All of a sudden the foreign media were bringing home the 'truths' of how sports products sold in the United States, often by famous brands, were manufactured. Sialkot, producing almost 90 per cent of the world's footballs at this point, was brought to center-stage. The movement to end child labour coalesced around football manufacturers in the *Foul Ball Campaign*, a lobbying effort that relied on dramatic claims and denunciations. 'Children would no longer kick around the balls made by impoverished children half a world away', stated Dan McCurry, the director of the football campaign (World Traveller Internet Website). The campaign garnered considerable publicity. Damning estimates began to appear of child labour in Pakistan's football manufacturing industry. Many of the charges, however, were based on erroneous information, but the multinationals were threatened with a serious tarnishing of their brand names.

Almost immediately the brands' manufacturing partners in Sialkot began to feel the pressure. Khwaja Zakaullah, head of Capitol Sports, one of Sialkot's largest football manufacturers, related to me how he was first confronted with the issue of child labour in the Sialkot football industry:

One day I received a frantic phone call from an American business associate and customer. He told me that he had seen a report on the news in which it had been claimed that child labour was being used in the manufacture of footballs made in Sialkot. He asked me whether this was true and whether children were stitching any of our footballs. I didn't answer immediately because the question had taken me aback. We didn't know who was stitching the footballs. All our work was sub-contracted out by our makers[5] to the villages surrounding Sialkot city and then redelivered to our factories as a completed product. We had never thought about who stitched the footballs.

However, the foreign media had unearthed what appeared to be a major story. From a small town not much heard of outside Pakistan, Sialkot rapidly gained notoriety. For the local population, it was an unwelcome intrusion as foreign journalists, usually openly and somewhat insensitively, attempted to draw out newsworthy stories.

Entering an arena that had long been the concern of a few politicians and professionals in international organisations, suddenly scores of activists became concerned about working children. Armies of reporters, some of them celebrities in their own right, joined the cause, scouring the Third World for examples of abuse and exploitation of children; their harrowing tales of brushes with mysterious thugs, some clad like policemen, lent them credibility and 'élan'. (One Step Forward, Two Steps Back, *Financial Times*, Robert Crawford).

Often they preferred to disguise themselves as buyers looking for the best possible deals. I was told of one American couple that masqueraded as representatives of a foreign NGO. On the pretext of instituting income generation schemes for the community, the couple surreptitiously filmed children stitching footballs. Their mission accomplished, they were gone before dawn the following day. Another local Sialkoti complained of a local NGO having done much the same and then having sold the documentary to a foreign news network. 'These people have sold us out', he stated angrily. The deception of journalists and NGOs, the realisation that every move was being watched, and the knowledge that being seen in conversation with 'outsiders' would lead to the assumption that you too were passing on sensitive information and therefore betraying Sialkot, led to an atmosphere of mistrust and unease amongst local communities. Communities closed ranks, fearing the loss of their jobs.

The most damaging journalistic pieces came in a flurry one after another and turned out to be the 'first-hand accounts' from journalists who had visited Sialkot. In February 1996 Jonathan Silvers, an American journalist and TV producer, wrote an article entitled 'Child Labour in Pakistan' for the *Atlantic Monthly* magazine. The article starts with the description of a father 'selling' his child as a bonded worker in the carpet industry. The text is littered with the sinister comments of employers: 'children are cheaper to run than tractors and smarter than oxen,' says one *zamindar*. At another point, Silvers quotes an official of the Pakistan Manufacturers and Exporters Association as saying: 'The memory of Western consumers is brief and our enemies' meagre resources cannot sustain their destructive campaign for long.' But it is the section on the football industry that is most damning.

> Soon after I arrived in Pakistan, I arranged a trip to a town whose major factories were rumoured to enslave very young children. I found myself hoping during the journey there that the children I saw working in the fields, on the roads, at the market places would prepare me for the worst. They did not. No amount of preparation could have lessened the shock and revulsion I felt on entering a sporting goods factory in the town of Sialkot.

Silvers (see quotation at start of chapter 1) goes on to relate how children stitch footballs eighty hours a week for the equivalent of $1.20 a day. Furthermore, in the event of minor 'infractions' by the child — speaking to strangers outside the factory, complaining of ill treatment to their parents, taking more than the allowed 30 minutes for a meal break or speaking while working, they are 'hung upside down by their knees and starved, caned or lashed.'

A few months later, Pulitzer Prize winning journalist Sydney Schanberg also visited Sialkot, producing an article for *Life* magazine entitled 'Six cents an hour: On the Playgrounds of America, every kid's goal is to score. In Pakistan, where children stitch footballs for six cents an hour, the goal is to survive.'

Like Silvers, Schanberg also discusses bonded labour, but this time he finds the *peshgi*[6] system as common in the football industry as 'the flies that swarm about the faces of workers'. He goes on to reveal that 'children as young as six are bought from their parents for as little as $15, sold and resold like furniture, branded, beaten, blinded as punishment for wanting to go home, rendered speechless by the trauma of their enslavement.' (S. Schanberg, 1996).

Both articles are emotionally charged reports that aim to shock the reader. They are also damning accounts of the conditions in which children were said to be working. Yet, despite the writers having visited Sialkot and interviewed respondents, the articles are patently inaccurate and as a result all the more damaging. I would not for a moment consider that these journalists and others in their position were fabricating stories. Some concession must be made for the fact that a journalistic piece has to capture the attention of the target audience for, as La Fontaine (1986) points out, the 'Western' public has become familiar with an imagery of extremity at the expense of understanding. But setting aside allowances for the sensationalisation of material, there are other reasons why such a representation emerged.

THE SIALKOT STEREOTYPE

Mitchell states that the West has come to live 'as though the world were divided in this way into two: into a realm of mere representations and a realm of the real, with exhibitions and an external reality, into an order of mere models, descriptions or copies, and an order of the original' (Mitchell 1988, 32). In other words we have Western societies and Western representations of other societies. The Third World and its people exist 'out there' to be known through theories and intervened upon from the outside. In the case of Pakistan, the representation of child labour drew strength from similar representations of developing world countries further sustaining 'the reality that feeds such an image' (Parpart 1995, 262). Discussion centred on modernisation theory's typical characterisation of traditional societies as being particularistic, unmotivated to profit and seeped in tradition. By contrast was the ideal: the modern society at the other end of the evolutionary scale—secular, universalistic, and profit-motivated. There was a tendency to use the most extreme examples to highlight the continued existence of 'repressive' traditions that had survived into the modern age. In the case of child labour in Pakistan, this usually meant bonded labour or categories of work that shared some features of forced labour. Specific instances of working children mingled with powerful images of poverty and underdevelopment to produce the typical representation of child labourers in Pakistan:

> At dawn each day 10 year old Kanji is kicked awake by the field managers and made to give fodder to the cattle. He works all day herding cattle. 'I experience a lot of heat, hunger and tiredness. If I am lucky, I find a piece

of stale bread, otherwise I pass the whole day without food.' At night he is locked in a dirty cell with a tattered blanket as his bed. 'I have never been paid for my labour because I am a slave and their property. With my own eyes I have seen my mother and father tortured mercilessly by the zamindar and his henchmen. But I could only remain silent. I too have suffered beatings and filthy abuse. Children my age are playing with other children and I would rather die than lead this awful life.' (Taken from Anti-Slavery International Website).

The use of extreme examples to highlight repressive indigenous traditions is particularly noticeable in the use of the concept of bonded labour in Sialkot. Schanberg clearly implies that 'bonded labour' is common in Sialkot's football industry by referring to the widespread incidence of the *peshgi* system. However, while there is clearly a system of offering and taking advances, (referred to as *peshgi*), in practice in the industry, to see this as leading to bonded labour, in the sense that Schanberg implies, is incorrect. In Sialkot, *peshgi* refers to the advance of money taken by football stitchers from a sub-contractor. This is generally a small amount—as wages for a single football were rarely higher than Rs. 30[7] (£0.35) per ball—and *peshgis* usually covered the 6-8 footballs given to a family to stitch. There is no question of large amounts of money being advanced to stitchers, as in the case of carpet weaving, for example, where a single carpet may take months to prepare and will therefore involve much higher *peshgis*. The larger amount of money involved in carpet weaving can lead to situations in which a family becomes heavily indebted to an employer, thereby setting up a scenario where persons can be bonded to provide labour for years until the debt is paid off. In the most extreme cases, this debt may not be paid off in the lifetime of the worker and may then transfer to the worker's children. In some cases children may be 'pledged' in place of the outstanding loan. This is what Schanberg means when he refers to the *peshgi* system.

However, in Sialkot, I came across few heavily indebted families and no examples of the kind of 'bonded' labour that does exist in other parts of Pakistan. Instead, football stitchers often informed me that sub-contractors were only entertained *if* they had *peshgis* to offer. Advances on wages would usually be used to assist in purchasing goods for general household consumption. While *peshgis* are a feature of the industry, the characteristic of these advances is that they tend to be small and do not have the 'strings attached' that bonded labour involves. Being 'bound' to a particular sub-contractor sometimes meant that the stitchers were obliged to give priority to that contractor's work. This occasionally means that stitchers lose out on higher rates of pay because they have become 'bound' to a particular sub-contractor. However, it was also fairly common for a stitcher to take out an advance from one sub-contractor to return the advance of another sub-contractor, thereby freeing himself to take advantage of a better wage rate. But the fact that the term *'peshgi'* implies one party advancing money to another party led automatically to the assumption that this was a case of bonded labour in the extreme sense of the term.

The *peshgi* system in the football industry is not the result of a 'traditional rural custom' imported to an industrial setting. Part of the reason for this is that Sialkot was never under the influence of large landholders. Landholdings were relatively small, and with the long history of industry in Sialkot, workers were less dependent on land, and therefore landowners, in order to make a living. Consequently, the feudal system that dominates parts of Southern Punjab and Sindh was never strong in the region. As a result, there appears to be no evidence of bonded labour in any of the work based in Sialkot. The *peshgi* system in the football industry in fact emerged in response to the decentralisation of the industry. Both the skill for stitching, and the labour, was plentiful and free, i.e. not bound by a contract. In order to maintain a flexible workforce which could be contracted or bound when demand required, employers resorted to offering advances. Thus, the *peshgi* offered in Sialkot is an effort to attract and retain labour within a competitive market.

WHICH REALITY IS 'REAL'?

Development theory in general, with its stress on linear growth, seeks to reduce the complexity of the social world to more simplified models. In this case it led to the formation of this 'western' representation or stereotype of child labour and, as Hall (1992, 308) points out, stereotypes are based on the collapsing of complex differences into a simple cardboard cut-out. But while this representation may provide a description of life for some children in Pakistan, it is only part of the story, and it is certainly not the only story. Nevertheless, this was the image that emerged and came to define the dominant discourse on child labour in Pakistan. A young child, working long hours, for little or no pay, in many cases bonded to an unscrupulous and merciless employer.

Robbed of their childhood, a time which should be devoted to being loved, cherished, educated and nourished, these unfortunate children are forced to prematurely inhabit the adult world. Furthermore, these children are seen as being exclusively located in the developing world. Yet, picture this:

> Ten year old children get up before dawn every morning and go to work. They are paid by the piece, not guaranteed an hourly wage. They get no benefits. And they work seven days a week, year round, with no vacation unless they can find someone to take their place. (David R. Henderson, 1996)

The above passage does not refer to a developing country. The work described is undertaken by children in the United States. The job is newspaper delivery. But while the image of the child labourer in Asia or Africa invariably involves association with extreme poverty, exploitation and barbaric customs and is presented by the development discourse as a reality, the second image, as illustrated in the above quote, is rarely invoked. This, despite evidence that child labour exists in developed countries as well as developing countries, albeit not on the same scale.[8] Morrow (1992) points out that recent research in the United Kingdom has shown that up to a third of secondary school children work illegal hours (too late, too early) in poor conditions or forbidden occupations. She goes on to state that while newspaper delivery, for example, is widely viewed in developed countries as a healthy way to earn pocket money and establish good working habits, it has been associated with illegal working hours, road accidents, sexual abuse and skeletal deformities from carrying heavy loads. In fact, Morrow's use of terms such as sexual abuse, skeletal deformities and heavy loads immediately conjures up images of children working as prostitutes in South-East Asia or Brazil, or carrying bricks in India. That they are being used to describe conditions in a developed country comes as a shock to those who assume that the West cannot treat its children in the same way as the 'less advanced' developing world. As Ennew notes, childhood becomes a valuable commodity in the power structure between developed and developing countries (Montgomery 2000, 14). It is because of this that hardships experienced by young people in developing countries are represented as a deplorable breach of childhood, while in developed countries similar hardships do not allowed to call into question Western society's commitment to its children. Therefore there exists the belief in the reality of bonded child labour in the developing world and the perceived absence of child labour in the West.

Apart from the influence of a stereotype of child labour that is dominant in the minds of the travelling journalists, there are further reasons why this representation of reality is not challenged. Chambers (1983) argues that for journalists the possibility of relaying misrepresented information is increased through a number of factors. Firstly, having had to persuade their editors that their proposed visit is worthwhile, they must make sure to get a story. This usually means going to an atypical place where there is either a project or a disaster. Secondly, journalists are even more pressed for time working with 'hot off the press' deadlines and exclusives than are development workers. They must find what they want quickly and write up immediately, often imposing meanings on the replies to what is asked. Checking information is difficult 'and with rural people who are unlikely to read what is written, let alone sue, the incentive to check is low. It is the one-off rushed and unconfirmed interview which appears in quotation marks in the newspaper article' (Chambers 1983, 10). In addition, while rushing may lead, as Chambers points out, to the poorest and most silent groups being overlooked, it can also result in taking on only the views of the poorest or some particular interest group. This in itself can produce a misinterpretation of social reality.

Chambers also points out that journalists frequently have to labour under the notorious difficulties and distortions of relying on interpreters, of being taken on conducted tours, and of misleading responses from those met. Local contacts tend to colour the views of their guests, and the ways in which outsiders are perceived tends to influence how reality is represented to them. As Mosse (1994) emphasises, local knowledge in development projects is shaped by the perceptions of project workers and their ambitions. There is a tendency to exaggerate problems and figures in order to shock the unsuspecting foreigner. Chambers refers to this as the 'self-sustaining myth'. He states that power relations can lead to mutual deception by 'uppers' and 'lowers'—i.e. by 'outsiders' and villagers. Inadvertent ventriloquism occurs when 'uppers' are told what 'lowers' think they want to hear. Myths presented by villagers for reasons fuelled by hope of gain, fear of penalty, or self-respect and self-identity, can be accepted and disseminated by outsiders as the reality. In the case of Silvers, his sympathy for the NGO that accompanied him in his travels, again the controversial BLLF, is apparent. Some of the most serious accusations, such as the torture rooms, are completely unsubstantiated and appear more to be the exaggerated accounts employed by NGOs and guides who wish to impress upon their foreign visitor the gravity of their own struggles.

In such cases the journalist is pre-prepared and acutely aware of what is needed to produce the required hard-hitting story. There is little time for preconceived ideas to be challenged and modified. More often than not, if you look hard enough for something, you will find it in one form or another. It is clear in Silvers' article that he is on constant 'alert' for children—and he finds them: 'I have entered a land populated and run by children... adults are in short supply' (1996).

The publishing of these articles in the Western press led to a strengthening of stereotypes and a substantiation of a representation of reality based on those stereotypes. However, it is not difficult to illustrate how tenuous that representation can be. The articles by Silvers and Schanberg highlight the pain of the children and in keeping with the Western ideal, the assumption is that children would much rather be in school than at work, and that childhood is a time of carefree abandon, a time when children should not be working but should be at school.

> Would you like to go to school?' I asked Shakeel who is eight. 'Anji', he says. But he speaks in a whisper, his head lowered, trying not to anger his boss. 'Why can't you go to school?' He does not answer. I ask him again gently, and his eyes fill with tears. He scurries back to his anvil and starts filing rapidly, turning his face away. Yes it's a different culture, but a child's pain is the same everywhere. (S. Schanberg 1996).

The implication in the above extract is that the child was being prevented from going to school because he was employed and was upset as a result. I was guilty of carrying out a similar conversation with a young girl stitcher whom I interviewed early on in my fieldwork. My intention was to try to ascertain why children stitched footballs and particularly wanted the 'voice of the informant' to elaborate on this. In the passage below, I reproduce my original field notes from that interview.

> Lubna is 13 years old and lives some 35 km from Sialkot city centre in a village called Mundey ke Beriyan. About five years ago, her father, the family's sole breadwinner, committed suicide, leaving the family of seven (Lubna's mother, her 3 sisters and 2 brothers) with no source of income.

The sisters began stitching footballs and managed to survive on the income from it. When I interviewed Lubna, she came across as a shy but bright girl. Lubna had joined the non-formal school that had recently been set up in her village. Prior to this she had never been to school. Government schools were too expensive—fees have to be paid and there is the additional cost of books, uniforms and stationery. Also school hours were long and inflexible. More importantly, Lubna had heard that the teacher was often absent and when she did come she would make the children do chores for her. The non-formal school was free and they provided books as well. You did not have to wear a uniform and the teacher was from her own village. Lubna was a good student and was happy to be at school, but it was important for her to continue stitching. When I asked Lubna why she stitched, she became abruptly quiet. I asked as quietly as Mr. Schanberg supposed he did and got a similar response.[9] Lubna began sobbing. I changed the subject and she regained her composure, but I had my answer and it troubled me. Why you stitch footballs was a sensitive question—for some more so than others. Lubna came from an extremely poor family—a family that had lost their source of stability and support. Not only was the death of her father a tragic personal loss, it was likely to consign Lubna and her family to a life of insecurity. From all that Lubna had told me, she and her sisters were able to make ends meet through the income received from football stitching. Sometimes when they did not get enough material to stitch, their neighbours would help out by sending food across. It was obvious why she stitched and yet I had wanted her to spell it out. 'You know that I am poor, you can see from my clothes and where I live and the work that I do that I am poor. Now you want me to say it to you as well?' Lubna never stated this out loud but her silence and tears betrayed her feelings.

Did the boy interviewed by Sydney Schanberg burst into tears because he was not going to school or because a foreign man, obviously from a 'different world' was quizzing him on his life, microphone and camera in hand, and with the boy's employer looking on? Did Schanberg really understand the pain of the child or was he part of that pain? Through the above example I have attempted to show how different perspectives on the part of the interviewer can lead to very dissimilar interpretations of a similar situation. As a further example of perspectives and preconceived notions colouring understanding, consider the two following passages:

Passage 1

The room was dark and airless. Such light as there was came from a single ceiling fixture, two of its four bulbs burned out. A thermometer read 105 degrees and the mud walls were hot to touch. A window promised some relief, but it was closed against fabric eating insects.

Passage 2

I jumped over open drains overflowing with human excrement. Rubbish lay strewn in haphazard heaps around a large pool of stagnant water and sewage. A few metres from this was a small compound. Inside the compound a buffalo was tethered to a peg along with its fodder. Against the metre high wall were heaps of dung left out to dry in the baking hot sun. To one side was a narrow room with a single small window. There was no ceiling fan and the single bulb was not switched on. Some 30 children sat cramped together. An ominous cane stood against the front wall. Disobedience or misbehaviour would not be tolerated. The children sat quietly in fear in the stifling heat waiting for the ordeal to finish.

Despite the similarity of the two situations, they refer to two quite distinct environments. However, the conditions in one are generally condoned, and in the other, condemned. Passage 1 is taken from Silvers' description of a carpet workshop employing children. Passage 2 is again from field notes that I took while visiting a government school in Sialkot. The experience of children in schools can be as terrifying as working as a child labourer and often worse. But it is usually taken for granted that children will be better off in school, and that they themselves would prefer to be there rather than working as stitchers or weavers. It is also unrealistic to expect that living standards, like standards of childhood, are the same across the globe. In Europe or America it would be inconceivable that people would still live in houses made of mud or that animals would share living space with humans. But in Sialkot, mud houses are environmentally friendly and cheap to build. The animals provide fresh dairy products and the dung is dried and used as a source of fuel. There may not be a toilet in the house but most people use their fields. The key point is that many Sialkotis do not perceive themselves as living in a physically oppressive or demeaning environment. Comparing culturally specific environments will always throw up the problem of what yardstick is used in the evaluating process. In this case, comparing the conditions in Sialkot to those in developed countries only encourages the formation of a misleading portrayal.

How particular representations of reality gain the currency of 'truth' in public discourse and dominate certain discourses, whilst other alternative representations are marginalized, becoming the focus of resistance to the dominant representation, stems from the dynamics of discourse and power. Claude Alvares (1992, 230) summarising Foucault's argument in the *Order of Discourse* (1971) states that knowledge is power, but that power is also knowledge. Power decides what is and what is not knowledge. From this, areas of developmental knowledge or expertise can be deconstructed as historically or politically specific constructions of reality, which are more to do with the exercise of power in particular historical contexts than presenting 'objective' realities (Gardner and Lewis 1996, 71). Unfortunately, the articles in the *Atlantic Monthly* and *Life Magazine* were widely read, particularly in the United States, and while they may have been unintentionally misleading, they led to the perpetuation and domination of a particular image of child labour in which a simple stereotype or representation tarred a complex range of activities with the same brush. Much of the foreign press picked up on this image and projected it further. The result was the dominance of a specific representation of reality and the discourse of child labour being defined by this particular representation.

As more and more of the international press picked up on stories, now coming thick and fast out of Sialkot, the reporting became more sensational and the facts more obtuse. An 'investigation' by a British weekly newspaper described children working in surgical goods factories in Sialkot as having their bodies deformed by working 13 hours a day in cramped, sweltering workshops in the 'industrial hell holes of Punjab'. Pushing the 'helpless' image of the child beyond previous limits, the report stripped the children of any dignity, reducing them physically and mentally to the level of animals, 'Their years of work have stunted their physical and mental growth and they shy away from daylight. Lack of education means that they have a vocabulary of only a few words and they respond to adults by grunting like animals.' This was what the representation of Sialkot had become.

'Perceptions are reality', Geertz stated in his book *The Interpretation of Cultures* (1973). When these perceptions are firmly held, they express and give rise to deep, powerful, comprehensive and lasting beliefs, attitudes and behaviour. In this case, the perceptions of the

Western media quickly came to define the discourse of child labour in Sialkot and therefore the 'reality' of Sialkot.

THE CONSTRUCTED REALITY — A BASIS FOR LEGITIMISING INTERVENTION

This representation of child labour in Sialkot became the foundation for prolonged investigations by NGOs, denunciations by foreign politicians and boycott threats from foreign activists. Even more damaging was that this image became the basis for international organisations, policy makers, social institutions and individuals who had been 'empowered' to intervene in the lives of children and their families, to do so on the basis of obviously unclear and arbitrary knowledge about the reality of these children's lives. As Brock et al. point out, discourses not only ascribe moral authority to particular actors, but also 'circumscribe the boundaries of action' for those actors and legitimise particular forms of intervention (Brock et al., 2001, 5-6).

The particular representation of reality, based on the emerging dominant discourse, may have formed the basis for the proposed intervention, but interventions drawn up on the basis of this constructed reality are unlikely to produce positive results. Bonded labour, referred to in the 'extreme' sense of forced labour to pay off an outstanding debt, requires that immediate action be taken to free labourers. But not all working children are unfree labourers. In fact, bonded labour constitutes only a small percentage of the work activities that children undertake. While other forms of child work may also be exploitative, remedial action based on a bonded labour scenario may well lead to further deterioration of conditions for children, as was the case in the Bangladesh garment industry example, where dismissed children undertaking relatively simple tasks were forced to work in far more hazardous conditions in the informal economy. In Bangladesh, one representation of reality, the dominant one, insisted that removing children from working in the garment industry was a step towards eradicating underdevelopment and poverty. The other representation of reality was the outcome of the child workers themselves arguing, some of them in a petition to the press, that light factory work combined with attending school for 2-3 hours a day was the best solution to their poverty (James, Jenks and Prout 1998, 111-112). But dominant discourses work by defining terms of reference and by disallowing or marginalizing others. For that reason, the reality was the launch of a campaign, followed by the project to eradicate child labour from the garment industry.

REACTION AND RESISTANCE

The reaction in Sialkot was resistance and anger at the 'imposition' of this reality, and a growing resentment against what was seen as a 'breach of sovereignty', in which developed nations had appointed themselves to police others without understanding the many complex cultural and economic issues involved (Boyden 1997, 220-221). Furthermore, it was felt that foreign interference and pressure—wielded under the guise of development involving the implementation of a programme to eradicate child labour and through the imposition of conventions and clauses that promote 'universal' norms—had led to Pakistan and Sialkot losing control over their own affairs. The backing of these 'rules and regulations', drawn up in the West and based on Western norms, and imposed by the threat of sanctions, made society in Pakistan react as if the country's sovereignty had been impinged upon. As global and local norms came into closer contact, the conflict between the two models led to a backlash against what were seen as neo-colonial methods of exerting control over developing countries.

When I arrived in the field in 1999, I was somewhat taken aback by the pervasiveness of the feeling that Pakistan was the target of a conspiracy. From academics to government officials to the man on the street and the woman in her home—they all saw Pakistan as being on the receiving end of a calculated plan to destroy the country's economy and to make it completely dependent on aid hand-outs from the West. This could be described as an example of a marginalized counter-representation, serving as a source of resistance to the dominant discourse. While this counter representation may not yet be considered a fully-fledged rival discourse, these strands of opposition to Western norms and values are attaching themselves to more powerful strategies of resistance that have crystallised in an anti-Western discourse, which is increasingly manifesting itself in the form described as 'Islamic fundamentalism'. Escobar (1995, 217) in fact predicts that the failure of the Western development discourse may lead to a re-emergence of new fundamentalisms as competing discourses.

It was for this reason that the child labour issue was often seen as part of an Indian-Jewish conspiracy. It was for this reason that Ehsanullah Khan was branded a traitor to the country and it was for this reason that Western reporting was seen as anti-Pakistan. Even Najmuddin Najmi, who had spoken so eloquently and honestly about the failure of society and the government to tackle the issue of child labour in Pakistan, insisted that the Western world was bent upon showing that Pakistan was a failed state:

> Pakistan is singled out in its dealings with the international community, and issues like religious fundamentalism and child labour are exploited. The idea is to undermine, blackmail and weaken Pakistan. During the Cold War, we were a key ally of the West. They gave us arms and funding. Now the cold war is over and we are no longer needed.

The most vocal informants were Sialkot's industrialists. Many pointed to clear evidence of victimisation. Pakistan's market share in the football trade dropped from 93 per cent to 73 per cent between 1996 and 2000. In the United States, the decline was more rapid—from 65 per cent in 1997 to 45 per cent in 1998—possibly implying the greater affect of adverse publicity in the United States.[10] Though they were willing to do whatever the West required in order to survive, manufacturers chafed at what they saw as foreign standards imposed on them by outsiders ignorant of Pakistani realities. The following was stated by Ali Shabbir, one of the new generation of Sialkot's industrialists. His grandfather established a sports goods factory in Sialkot soon after Independence in 1947. Since then the original factory has spawned two further factories, each run by a grandson of the founder.

> The West has huge double standards. All these programmes for children, it is all one big tamasha [performance]. They have managed to develop their own nations, but when it comes to us, they want to keep us in chains. The U.S. is a nation with a history of genocide and slavery and they suddenly feel sympathy with the children of Pakistan. Now they are the champions of peoples' rights. But when I ask my buyers to make concessions over the rates they will pay, they refuse.
>
>   You know when I went to Dubai, a friend took me to the races. There they had camel racing where all the jockeys are children often kidnapped from Pakistan and Bangladesh. As the camel starts to run, the terrified screams of the child make the camel run faster and faster. You know nearly

everyone in the audience was a foreigner or an Arab. They never say anything then, do they? Why don't they pressurise the Arabs? Instead, they focus on Sialkot and its footballs. Even in football stitching, the international community is able to pressurise Pakistan, but they can never bring the same pressure to bear on China or India. See, in India they have more child labourers than Pakistan, but they have not allowed any outsiders to monitor their factories. In China, they have been making footballs with child labour and prison labour. But they don't let anyone enter their factories. They say give us the order and we will give you the goods. Don't ask questions. The U.S. just wants increased trade with India and China. That is why they are trying to destroy our industries. Nowadays, warfare is not a matter of guns and tanks. It is fought through winning markets. Our competitors have played up this whole child labour issue. India is competing with us in the sports industry and they have a very strong media. So they spread stories about abuses in Sialkot. Now we are under the microscope and have a programme against child labour in place. The media campaign has succeeded in raising our prices and subsequently India and China have both increased their market shares.

Several industrialists questioned the ban on children stitching footballs at home while children in the United States delivered newspapers or worked in supermarkets or restaurants on a part-time basis. They saw little difference between the two situations. Many industrialists specifically drew my attention to reports of child labour abuses in the West. Two photocopies of reports were thrust into my hands by Khwaja Zakaullah. One stated that 5,000 child labour grievances a year were filed with the U.S. Department of Labour. The second press release stated the findings of a British based research group that had found 'almost Dickensian conditions in which two million school-age children had some form of part-time job and in some cases worked up to 29 hours a week for 33 pence a day' (*Dawn*, 12 February 1998). The report further found that 25 per cene of working children were under the legal age of 13. 'The West can't look after their own children but they still find time to worry about ours,' Zakaullah commented sarcastically. There was a definite view that the football sector had been unfairly targeted—primarily through biased media reporting, and then from the threatened sanctions and remedial programmes that were the outcome of the campaign centred around the media drive.

While the views of the stitchers and their children form the focus of the entire study, (and will be covered in detail in subsequent chapters), I was struck by the degree to which football stitchers, particularly in the less remote regions of Sialkot district, were aware of the complex intrigues that lay behind the child labour issue. As many as one in four felt that the media's description of child labour in the international press had caused a decline in orders. Many complained of an unfair targeting of Sialkot's world-class industries, pointing out that no remedial measures had been instituted against India, for example. Outsiders were jealous of the fame and skill of Sialkot. The fact that Sialkotis had a strong sense of 'owning' football stitching as an exclusively Sialkoti skill deepened the feeling that Sialkot was being targeted. There was anger at being prevented from earning a livelihood and bewilderment at the severity of the response against children stitching footballs. Nazir Ahmed, a middle-aged football stitcher who had been stitching for almost two decades, echoed the opinion of the majority of football stitchers that I met in Sialkot, when he angrily complained about the project to remove children from the stitching labour force:

> They want to destroy our skill. For generations we have produced sports equipment here. Sialkot's footballs are famous the world over. If our children do not learn, our skill will die. Football stitching allowed us to gain an extra income. We were able to improve our standard of living. Now not only children, but also their parents are being denied the chance to earn a livelihood.

The response was similar across the 'stitcher spectrum'. Women and even child stitchers resented the enforced reduction in their choices. When I asked Nazir's fourteen-year-old son, Omar, why he thought the campaign against football stitching was being implemented in Sialkot, his answer was direct and highlights the gap between two increasingly divergent realities.

> We used to be able to stitch footballs when we needed to. Now there are no footballs coming to the homes for stitching. Why have they stopped our rozi-roti [means of living]? I don't know. They must hate us. We are poor and not well educated. Maybe it is because we are Muslims and people in the West are against Muslims. That is why they don't want Sialkot's name to be at the top.

CHANGING REALITIES

The first signs that the now entrenched dominant discourse and representation of child labour in Sialkot was beginning to change significantly came about four months *after* the project to eliminate child labour from the football manufacturing industry was drawn up and instituted. Save the Children's[11] baseline study for the project, *The Voices of Children* (1997), clarified a number of misconceptions that apparently had been perpetuated by what David Husselbee, the head of Save the Children's Sialkot programme, described as 'shoddy and exaggerated reporting'. (Crawford, 1999).

For the first time, a detailed, Sialkot football industry specific survey had been undertaken. The findings openly contradicted earlier assumptions. For example, bonded child labourers exist in parts of Pakistan but there was no evidence of them in the football industry. Child labour may prevent children from attending school but again this was not necessarily the case in Sialkot. The Save the Children (SCF) report found that children often stitched on a part time basis to pay for school fees. Working conditions in many industries were hazardous, but in Sialkot's football industry children overwhelmingly worked at home under parental supervision. Weaving carpets, working in the surgical goods manufacturing sector or in brick kilns poses a serious threat to the health of children. The SCF report found football stitching not to be a hazardous profession. Early accounts of child labour in Pakistan had taken little account of the fact that the category of working children covers a spectrum that differs substantially in working conditions, poverty levels and types of work undertaken. Lumping all types of child work under the generic media stereotype created a particular representation of reality. But while the findings may have led to a reappraisal of the child labour discourse in Sialkot, there was no change in the way that the project, planned on the basis of earlier information, was designed or implemented. The reasons for this are looked at in chapter 5 of the study.

Later journalists also found little evidence of the intimidatory thugs or torture chambers so vividly described in earlier accounts of Sialkot's industries. When I interviewed Dr Robert Crawford, who had undertaken a case study on Sialkot's sports industry for the French Business School, INSEAD he related how articles like those written by Silvers and Schanberg had made him extremely apprehensive of travelling to Sialkot. Prepared for being assailed by gangs of ruffians he was instead pleasantly surprised. 'Rather than the violent, closed and grim situation that I had feared, I found Sialkot to be a place full of hope and energy.' This was a far cry from the Sialkot of Silvers or Schanberg. Similarly, Michael Sheridan, a photographer and filmmaker who made a documentary on the views of working children in Sialkot, wrote in his diary:

> When I was first asked to make a documentary about children stitching footballs in Sialkot, Pakistan, I conjured up the image most of us have when we hear the words 'child labour'. I saw young children working long painful hours in dark, dirty conditions. I thought of evil and greedy manufacturers, corrupt government officials, and multinationals making an easy buck. My night of reading has opened my eyes to the complexities of the problem. As I've learned repeatedly in ten years of humanitarian work, the problems faced by the poor and hungry are not usually as easy to understand as we think. (Taken from Michael Sheridan's Video Diary, Save the Children Website, www.savethechildren.org.uk).

Khwaja Zakaullah of Capitol Sports acknowledges the debt that Sialkot's sports manufacturers owed to SCF, whom they saw as providing an impartial account of the situation on the ground. However, he chafed at the fact that, particularly in the United States, 'misinformation' continued to dictate policy. 'During one meeting with a group of Congressmen, I was constantly interrogated about child stitchers as young as three years. Anyone who knows anything about football stitching will know that this is absolutely not physically possible' Zakaullah told me.

The issue returns to Hajer's (1995, 59) concept of discursive hegemony where representations of reality conflict with one another in an attempt to impose a particular definition of reality. Alternatively, we can employ Hobart's (1993,12) view of coexistent discourses, wherein the conflict between the 'representations of reality' can be seen as the struggle between what Hobart refers to as the professional, local and national discourses of development. In the examination of child labour in Pakistan and Sialkot the corresponding categories would be the Western discourse on child labour (professional), the Sialkoti (local) discourse and the Pakistan Government (national) discourse. All three discourses have been examined in these first two chapters and the local discourse, in particular, will be looked at in greater detail in the following chapters. However, in order to understand which discourse or representation of reality becomes dominant we again turn to

Foucault. In his analysis of power and knowledge, Foucault (1971) concluded that it was power rather than truth that defined knowledge. Similarly, Hall (1992, 295) points out that those who produced the discourses also had the power to make them true. The latest re-definition of the reality of working children in Sialkot took place at the 1999 annual ILO Conference during which President Clinton made the observation that has been used as a quote at the start of chapter 1:

> Today the work has been taken up by women in 80 poor villages in Pakistan, giving them new employment and their families new stabilities. Meanwhile, their children have started to go to school, so that when they come of age, they will be able to do better jobs raising the standards of living of their families, their villages and their nation. I thank all who were involved in this endeavour and ask others to follow in their lead. (ILO Conference, June 18 1999).

In a matter of minutes Bill Clinton had again changed the reality of child labour in Sialkot's football industry in the public discourse. But as Mitchell (1988) has shown in his deconstruction of development in Egypt, often the very reality that is constructed and then reconstructed is misleading, and the discourses, assumptions and figures on which it is based can be examined and re-interpreted to reveal a very different picture. The language of underdevelopment, of chaos, crisis, and backward indigenous customs creates an urgent need for intervention and management.[12] Silvers' quote, with which chapter 1 begins, represents the construction that necessitates intervention. Once this intervention is implemented, as in Sialkot, the object becomes one of managing the rehabilitation. This is exemplified by the reality of child labour in the football manufacturing industry of Sialkot, followed by the intervention, and then the road to prosperity and recovery, as highlighted by the Clinton quote. The pendulum swings from media reports of torture chambers and bonded labour to women's employment and school-going children. This reaffirms the success of development and our faith in it as the primary path to progress. But in both cases, the supposed beneficiaries have come under increased pressure. When child labour was reported as rife, journalists searched for stories that provided a particular representation of working children based on predominant stereotypes and Western values. Now another representation of child labour has constructed a reality where children are no longer stitching. Dominant interests decide which of the two discourses are seen as 'true'. In the midst of the struggle between the discourses are the experiences of those who inhabit these realities in this case the child stitchers and their families. Invariably, this group is the one without the power to define their own reality in the public discourse, and this inability to make their voices heard lies at the heart of how the programme to remove children from the football industry's labour force has affected them. As Mitchell concludes, the solutions that follow are not just technological and managerial, but social and political (Mitchell 1995, 130). Hence the subsuming of one reality by another. As a result, the supposed beneficiaries of 'development' become the objects for the application of power rather than the subjects experiencing and responding to the exercise of that power. That, then, takes us back to the start of chapter 1—development's power to transform old worlds and to imagine new ones.

NOTES

1. The Employment of Children Act in 1991—the first child labour related law to be passed since 1969, followed by the Bonded Labour Abolition Act of 1992 (Anees Jillani, 1997).
2. The 1992 Child Labour Deterrence Act was popularly known as the Harkin Bill after the proposing US Senator, Tom Harkin.
3. UNICEF (1997).
4. Figures from Government of Pakistan, 1996.
5. Local term for sub-contractor.
6. The term *peshgi* refers to an advance of money and the *peshgi* system therefore implies a bonded labour system.
7. Current exchange rate: £1 = Pakistan Rs. 90.
8. See for example Fyfe (1989), Morrow (1992), Dorman (2001).
9. This sentence was not part of the original field notes.
10. Figures from E. Cummins (2000).
11. Save the Children Fund (SCF) is an international NGO working with football stitchers in Sialkot. They were closely involved in the Sialkot football-stitching project.
12. Hobart (1993, 2) refers to this process as being 'agentive'—i.e. depicting a state of affairs that requires action or intervention of some kind.

3

POWER AND AUTHORITY IN THE FIELD

SIALKOT BOUND—INTRODUCING THE FIELD SITE

Having spent the best part of a month in the capital city of Islamabad organising my stay in the field, I was ready to proceed to the fieldwork site. Located in the north-east of Pakistan's most populous province, Punjab, Sialkot is approximately 220 km from Islamabad. The drive was estimated at between four and six hours depending on traffic. My intention was to get there before sunset, so I departed in the early morning. Driving becomes considerably more difficult as dusk falls. To compound the difficulties, not only had I never been to Sialkot, but a pit stop at a mechanic's on the way extended to almost six hours, and it was not until 4 p.m. that I was able to resume my journey.

Sialkot is not situated directly adjacent to the new 8-lane motorway that connects Islamabad and the provincial capital, Lahore. Instead, one has to drive along the famous Grand Trunk (GT) Road described by Kipling in his book *Kim* as being 'such a river of life as exists nowhere else in the world'. A less romanticised account is given by Sir Malcolm Darling, a senior British officer in the Indian Civil Service: 'The road was pleasanter in the days of Kim, and though untarred, it could not have been dustier, for as lorry met lorry, both were forced onto the nearby earthy tracks on either side and the air became thick as London fog' (Darling 1934, 72).

The road is now tarred, but apart from a massive increase in traffic not much else has changed, including the dustiness and the habit of larger vehicles forcing others off the road. Within an hour of leaving Islamabad, I had passed the town of Gujar Khan, from where I was to learn later that a *biraderi* (patrilineage) of *lohars* (blacksmiths) had migrated to Sialkot over a hundred years ago. They settled in Sialkot in a village called Kotli Loharan (literally 'abode of the blacksmiths', no.56)[1] [see map of Sialkot] and distinguished themselves during British times for the excellence of their damascened work. Later their skill formed the basis of Sialkot's surgical manufacturing goods industry and spread to a number of other villages, which again took the inspiration for their names from the occupation of their inhabitants, notably Talwaran Mughlan (Sword of the Mughals, no. 15) [see map of Sialkot] and Talwaran Rajputan (Sword of the Rajputs, no. 89). Towns either side of the GT road have grown rapidly due to their [see map of Sialkot] proximity to the main commercial transport artery. On entering a new town, the road on either side becomes surrounded by colourful local bazaars selling fruits, vegetables, chickens, meat and locally made handicrafts. Roadside restaurants known as *khokhas*, particularly popular with truckers, sell a variety of freshly made dishes, usually a *daal* (lentils), a couple of vegetarian dishes and a meat dish. To complete the menu, there is the excessively sweet, milky tea. In winter, trade is further bolstered by the sale of hot *samosas* and *gajar ka halva* (a dessert made of carrots and cream). In summer locally made ice-cream called *kulfi* makes a welcome appearance.

The villages dotted round the town of Gujar Khan form the rural hinterland of the district. Many villagers work in the town but prefer to live in their villages, commuting into town every morning. There is a reluctance to move from ancestral family lands, which are seen as providing men with their identity. For women, because marriage is patrilocal, the attachment to land is not as strong. But the 'roots of men' should not be severed from the land from where they came. Even those who migrate tend to return to their ancestral villages or, in the event of those migrating to countries as far as the United Kingdom, at least maintain the 'myth of return'.

As a result, all those who have land tend to retain small agricultural fields in the villages. Wage work in the urban areas complements any income received from agricultural work. Punjabis, of all the ethnic groups in Pakistan, are said to show the closest attachment to their *zameen* (land). A history of settlement in this fertile land has led to this long standing relationship, so much so that the land is often seen and referred to as '*maa*', the 'mother'. If the Pathan from the Frontier province is seen as the indomitable warrior, the *Muhajir* as the urbane professional, the overwhelming image of the Punjabi is that of the 'son of the soil'.

The pattern of concentrated urban commercial activity around the main road with the more rural, residential base at a distance surrounding the urban core is repeated for other towns along the GT road. Apart from the bazaars lining the roadside, the most common sights are the numerous automobile workshops catering to the many breakdowns that occur on the road. Almost all the mechanics are taught entirely 'on the job', many having learned their skill as part of an apprenticeship that sees boys starting work from as early an age as eight. At that point the boys, known as *shagirds* (apprentices) usually carry out simple chores, filling tyres with air, fetching tea for the *ustaad* (expert) and cleaning the cars once they have been repaired. Apart from lunch, the 'apprentices' will rarely receive any further benefits and will unlikely be paid more than Rs. 20 to Rs. 30 per day (£0.20-0.30). In time, the young worker will increasingly be given more complex tasks to tackle. Two to three years into his training the apprentice will start earning a monthly salary and his aim, like those before him, will be to reach the rank of master mechanic. The cycle then repeats itself with a new generation of *ustaads* and *shagirds*.

For many parents and their children this may not represent an ideal career, but it allows the children the 'luxury' of two meals a day, and in a country where schools have failed to attract or retain large numbers of students, it is often viewed as the best alternative. This 'traditional' form of 'education', or socialisation as anthropologists have termed it, involves learning by 'observing' and 'doing'. Football stitching follows a similar pattern, as will be examined in subsequent chapters. While I was not entering what Silvers had described as a land populated and run by children, it was a land where children participated more openly in the sphere of work, rather than being excluded from the work place as in the West.

Summer had not yet come to an end but the sun was beginning to set earlier, so that by dusk I was only half-way to Sialkot, having passed through the towns of Jhelum, Lala Musa and Kharian. Jhelum is famous for being the place where Alexander the Great defeated Porus. Later Jhelum, like Kharian, became a British cantonment town and still retains its old military character with army academies, barracks, life-sized model tanks and other armaments, all part of the town's monuments. Lala Musa has the slightly less flattering distinction of being the centre of 'fake' merchandise, toys, batteries and electrical items are all made in Lala Musa but with a bit of imagination in the labelling process they are effectively made in the USA. I had heard stories of how manufacturers in Lala Musa label their goods '*made in lalamUSA*—the lalam written in very small print and the USA in bold.

I admit to not believing these accounts until I purchased a set of batteries at the town to see for myself. They were 'Made in Ialam USA'. After a short break for tea, I was off again, my speed slowing considerably as night fell.

PUNJAB'S INDUSTRIAL BELT

Leaving Kharian behind and passing through numerous smaller towns, I entered the city of Gujrat, one of the main industrial cities in Punjab's north-eastern industrial belt. Gujrat has made a reputation for itself as a producer of furniture and electric fans, both the ceiling and tabletop variety. Crossing over the river Chenab, one of the five rivers that run through the Punjab,[2] the GT road carries on towards Gujranwala and on to the provincial capital, Lahore, which, with a population of five million, is Pakistan's second largest city and its cultural and historical centre. Gujranwala borders Sialkot district on the west and south-west and has become the hub of industrial activity in ceramics, iron safes and copper, brass and aluminium utensils.

Both Gujrat and Gujranwala, unlike Sialkot, have developed medium and large-scale industry. Sialkot's industry has remained focussed on small-scale industrial units based almost entirely on local Sialkoti entrepreneurs who emerged from the ranks of the artisans to become the industrialists of today.[3] In contrast, Punjab's other industrial areas had their economic development fuelled by Muslim industrialists who migrated from India at Partition. Very few settled in Sialkot,[4] the primary reason being the district's proximity to the disputed border with India. A second reason given is that Lahore, Gujranwala and Faisalabad, Punjab's other large industrial centres, had already developed their small and medium scale industry and this provided entrepreneurs more opportunities to start up economic activity. In addition, migrating entrepreneurs were usually 'compensated' for loss of livelihood resulting from migration by being given businesses left behind by Sikhs and Hindus who moved to India. Sialkot, in contrast, was the centre of a cottage industry, and this meant fewer opportunities for outsiders, for despite the departure of the Sikh and Hindu entrepreneurial class, the majority of workers remained behind, continuing to work at home or in small groups. As a result there were not many 'establishments' that remained unoccupied.

The minimal change in the composition of Sialkot's population meant that industry continued to be based on the indigenous artisan class. This was a unique feature of industry in Sialkot and it led to a strong feeling of local ownership of those industries and skills associated with them. The ingenuity of the Sialkoti craftsmen, their mastery of specialist skills and their spirit of enterprise is deeply ingrained in the minds of Sialkotis and is reflected in the many tales of the 'legendary' craftsmen of Sialkot. For example, it was a common retort by respondents during my field interviews that all the cutlery and surgical goods made in Sialkot had 'made in England' stamped on them but were in fact crafted by Sialkot's blacksmiths. I was told (On more than one occasion) the legend of the worker from Kotli Loharan who built a steam engine on his own, only to have his hands cut off by the British for fear that their own industry could face competition from the extraordinarily skilled blacksmiths of Kotli Loharan. There are also many stories of the legendary *mochi* (cobbler) who when asked to repair a football by an English priest, not only repaired it but also made several new ones from leather left over from his work with leather saddles. The sports industry in Sialkot is said to have its genesis here. The skill of the Sialkoti craftsmen has become part of the folklore surrounding the success of the industry in Sialkot indicating the importance of the historical dimension of craftsmanship in Sialkot.

To reach Sialkot, one must part company with the GT road having crossed the River Chenab. A smaller road veers off the Gujranwala-bound GT road towards Wazirabad and finally Sialkot. Wazirabad itself has a long history in medium and small-scale manufacturing producing quality cutlery and crockery.

The forty-five kilometres to Sialkot city, via Wazirabad, takes another hour. The 'detour' represents an important turn. Northern Punjab's industrial belt consisting of Gujarat, Gujranwala and Lahore, are all serviced by the GT road, and their location along this main artery is an important advantage that Sialkot lacks. Furthermore, there is no airport in this export oriented industrial cluster. However, an airport funded by Sialkot's business community is under construction. Again the proximity to the Indian border is a factor. The plains of Sialkot slope down from the uplands of the Himalayas, and its north-eastern border is shared with the disputed territory of Kashmir. On a clear day one can see the Himalayan peaks and the Indian military watchtowers on them. In the 1965 war, the village of Chawinda (No.115) in Sialkot was apparently the site for the largest tank battle since the Second World War. As the Indian army advanced into the district they were held back by Pakistani soldiers allegedly tying bombs to themselves and crawling under Indian tanks. Even today the villages along the border are prone to shelling as Indian and Pakistani troops exchange fire. As a consequence of its sensitive location there has been little government investment or support, making the success of its industry all the more celebrated.

SIALKOT

There was considerably less traffic on the Wazirabad-Sialkot road but the road's condition had deteriorated alarmingly from the chaotic but relatively well-maintained GT road. Darkness had fallen by the time I passed a police checkpoint sign that signalled entry into Sialkot district. It did not need to—every 100 meters or so there were signs pointing off the road towards 'Stitching Centres'. The influence of football stitching was immediately evident. Starting in the 1970s Sialkot had risen to become the hub of the world's football manufacturing industry by the early 1990s, producing three out of four footballs manufactured worldwide. Fifteen kilometres further on I read a signboard for Sambrial Dry Port. This is the depot from where all Sialkot's manufactures are exported. At the dry port, five or six massive trucks marked SDPT (Sialkot Dry Port Trust) were parked at the roadside. On one side a building marked Duty Free Shop was visible. On the opposite side lay the port itself. From the little I could see through the locked gates, crates of packed material stood ready for onward loading.

Sambrial (no. 51) falls in the Daska *tehsil*[5] of Sialkot district. There are two further *tehsil*s making up the district, Sialkot *tehsil* and Pasrur *tehsil*. Sialkot *tehsil* (population 1.2 million) is the most populous and urbanised, followed by Daska (population 860,611), and Pasrur (population 611, 871). Taken together the district's population stands at just over 2.7 million.[6] Daska's larger towns, like Sambrial and Begowala Jhamut (no. 54) are situated along the main road which continues on to Sialkot city (See Map of Sialkot). The surrounding villages in the *tehsil* are connected to this main road via un-metalled tracks. These approach roads often become impassable during the monsoon season (July–September), making contact with the villages difficult. The agricultural lands of Daska are amongst the most fertile of the region, and the installation of tube wells to exploit the sub-soil water led not only to increases in the production of seasonal crops, but also to the start of a cottage industry in the manufacture of diesel engines and accessories. Sialkot district, along with its tradition in cottage industries, is also renowned for the production of the famed *basmati* variety of rice.

Leaving Sambrial I was suddenly struck by a foul, acrid smell. My headlights caught pools of fluorescent red liquid on either side of the road. In the background was what looked like a large factory. On closer inspection it turned out to be a leather manufacturing plant. Sialkot has a long history in making leather products starting with saddles made in colonial times. Recently, the industry has grown rapidly and manufactured items include sports goods, leather jackets, gloves and motorcycle apparel. But the enlargement in production has meant a consequent increase in the toxic waste produced during the tanning process. Recent studies on leather tanning factories in another part of Punjab (Kasur) have revealed high levels of cancer and Hepatitis B amongst workers and local inhabitants. I was later informed that Sialkot was suffering similarly and that a recent United Nations report had stated that within five years every person in Sialkot city would be affected by waste from the tanneries. There is a plan to move the tanneries away from the city to a separate site where a proper filtration and waste unit can be set up but until that is implemented tannery waste is a serious concern.

Sialkot city is barely five kilometres from this spot, but luckily the toxic smell was no longer evident. On entering Sialkot city, there were some signs of lighting and life. One major road, which appeared to pass through the heart of the city, was being re-laid. The drive to Sialkot after the turn-off from the GT road had been dark and isolated throughout. Most villages were at some distance from the road and small towns like Sambrial had long since closed up for the night. Sialkot city was still awake at 10 p.m. A few tea stalls and roadside restaurants were serving people, but I had been told that Sialkot was a city that worked hard during the day and closed up soon after nightfall. Much of this was a reflection of the fact that many of the labourers working in the city come from the surrounding villages, swelling the city's population of 400,000 to considerably more during the day. Having commuted early in the morning, most workers return home at the end of the day.

Coming into Sialkot may be time-consuming and relatively expensive in terms of daily transport costs but the city provides a wider range of employment than the rural areas, particularly in times when rice and wheat crops are not being sown. Living in the city, though, is more expensive than in the villages where food and accommodation in particular are cheaper. There is also the desire to own and maintain the family land.

Eventually I stumbled onto the field residence of the NGO with whom I had arranged accommodation in Sialkot. The city is the birthplace of two of Pakistan's most famous poets, the revolutionary Faiz Ahmed Faiz and the Cambridge-educated philosopher-poet, Muhammad Iqbal, who in 1930 envisioned the concept of Pakistan as a separate nation state for the Muslims of the subcontinent. Today, Iqbal's old house, located in the bustling centre of Sialkot city, has been transformed into a modest museum and library. In the following days, the curator at *Iqbal Manzil*, Rana Naeem would hold me enthralled, relating tales of the early history of Sialkot. Over a succession of lunches, usually consisting of *pullao* (rice and meat) brought from a nearby restaurant, Naeem would pull out books, documents and gazetteers to help piece together a picture of early Sialkot.

[I] [learned that] Sialkot is an ancient city and district. There have been people settled here for centuries—and there were, till Independence, many religions represented here. The Sikhs have always seen Sialkot as a holy place and every year they come from across the world to pay homage at the temple of Guru Baba Nanek—the founder of their religion. There are also several shrines of Sufis (Muslim Saints), the [best] known being the mosque and shrine of Imam Sahib. It is one of the oldest strongholds of the Muslim religion and is held in great reverence throughout Punjab. But the earliest accounts of Sialkot appear in the ancient Hindu religious epics, the Mahabharat and the Ramayana, during which the city is described as flourishing until floods left the entire area under water and uninhabited for a thousand years. Sialkot was re-discovered by the Hindu warrior tribe, the Kshatriya, and rose to become their political and military, centre until Alexander the Great laid siege to it and subsequently razed it to the ground.[7] After that, the city's next resurgence came under the Mauryan Emperor, Ashoka,[8] during whose reign the city became a centre of Buddhist learning. Following further upheavals and invasions, notably by the Huns and the Central Asian invader, Mahmud Ghaznavi, Sialkot's fortunes continued to ebb and flow, until the onset of the Mughal Empire.[9] The stability that followed allowed the city to rebuild. Then Sialkot started becoming a famous industrial centre.

Rana Naeem talked endlessly, thrilled at having found someone interested in his 'home town', and whom he could impress with his knowledge. As he appeared to have few occasions to flaunt his expertise he ensured that my lunches with him lasted late into the afternoons. He somewhat reluctantly photocopied material for me, provided me with several important contacts in Sialkot and invited me back on numerous occasions. I found later that his reluctance to photocopy material was based on the fact that most of his 'inside' accounts of Sialkot were gleaned from the material he photocopied for me. Nevertheless, it did mean that 'his' information was generally backed up by historical accounts of the region.[10]

Back in my bedroom, as I stared out of my curtainless window, the monsoon air was still warm and moist, but a ceiling fan made it less oppressive. In winter it would get much colder, dropping to almost freezing in a few months, and there would be the thick fog that envelopes this part of Punjab for two to three weeks. Just outside the house I could see the local railway station. Every morning a crowded train would stop here bringing daily-wage commuters to the numerous industrial workshops that have been part of Sialkot's history for so long, and which are still dotted around the city today. I would find that Sialkot city was the focal point of the football industry but the industry's structure had meant that the work areas had pushed their way 'out' into the surrounding villages. Unlike the commuters streaming into Sialkot city, my fieldwork would take me in the opposite direction—to the outlying villages that provide the labour for football stitching.

FIELDWORK

As well as introducing the field site, the current chapter deals with how fieldwork was undertaken, and how the background and structure of organisations involved in the project to eradicate child labour from the football stitching industry influenced the nature of the information they gathered.

BUNYAD

Apart from the personal desire to analyse child labour per se, one of the reasons for choosing the particular field site was the extensive personal contacts that I could build upon in Sialkot—from industrialists to football stitchers. This becomes all the more important when keeping in mind that the sensitive nature of child labour makes eliciting information on the topic particularly problematic without an entry point. This crucial entry point for me was Bunyad, the organisation most closely involved at the 'grassroots' with football stitchers.

My association with Bunyad and its field councillors was invaluable, both in the initial entry into the villages where I undertook fieldwork, and subsequently, when I would search for more of the 'insider' accounts from informants. Effectively, my new 'colleagues' at Bunyad became research assistants, and rapidly familiarised me with Sialkot through providing vital contextual information about the villages, local culture and subtleties of language. Furthermore, they acted as 'ambassadors at large, introducing fieldworkers to the local community and discreetly explaining the presence to people who might be too shy or suspicious to ask directly' (Devereux and Hoddinott 1992, 26).

Thus the association with Bunyad literally opened up the field for me, not only in terms of football stitchers, but also in terms of examining the development organisations involved in the wider process. Without this backing, I doubt if I would have been able to get access to, for example, Qayyum, the owner of the independent home factory, or to Iftikhar Shah, the contractor responsible for keeping strangers like myself out of the stitching centre of which he was in charge. I also doubt that I would have received the same cooperation from the adult stitchers who became my informants, or the football manufacturers I interviewed.

Within my first week in the field, I realised that one of my most basic assumptions concerning fieldwork methodology needed to be adjusted. Sialkot city would not be the focus of my activities. The football industry was based in the city, but by the 1970s had decentralised to the surrounding villages. A further realisation hit me, when I spent an hour on the back of a motorbike travelling to one of the most far-flung villages in the district. Sialkot district measures 3,016 square kilometres and some villages lie more than 35 km from the city centre and are accessible only by motorbike. This research was not going to follow traditional South Asian village anthropology that used intensive village- based studies as their focus.[11] Instead, I travelled from one end of the district to the other. My 'research community' was bound only by the proviso that there were children stitching footballs in a particular place, thereby making the fieldwork *process*-based rather than *place*-based. The process in this case was stitching footballs, and it was Sialkoti stitching rather than a particular location that formed the unit of my analysis.

As football stitching had spread to include almost all of Sialkot's approximately 1500 villages, I decided to concentrate on those villages where Bunyad had identified concentrations of stitchers, and had accordingly established non-formal schools, as my focal locations. These villages were spread evenly through Sialkot's three *tehsils* — Pasrur, Daska and Sialkot. In the course of fieldwork I also managed to visit a number of villages where schools had not been established. This provided additional and often contrasting information to that gathered from the sample villages. However, the majority of the information gathering was focused in villages where existing contacts had been built up primarily through the NGOs that were involved with setting up of schools. From the core group of child stitchers placed in the non-formal schools, I traced linkages to their parents, as well as looser ties to other members of the village. The schools also provided links to children who had dropped out. This was an important group, as some children had found alternate work, and interviewing them provided vital information on the decision-making process of those children who chose to work rather than stay in school. Once respondents were identified and entry gained, the effort became one of gathering information from children and parents, as well as those more directly involved in the business side of the industry, primarily the sub-contractors and industrialists.

My 'acceptance' by villagers, assisted greatly by my association with a familiar local institution involved in football stitching, was also aided by the fact that I was to spend a year doing fieldwork. Many of my informants, starting with my four 'research assistants' from Bunyad, seemed almost flattered that I was spending a year in Sialkot, away from the 'luxuries' of England, in order to learn about their project and way of life. Secondly, my (not pre-meditated) strategy of, to use Spradley's term, 'maintaining naiveté' — the skill of being a novice — was also useful. In this I was perhaps helped, like Gans, by 'what seems to be an honest face, a visible earnestness about wanting to do research, and a quiet demeanour that perhaps tells people that I will not be a threat to them' (Gans 1982, 57). In the environment of mistrust that was prevalent in Sialkot at the time of my undertaking fieldwork and with the sole purpose of apparently discovering the hidden principles of another way of life (Spradley 1979, 4), the role of novice assisted in reducing the 'threat' factor and facilitated frank discussions with informants.

Therefore, one of the key components of my fieldwork strategy revolved around stating clearly my need to understand, from the point of view of the football stitchers, what they felt about the external imposition of a programme that directly targeted their way of life. I felt this was the best approach to encourage respondents, to see this as an opportunity for them to talk and for me to listen and learn. Often this meant spending hours being 'held hostage', as in the case of Rana Naeem, giving an informant the chance to express his views on a range of subjects. Admittedly, there were occasions where we talked more about Shahid Afridi's batting and less on the effects of the decline in football stitching work. But on other occasions I was told about the continued involvement of children in the industry, despite the programme. This series of unstructured interviews, described by Spradley (1979) as a series of friendly conversations into which the researcher slowly introduces new elements to assist informants to respond as informants, became an invaluable source of field data.

Thus, the specific environment of mistrust in Sialkot, largely influenced by the events discussed in the previous two chapters, meant that my methodology was adjusted to ensure that engendering trust was the foundation of any information. However, this proviso did impose certain restrictions on fieldwork.

At the outset, the fact that I was dealing with a large and dispersed population meant that trust-building had to be negotiated on an almost daily basis. Furthermore, and related to research ethics, throughout the fieldwork I felt the intrusiveness of anthropological examination weighing heavily on my mind. Encroaching on another's way of life involves the encroached giving up part of their space and risking losing control of how they are represented. I was acutely aware that in Sialkot, informants went out of their way to volunteer information to me. Some of this information was sensitive and divulging it may have had repercussions for them. In addition, I had little or nothing to offer them in return. In this situation I decided that, even as a token gesture towards the integrity of the researcher-informant relationship, I would abandon all use of cameras and dictaphones. This had a beneficial effect on my interviews, in that informants felt more comfortable without the intrusiveness of cameras or tape recorders. Moreover, the awkwardness of asking for a photograph, or if a conversation could be taped, was then avoided. This was important not so much because of my discomfort at asking for photographs or taping conversations, but because I felt that having volunteered so much information already, asking for more in the form of photographs or taped conversations would be going beyond my own limits as a researcher. Yet, on the few early occasions that I did ask whether I could take a photograph, there were no refusals, only a slight hesitation. Nevertheless, I felt that this was overly exploitative of my informants and would have a negative impact on the quality of information volunteered. In fact, in an effort to promote as relaxed an atmosphere as possible during interviews, I also abandoned the use of note-taking during informal conversations with informants. Instead, I would write up the conversations upon on the returning to my room following a day in the field.

Some of the effects of the constraints imposed by my chosen methodology can be seen in the thesis. For example, there are few substantial, direct quotations from informants, mainly because I had no recorded interviews. Nevertheless, I believe that the 'compromise' in one area impacted positively on the research as a whole.

It is also worth pointing out that interviewing children requires different approaches to those involving adults. However, while I had undertaken some pre-fieldwork research on methodologies for interviewing children (James and Prout, 1998, James, Jenks and Prout, 1998, Toren 1993), in the field I relied largely on my general approach of reducing the 'threat' factor of the researcher. Winning the trust of child informants is crucial to gaining genuine information from them, and I found that my position as a young fieldworker helped reduce the distance between adult researcher and child informant. Furthermore, regular participation with children in events such as school plays, singing contests, sports events and traditional games, and perhaps, best of all, invitations to judge cookery contests at schools, was extremely beneficial in enhancing my rapport with both children and community members.

Having gained an enviable level of access, I was soon to find that many pre-conceived ideas that were part of my own upbringing were to be challenged. I began my research taking for granted the fact that all child work was abhorrent and damaging for children, that education represented the only antidote to child labour, and that the two were mutually exclusive activities. Moreover, I shared the belief that parents behaved 'irrationally' by having large families and then sending their children to work rather than school. Furthermore, there has been little anthropological study done in Sialkot. The recent initiatives against child labour had meant a proliferation of rapid assessment surveys, short-term studies and situation analyses. However, these writings have tended to remain within international development agency and NGO circles. More accessible were the journalistic pieces discussed in Chapter 2. With little other direct information available, my earliest impressions were dominated by the representation of Sialkot examined in the previous chapter and it was this that formed the basis of my planned methodology. Two of the most influential articles specifically concerning child labour in Sialkot's sports industry—(S. Schanberg and J. Silvers—discussed in chapters 1 and 2)—were typical of early writings on child labour in Pakistan, for example.

> In recent months, Western journalists had been threatened and assaulted for reporting on child labour in this still feudal society, particularly in those industries where legions of small children toil for 60 cents a day to make products for export to the US and other developed countries. (Schanberg 1996).

Silvers' article had similarly mentioned an attack on a Norwegian trade union delegation as they visited a sports factory. The delegation's guide and cameraman were apparently severely beaten by armed men believed to be working for the sports factory being inspected. In addition to these reports was the violent death of Iqbal Masih, the child labourer turned human rights activist. Whether or not the accounts were correct, my most immediate concerns regarding fieldwork were linked to the element of danger that had been highlighted by Silvers and Schanberg, and by the murder of Iqbal Masih.

Apart from my own uneasiness, the second issue influencing fieldwork methodology was a direct outcome of the way the discourse on child labour in Sialkot developed through media reporting and subsequent pressure on Sialkot over the involvement of children in its export industries. The growing resentment ensuing from what was locally seen as the imposition of an external reality, leading to interference in Sialkot's affairs, left target informants suspicious and occasionally hostile to outsiders. Business had been adversely affected and this had negative repercussions on both local industrialists and stitchers. The foreign media had, in many local eyes, sensationalised events to create undue hysteria against Sialkot's world famous sports goods industry. More practically, all this attention was affecting the livelihood of workers. In such an environment, suspicion and mistrust of outsiders was running high. Earlier studies on child labour had noted that workers and villagers had been reluctant to reveal information about working children. A survey carried out in Sialkot by Save the Children (1997) reported that villagers had been told by sub-contractors not to talk about working children to researchers, and many workers feared the loss of jobs and livelihoods. It was this environment that I faced on arrival in Sialkot, and it was these conditions that dictated the method of subsequent fieldwork.

Not surprisingly, in the given environment, it was essential that a considerable effort be made towards establishing trust on both sides. Without trust I would not have the confidence to ask the necessary sensitive questions. Similarly, without trust my respondents would, at best, pay lip service to my queries, leaving me with access to only surface level information. In this crucial period of building trust and in the subsequent information gathering period I was helped immeasurably by my association with Bunyad, and through the positive relationship that the NGO's fieldworkers had developed with child stitchers and their families. I believe, and aim to show in the following pages, that this rapport between the two groups could be attributed to the ideology of the NGO, the social background of the fieldworkers and their resulting attitudes towards the 'community'.

ORGANISATIONAL IDEOLOGY

Pottier (1993) points out that project ethnography must focus on the internal functioning of development organisations themselves, 'in particular on their ideologies; the modes adopted for decision making and the practice of personnel recruitment' (Pottier 1993, 7). In this second part of the chapter, I will attempt to show how the different ideologies, internal hierarchies, training techniques and office cultures of two of the main organisations involved in the project to prevent children from stitching footballs influenced not only the nature of the information they collected but also the discourse on child labour in Sialkot, and the subsequent implementation of the programme. On the one hand, it led to a more harmonious and positive relationship that benefited my own fieldwork; on the other, it discouraged the receptivity, patience, open mindedness and respect for the opinions of others that active participation demands, leading eventually to a marginalisation of the target 'beneficiaries'. The stitcher's views became no more than legitimising inputs. A deconstruction of the rhetoric of policy reveals the self-interest and power relations that underpin and dictate the direction that the emerging discourse on child labour took. Ultimately, the power of one organisation over the other led to a 'discourse coalition', which again was based on a representation of reality that had more to do with the organisation's own survival than with the reality of football stitchers. If the first two chapters were about the development of a dominant discourse and a constructed reality, this chapter examines how the agents that propagate that discourse—the international development organisations—maintain that particular dominant representation of reality, even though it may lead to a marginalisation of the supposed beneficiaries of 'development'. In Sialkot, the organisational structure of the international organisation, the information gathered and the analysis of this information was all geared towards the survival of the organisation and maintaining the imposed representation of reality rather than challenging it.

INFORMAL AND ANTI-BUREAUCRATIC—THE BUNYAD ORGANISATIONAL IDEOLOGY

It could be argued that Bunyad promoted an unprofessional approach that led to ad-hocism and haphazardness in policy. But as Nicholson (1994, 75) points out in her examination of the fit between bureaucracies and indigenous systems in Papua New Guinea, there are demonstrable benefits in confusion and uncertainty, particularly in the room it gives managers to manoeuvre. In Bunyad, employees were usually employed through being recommended by fellow staff members. There was no structured recruitment drive, and interviews, if they were held, tended to be brief and informal. The Bunyad workers were committed, if anything, to anti-bureaucratic, egalitarian forms of organisation. As such they exhibited the reverse of Weber's description of formal bureaucracy: there was no system of 'graded authority'; very little in the way of 'expert training', a rather fluid attitude towards rules, and a minimum number of written documents of the sort Weber had in mind in his analysis of bureaucracies. On the other hand, with the low salaries being offered, it was likely that only those with some commitment to Bunyad's aims, or those who saw it as part of a career in social work, would be interested in taking up a position. Field positions were demanding and required dedication and hard work. It was rare for Bunyad's field workers to return home before 6 pm having started at 8 in the morning. Anyone finding this routine difficult did not remain with the organisation long. My four research assistants had been with Bunyad for over two years, and while they undoubtedly found the pay insufficient, they saw this as a trade-off for being employed in a line of work that provided a high degree of 'job satisfaction'.

These individuals were not highly educated. They were not trained in methods of 'community participation' or 'mobilisation'. Nor did they have any knowledge of the various participatory techniques that are the hallmark of current Western models of NGOs. This finding is consistent with Hailey's (2001) conclusion that participatory technologies such as Rapid Rural Appraisal (RRA), Participatory Rural Assessment (PRA) and Participatory Learning Analysis (PLA), and their associated tools and techniques may be of less consequence than the development literature suggests. Instead there appears to be a much greater reliance on personal engagement in order to shape decisions, operational issues and programme design.

> In reviewing evidence from South Asian NGOs it has been striking how important informal, personal interaction has been... staff appear to have engaged with, and listened to, the communities with whom they work in an unstructured, informal manner. This highly personalised interaction has clearly shaped their programmes, and created a bond of trust between key staff and the communities with whom they work. (Hailey 2001, 88-9).

Bunyad's work strategy was based on these principles and contrasts markedly with what Hailey (2001, 89) dubs the 'tyrannical' and 'formulaic' nature of participative technologies of organisations, such as Bunyad's funding agency, the International Labour Organisation. Furthermore, the manner in which Bunyad developed this relationship is indicative of the attitudes that Bunyad's staff held towards those they were working with. But this close relationship did not emerge overnight. It required considerable effort as Aslam, one of Bunyad's field councillors, explained to me:

> At the start of the project we hadn't received any funding from the ILO. As a result we did not have motorcycles to go round the villages. I used to walk from village to village trying to persuade parents to send their children to

school. We went from door to door in every village. We called group meetings and spoke to village elders. Initially they were extremely hostile towards us because they felt we were responsible for the decline in stitching work. But slowly the schools started attracting students and people realised that we were genuinely trying to minimise the effects of a decline in stitching work. Now, after two years, I know nearly all the people in the thirty villages that I cover. They have come to accept us because week after week, rain or shine, they see us bringing books for schools, supporting the teachers and they see their children receiving some basic education.

The NGO staff invested considerable time, emotion and energy building up relationships of trust and shared understanding between themselves and local people. The relationship between Bunyad and the villagers they worked with was founded on regular contact, personal ties, shared beliefs, and mutual dialogue. Bunyad's dedication and commitment lay at the root of their enviable rapport with the villagers.

The councillors rarely conveyed an air of superiority or power over the villagers with whom they worked. Nor was there an environment of reprimand or punishment. If children did not attend school, efforts were made to find out why this was so. But whatever course of action was taken was done in consultation with the parents and the children concerned. The only group who were regularly pushed to maintain a basic standard were the teachers. As Mohammed Aslam pointed out, the councillors had to visit villages, where schools had been established, on an almost daily basis. This regular contact meant a certain accountability to the villagers and the development of a relationship, requiring give and take on both sides. A relationship also implies that both sides have a degree of understanding and empathy with one another. There is a feeling of participation *with* rather than separation *from*.

The attitude of the NGO workers, and their backgrounds, allowed a distrustful group of 'beneficiaries' to accept and trust them as individuals, sincere in their attempts at guiding and mentoring them. It helped that Bunyad's fieldworkers came from rural backgrounds and were familiar with the way of life in villages. All of them had also grown up doing some work in their childhood and were unfamiliar with the Western construct of childhood. As a result there was no immediate internalised rejection of child work as a breach of an inviolable right. But more important was the absence of a patronising attitude that views indigenous processes and knowledge as inferior and unworthy of serious analysis. In its place was an openness to understanding the point of view of the 'beneficiaries', which was clearly helped by the fact that their views were not overly different from those of the fieldworkers. This promoted mutual understanding between the groups. Furthermore, it was a relationship that once established, was nurtured through the daily interactions that the councillors had with the children and wider social networks, as well as through their organisation of, and participation in, the frequent functions for students, teachers and villagers.

POWER AND AUTHORITY—THE ILO ORGANISATIONAL IDEOLOGY

The influence of the 'Bunyad ideology' and the attitudes of its staff members becomes clearest when contrasted with the ideology and approach of Bunyad's funding agency, the International Labour Organisation. In contrast to Bunyad, the ILO is the archetypal formal organisation with a bureaucratic organisational structure revolving around 'job descriptions, the hierarchy of decision-making, goals, rules and policies' (Wright 1994, 17). Weber argued that bureaucracies achieve rational efficiency through well-defined formal structures. Each bureaucracy administers its official duties through an explicit hierarchical system. Specified roles and statuses divide work into delimited spheres of professional competence. Theoretically, bureaucracies are independent of personalities; their leaders' and members' lives do not intrude in the work environment. Candidates are appointed on the basis of technical qualifications and their work roles are defined by a consistent set of abstract rules. Being a bureaucrat is a career, and promotion occurs in a regularised manner (Cohen and Britan, 1980, 10-11). The contrast with Bunyad's organisation is apparent and it is not surprising that the differing structures have produced different approaches.

The ILO was created in 1919, at the end of the First World War. It thereby preceded the formation of the United Nations by almost three decades. Over the decades, the ILO has developed a long-standing bureaucracy and, as Cohen and Britan point out, agencies with entrenched bureaucracies, such as the United Nations, 'often develop their own cultural orientations, goals, rituals, language and norms' (Cohen and Britan 1980, 19). Most studies of formal organisations have tended to concentrate on how individuals affect the organisation and less on how organisations affect the individual. But being in a bureaucracy engenders certain patterns of behaviour, cultural norms, and sets of shared, learned, and transmitted behaviours. It is the function of the organisation to pass on and reinforce this shared culture to its staff members so that this culture and ideology have a pervasive influence on the staff they surround.

The ILO's Pakistan headquarters are in the capital city, Islamabad. An imposing, newly constructed, three-storey complex stands in one of Islamabad's most prestigious locations. In the car park outside are numerous vehicles emblazoned with the ILO logo. A few of the shiniest and largest ones have drivers tending them. The entrance to the building is guarded by security officials, and entry without an appointment is not possible. Inside, the building is centrally air-conditioned and finished in marble. Senior staff have spacious single offices to themselves and there are several large conference rooms all furnished with specially imported furniture. The most senior posts are reserved for the foreign 'experts', transferred to Pakistan as part of the 'technical assistance' that international organisations provide host countries. Just beneath the foreign experts are the senior local staff. But as George and Sabelli (1994, 113) point out in their critique of the World Bank, 95 per cent of the Bank staff members from developing countries received all or part of their education in the developed world and will tend to be drawn from the elite groups that were discussed in the first chapter. Similarly, at the ILO, recruitment procedures are strict and highly competitive, with university level qualifications from a foreign university being particularly valuable. What we have in international organisations is a professional group representing the 'crème de la crème', all coming from similar educational and class backgrounds:

> Put in the same place several hundred people who have been trained in the same schools to think in the same way, recruit them precisely because they have excelled in this training, provide them further with high salaries and many benefits, give them power to impose their doctrines on hundreds of thousands of (by definition) ignorant people and you are unlikely to produce a climate of humility and tolerance. (George and Sabelli 1994, 102).

The transnational elite—comprised of people with particular backgrounds and beliefs that may or may not be shared by large segments of the outside society (Cohen and Britan 1980, 9) are therefore able to dominate policy, and their propensity for viewing local populations and their values as separate and inferior to their own, is constantly reinforced by the social milieu of the international organisation and the attitudes of those occupying the key positions.

The feeling of superiority is further reinforced by the associative power of the ILO as a foreign-based, international organization, with 'foreign experts' working for the development of the country. Included in its identity is this elevated status and, most importantly, its position as a donor. The most frequently cited constraint to the formation of an authentic partnership, with partner organisations or with communities, is control of money. The position as donor immediately produces an imbalance in power relations. Knowledge on the part of the staff members that they are employed by an internationally renowned organisation that is empowered to make or withhold eagerly desired loans is not conducive to humility. The ILO is a symbol of power and authority and by association with it, staff members assume these characteristics. As Lukes points out, 'once internalised, these norms influence them to think, feel and act in certain ways' (Lukes 1973: 15 in Wright and Shore 1997, 9). The organisation's identity is used to enhance and even replace the individual's identity. Even the drivers of the ILO vehicles feel it their right to use their position of authority. Hence, the occasions when drivers of diplomatic cars break traffic rules and then shout out, '*Yeh gaari* UN *ki hai*' (This is a UN car), implying that the same rules do not apply for international organisations and their personnel.

The ILO field office in Sialkot is less impressive than the country headquarters, but only comparatively. The same identification with the organisation remains in place. The feeling of superiority emanating from the international status of the ILO is, if anything, even stronger in a small city like Sialkot, where the exposure to similar organisations is less frequent than in the capital. This approach is highlighted by the attitude of ILO staff towards both their local NGO partner in the project and the targets of the project. Bunyad's 'junior' status in the partnership is based on the NGO's position as a recipient of funding from the ILO. The power unequivocally lies with the donor agency. At a physical level the difference between the two organisations is immediately apparent and reflected in the location and size of the respective field offices. Bunyad's Sialkot office consists of a single room and attached bathroom, located on the roof of the ILO building. Two desks, a few chairs and a cupboard is the sum of the furniture. There is a computer, but their request for a telephone line has been pending for several months, so that calls have to be received downstairs in the ILO office. There is no air-conditioning and the ceiling fan has almost no effect when the searing summer sun roasts the roof. By contrast, the ILO office downstairs is equipped with air-conditioning in every room, an array of telephone lines, internet facilities and wall-to-wall carpeting. A kitchen provides a canteen for staff members.

The difference in 'power' between the two organisations—highlighted by the material disparity between the two—was based upon a number of factors, the most important of which was the international/local organisation distinction and the fact that the ILO was funding Bunyad. Without continued ILO support, Bunyad would not be part of the project. This asymmetry was not only reflected and reinforced by the physical environment of the two organisations, but also translated into the arrogant attitude that most ILO staff members had towards not only their Bunyad counterparts, but also the 'project beneficiaries' with whom they were working. I believe that this attitude had a major impact on the way that the programme was administered and on the nature and quality of information gathered by the ILO personnel. It also led to a divergence in the approach towards what was professed to be a common cause—promoting the best interests of the children.

As described in Chapter 2, many Sialkotis resented the 'loss of control' of their own affairs, seeing it as unwarranted intervention by foreigners unfamiliar with Sialkot's social fabric. As 'not an outsider' (by virtue of being identified with Bunyad) and a fellow Pakistani, I was expected to better understand the problems faced by local 'communities'. This feeling of inclusiveness was strong in Sialkot, mainly as a result of the child labour eradication programme being seen as a foreign intervention—an effort funded and designed abroad, and implemented and monitored largely through an international organisation. As a result, the distinction between the 'foreign interventionist' group and the 'national' local group was strong and well-defined—strong enough, in fact, to exclude those local Pakistanis who worked with foreign organisations and were therefore associated with them. As a reflection of this distinction, villagers addressed the Bunyad field councillors as Aslam *bhai* (brother) or Razzaq *bhai* whereas ILO monitors were addressed with the far more distant *sahab* (sir).

The ILO monitors as well as senior staff come with the paraphernalia of an international organisation and this constantly reminds the hosts of the power and resources of the organisation, thereby immediately differentiating them from the project's beneficiaries. The ILO identity and the internalising of this identity by ILO staff members was sufficient to deprive them of their 'insider' status. One could therefore be Pakistani and even Sialkoti and still be an outsider. In fact, local Pakistanis who worked with international organisations were often resented. Furthermore, the hierarchical nature of the relationship between the groups meant that communication between them became not a two-way conversation, but a matter of the more powerful group— the one considered to have expert knowledge—giving information to the less powerful group.

In this environment, along with the field councillors, I was party to much of the 'hidden transcript' that manifested itself in the form of bitterness against foreign intervention and the ILO. Villagers talked of the ILO and its monitors with disdain, complaining that they would come in their big cars, with their *gora* (white) bosses to make sure that children were not working. 'We tell them what they want to hear and get rid of them quickly. They are happy with that. All they do is fill out forms and take them back to their offices', said Nazir Ahmed, the stitcher who had earlier complained bitterly about the reduction in footballs reaching homes. The sub-contractors of the various stitching centres were even more dismissive of the ILO monitors. From time to time (once every six weeks is the current lap time according to the ILO) the ILO monitors check designated units to ensure that no children[12] are working in the facility. It is an issue that rankles the sub-contractors and stitchers alike, not necessarily because they believe that children should be allowed to work, but because of the feeling that they are constantly under surveillance. A number of sub-contractors I spoke to chafed at what they perceived was the arrogant and officious attitude of the ILO monitors. Again, the surveillance nature of their work made them ideal candidates for resentment. The result was that they were seen simply as interferers bent upon causing problems. They rarely brought good news but could often be the bearers of reprimands and sanctions. 'These ILO monitors come once every two months, ask us whether any children have been working at the unit and then they disappear for the next two months,' smirked one of my sub-contractor informants with a degree of contempt. 'Even if there were any children, the whole village knows when they arrive and word gets round quickly'. Thus, it is not only development officials who ascribe ignorance to locals. The reverse also occurs.

The role played by ILO monitors also varies with the size of the stitching units. While the monitors felt confident to display their authority over smaller centres, often reprimanding the sub-contractors, they were far more circumspect in their dealings with larger units. At the larger centres, the ILO monitors were not able to enter unannounced and could only gain admission when allowed by the unit representative. Even then, their main function was to check a few records and then leave. On the few occasions that the monitors had complained about the presence of children in units, no action had been taken because the 'transgression' was explained usually through the provision of birth certificates showing that the children were over age, or that the children were not there for stitching but were in fact running the canteen.

During my stay in the field, an added point of tension developed between Bunyad and the ILO. It was also an example of how the rhetoric of policy and the official discourse masked the interplay of interests of individuals and organizations, and how these dynamics adversely affected the impact of the project on target populations. Bureaucratic disputes dictated how the programme was administered, so that it was often these tussles rather than responses to the needs of the people that determined programme implementation. It is to one of these tussles that I now turn.

CONFLICT AND RESOLUTION

In late 1999 the first stage of the project was coming to a close. This meant that the ILO would evaluate Bunyad's progress before deciding to renew their contract. Effectively, Bunyad was on 'probation' pending an end of year report. As rumour began to spread that some members at the ILO field office were 'against' Bunyad and would try and engineer the NGO's exit, communication between the two organisations became increasingly fraught. Behind the scenes a struggle developed between the ILO and Bunyad field offices, with ego hassles on both sides playing an important role. The result was an environment of mistrust and non-cooperation. Far from working together as a partnership, the organisations actively began trying to place hurdles in one another's paths. Any semblance of partnership—of working together towards a common goal—was overshadowed by the bureaucratic bickering that increasingly shaped the discourse of child stitchers in Sialkot.

The trading of 'misinformation' generated through the increasingly adversarial relationship between the two field offices became part of the statistics on child labour. The ILO version stressed that the poor standard of Bunyad's schools meant that children were either not enrolling in them, or were dropping out and rejoining the labour force. Bunyad insisted that the ILO used as a model only the very weakest schools that had been established.

The result was a suspension in funding and delays in the distribution of salaries for Bunyad's field officers and teachers in the schools. For the last two months of my fieldwork the field staff worked without wages, and with no indication that the project would continue. The uncertainty spilled over to the implementation of the project. Delays in salaries to teachers caused community members to speculate that the non-formal schools were to be closed down. Supplies to the schools were also disrupted and student achievement suffered. Furthermore, football stitchers complained that children had firstly been stopped from working and now the schools set up were also going to be shut down, leaving families and children with no options. It was Bunyad that lost face in the villages where they worked.

In retaliation, Bunyad manipulated attendance figures to show that its schools were exemplary and that the incidence of working children had declined dramatically. Any notion of highlighting the real situation and including, for example, reports of the resentment by football stitchers towards the imposed project—primarily due to the decline in income following a fall in home-based stitching (see chapters 4 and 5)—was discarded from fear that it would provide 'elements' in the ILO ammunition to remove Bunyad from the project. In fact, there was evidence from the field that pointed to weaknesses in programme design and implementation, which would ultimately have reflected poorly on both organizations.

As a result, either the information collected was inaccurate or, even when it was accurate, it was manipulated to cater to the interests of the organisations involved in the project. The project's survival depended on maintaining, or creating, sufficient ignorance about what was happening locally. As Gardner and Lewis point out, 'only statements which are useful to the development institutions concerned are therefore included in their reports; radical or pessimistic analyses are banished. The discourse is thus dynamically interrelated with development practice, affecting the actual design and implementation of projects' (Gardner and Lewis, 1996, 73). Therefore, dominant interests were able, through concealing parts of the social reality-even that generated by their own research methodologies-to manipulate the reality of others.

So, while a struggle had emerged between the agendas of the ILO and Bunyad field offices, this struggle was ultimately replaced by a 'discourse coalition' (Hajer, 1995). Both organisations were engaged in managing their own survival as well as trying to carry out the tasks assigned to them, and as Van Ufford (1993, 138) points out, these two aspects are often incompatible. The campaign to denigrate one another was therefore set aside in favour of the unproblematic continuation of the programme as a whole. It was the result of a political and discursive struggle that ultimately resulted in the production of a unified document highlighting the success of both organisations. The Bunyad figures were manipulated to show the success of the project—the number of children in schools showed an increase and correspondingly those involved in football stitching declined dramatically. At the same time, the ILO monitoring system was hailed as a model for other programmes and no mention was made of its shortcomings. Thus, as Moore (1996 in R. Werbner 1999, 132-133) points out, each project 'generates its own micro-politics over personnel, benefits, techniques, and objectives, and often over the very existence of the project'.

The requirements of the various development institutions ensured that the current reality, as drawn up at the end of the last chapter and reinforced by Bunyad and the ILO, is one of children in schools, free from labour and its harmful effects. This representation is the outcome of the power relations of those driving developmental programmes and as Escobar (1991, 674) points out, development institutions are part and parcel of how the world is put together so as to ensure a certain process of ruling. The outcome suited both Bunyad and the ILO as two of the agencies involved in the implementation of the programme. Funding for Bunyad continued for a further year. However, the ILO displayed, and reinforced its own authority, by contracting another NGO to 'share' the task of social protection along with Bunyad. The stitchers, in the midst of this struggle become Foucault's objectified persons, 'the objectified person is seen but he does not see; he is the object of information, never a subject of communication' (Foucault 1977, 200). The stitchers are the objects of information, to be acted upon bureaucratically, but who are not involved in the shaping of the information on themselves. They do not have the power (as conceived by Lukes (1974) to set agendas or manipulate conceptions of interest. The fact that this group lacks the power to make itself heard also means that there is very little knowledge about the way football stitchers, including children, view their own situation. They may be represented by dominant discourses based not on shared lives, problems and experiences but on external observations that are often mediated by a Western episteme and historicity. In the following two chapters, the attempt will be to illustrate what development has meant for those that it defines as objects, and from their point of view, so that it is children and their families that are moved to the centre of the analysis.

NOTES

1. Muslim migrants who moved to Pakistan from parts of present day India.
2. The word Punjab means 'five rivers' and refers to the rivers that flow through the province—the Ravi, the Beas, the Sutlej, the Chenab and the Jhelum.
3. For an account of this see *Culture, Class and Development in Pakistan*, Anita M. Weiss (1991).
4. Sialkot received the lowest percentage of refugee workers at only 21 per cent compared to an average of 49 per cent for Punjab. The cities of Faisalabad (70 per cent), Gujranwala (50 per cent), Multan (50 per cent) and Lahore (43 per cent) were dominated by migrants (Government of Pakistan census 1970, 2-3).
5. *Tehsil*—Smallest administrative unit of a district. Two or more *tehsil*s constitute a District and three or more districts form a Division. Sialkot comprises three *tehsil*s, Sialkot *tehsil*, Daska *tehsil* and Pasrur *tehsil*. I will attempt to clarify the usage of 'Sialkot' by referring separately to Sialkot city, Sialkot *tehsil* and Sialkot district. Where 'Sialkot' is used on its own, it will refer to the entire district of Sialkot.
6. Figures from District Census Report of Sialkot 1998, Government of Pakistan.
7. In 326 BC according to Ahmed Nabi Khan (1964).
8. 273 BC–237 BC.
9. 1527–1701 AD.
10. There is, in fact, very little in terms of specific recent historical accounts of Sialkot. Most accounts were written in the Colonial period though there are some accounts that go back as far as the time of Alexander the Great.
11. See, for example, Eglar (1960) or Kessinger (1974).
12. The ILO defined children in the football stitching project as those in the age range 5-14. For the purposes of this study I shall use the same age range (5-14) when referring to children.

4

FROM DISCOURSE TO IMPLEMENTATION
THE RESTRUCTURING OF THE FOOTBALL INDUSTRY

While the first three chapters dealt with the development of the discourse on child labour and a particular dominant representation of reality followed by the subsequent propagation of this reality through development institutions, this chapter examines the links between theory and practice. Development, according to Escobar (1995), links forms of knowledge (discourse) with the deployment of forms of power and intervention (the implemented programme). The concrete manifestation of the child labour discourse in Sialkot was the implementation of the programme to eliminate child labour from the football manufacturing industry. This chapter aims to show that just as dominant discourses work by setting up terms of reference and disallowing or marginalizing others, so their concrete forms function along the same principle—by instituting a particular model while marginalizing deviations from this model. The fact that the child labour discourse was based on a misleading and distant representation of reality will therefore lead to an intervention that is equally distant from the ground reality of the supposed beneficiaries of the project. As Hobart points out: 'There is an unbridgeable, but largely unappreciated gap between the neat rationality of development agencies' representations which imagine the world as ordered or manageable and the actualities of situated social practices, an incommensurability tidied away in sociological jargon as 'unintended consequences' (Hobart, 1993, 16). This chapter examines both the gap and the unintended consequences.

Located on Daska Road, one of the busiest roads radiating out of Sialkot city, are the headquarters of several of Sialkot's largest football manufacturers. Amongst them is the main stitching centre of Sublime Sports, suppliers of high quality footballs to the international sporting goods manufacturer, Adidas. A road sign points proudly to the *'Sublime Stitching Centre'*. From the exterior, a large double storey compound is evident but little else is visible over the high boundary wall. Outside, vehicles blaring horns career past at maniacal speeds, donkeys drag heavy loads and clouds of dust drift up from the roadside. The hustle, bustle and 'chaos' of everyday life contrasts starkly with the environment inside. On the other side of the gates, manicured lawns and sports fields for the use of employees are maintained by a team of gardeners. To one side is a large car park where a fleet of buses is parked. I was informed that these form the 'pick and drop' service for employees working at the centre. Everything is orderly and bound by a formal structure.

Entrance to the stitching centre was not possible until the *chowkidar* had announced my presence at the gate and my contact, Naeem Javed, the foreman at the centre, arrived to escort me inside. Within the building, posters of international sports stars contracted to Adidas, but unknown to most Pakistanis, are splashed on the walls. A code of conduct is written in both English and Urdu. The workplace area is designed on the principles of Fordism—separate tasks are carried out by separate teams of workers. One team stitches footballs, another checks for faults before either rejecting or passing the balls. The rejected balls are opened up and re-stitched by another set of stitchers. The passed balls are washed, tested for air pressure and then packed—all by separate teams. Finally, an on-site representative from Adidas randomly checks packed footballs.

As Naeem Javed showed me around, I could easily have forgotten that I was undertaking research on what had recently been an informal, cottage industry. The upper floor of the centre is equipped with a large canteen for workers. Naeem informed me that a gym and crèche facilities were planned in the near future. Sublime's major competitor, Saga Sports, the local partner for Nike, had already equipped six of its new centres with crèches, while its flagship headquarters comes with a cricket stadium large enough to rival the stadium built for international matches by the government. It was apparent that Sublime and Saga's Sialkot headquarters were inspired by the headquarters of their European and American partner organisations. In fact, Saga's managing director had informed me how impressed Saga Sports' founder, Khoorshid Soofi, had been when he had gone to Nike's Oregon base.

It was during this visit that Soofi and Nike's senior management developed the blueprint for Saga's child-labour-free stitching unit system. Soofi, while representing some of Sialkot's largest football manufacturers, presented this same plan to a group of international sports companies when Sialkot's football manufacturers were threatened by consumer boycotts and legal measures. The thrust of the programme was to 'save' the industry through the immediate implementation of a project to remove children working in the industry. This was to be accomplished through the 'formalisation' of stitching i.e. moving football stitching from homes into purpose built 'units' that could be monitored by personnel from the ILO—another partner in the programme. The plan was signed in February 1997 and came to be known as the Atlanta Agreement, on account of being signed in Atlanta. It was hastily accepted by the international and local companies who pledged that the football industry would be free of child labour within 18 months. According to ILO monitoring reports, by August 2000, 74 of Sialkot's 400 large,[1] medium and small-scale enterprises had joined the programme. By virtue of 'joining' the monitoring programme, manufacturers had to register with the ILO and undertake internal monitoring of their own units to ensure that no children were stitching footballs in their centres. They had also to provide details of all their stitching centres, so the ILO could undertake external monitoring. In return, members of the World Federation of the Sporting Goods Industry, covering all the major sports brands, pledged to favour vendors who did not use child labour and were registered under the programme. Tellingly, the assurance by the international brands was no more than a verbal commitment.

INFORMALISATION

The move towards formalising the industry was the first major structural change in the industry since the 1970s. After the Partition of the subcontinent in 1947 the sports industry rebuilt itself around men who owned small firms. Government policies from the 1960s onwards, in contrast, encouraged the establishment of large industrial units, sometimes employing hundreds of workers. Naeem Javed informed me that it was in the 1970s that a combination of factors led to a wide scale decentralisation of the football industry.

Football stitching for multi-national companies began in Sialkot when human rights activists in the West began campaigning against forced prison labour. Companies began sending the panels that make up a football to Sialkot for stitching. Before that Franco, in Spain, would have his prisoners stitch footballs. The jobs that cannot be done in the West anymore come to poor countries. But it was in the 1970s that the football boom began. Anwar Khwaja won the contract to produce 'Tango'—the official World Cup football for 1974. After that more and more companies began to come to Sialkot to have their footballs stitched here. At this point the majority of stitchers were men able to commute to Sialkot city, where manufacturing units were situated. Footballs were made almost entirely of pure leather and skilled workmen could stitch no more than 1-2 a day because of the tough material. Stitching these footballs required considerable skill and strength and only a small group of highly skilled men were involved in the trade. There was no input from women and children at this point.

It was also in the 1970s that Bhutto[2] came to power in Pakistan on the basis of an Islamic socialist manifesto.[3] In the years that followed, a tightening of labour laws and unions demanding increased representation, higher pay and better working conditions led to several organised strikes at Sialkot's factories. Industrialists saw trade union unrest as interference and misuse of power. 'All the time of the employers was being spent in court cases and no work was being done. So in order to circumvent this problem, we sent all our workers home and that is when home-based stitching emerged on a large scale' (Khwaja Zakaullah, Capitol Sports). Labour laws were not applicable to units employing less than ten full time workers and as a result factory owners decentralised their operations, thereby pre-empting the possibility of any further dissent. Work was increasingly done at home. The result was a return to a distributed cottage industry, relying not on a fixed labour force, but on a casual and cheap pool of workers. This also allowed industrialists to avoid large capital outlays, overheads and providing workers benefits such as medical coverage, educational benefits and old age pensions.

While decentralisation meant a reversion to 'cottage' roots, there were further developments that not only facilitated this move, but also led to a radical change in the composition of the workforce and the way that football stitching as an 'occupation' came to be viewed. Most important was the introduction of synthetic material to replace pure leather in football manufacturing. This allowed the production of three broad grades of footballs, known locally as *Vilayati, Lahori* and *Desi*.

As I looked at the sheets of different qualities of material at the Sublime stitching unit, Naeem Javed explained the differences.

> Basically there are three types of football—Vilayati, Lahori and Desi. In the past, footballs were made of pure leather and stitching them was very difficult. But in the late 1970s, PVC material began to be used for making footballs and soon leather was replaced completely. Now I don't think pure leather is used to make any footballs—even the highest quality ones. The synthetic material has many different qualities so it became possible to make different grades of football for different purposes. Today the highest quality football is called Vilayati. This is made of the highest quality PVC material from Japan. The Vilayati football is used in professional and club matches. The second quality ball is called Lahori and is made from a thick PVC material usually imported from South Korea. This is the lower end of the sporting ball market and is used by amateur clubs and in general sports retail. The lowest quality ball is known as Desi and this ball is not really a sporting product. It is made from thin PVC, which is often imported material as well. It is sold as a toy for children or as a promotional item. That is why Desi footballs are also called promotional balls. Only 20 per cent of footballs exported from Sialkot are Vilayati balls. The remaining 80 per cent are Desi and Lahori balls and many of these are manufactured by small manufacturers and not by big firms like Sublime. Adidas does not order any Desi balls.

Along with the introduction of synthetic material and the explosion in demand, equipment to ensure standardization of the panels that are stitched together to form a complete football also became available in Sialkot in the 1970s. This considerably improved the quality of footballs while making the task of manufacturing them easier, as it meant workers no longer needed to cut the panels, perforate their edges and then stitch them. All that was required was for the panels to be stitched together. Hand stitching was still favoured over machine stitching because of the cheapness of labour, and because hand-stitched balls were considered higher quality. Improved transport links with outlying villages meant that the panels could be cut at the Sialkot city based 'warehouses' and then sent to homes in villages for stitching. Once stitched, the footballs were collected and taken back to the warehouses for packaging and export.

Along with the move to home-based stitching, these factors—the improved transport links, the employer preference for a decentralised system, the increase in demand and the simplification of the stitching process through the introduction of machine cut panels, and softer (and therefore easier to stitch) material for lower quality footballs—meant that football stitching was no longer the preserve of patrilineages or *biraderis* of highly skilled artisans.

BIRADERIS

The relationship between *biraderi* and caste, or *zaat* as it is locally known, is complex, and is further complicated by discussion over whether caste even exists in Muslim societies. Without going into details of this[4] debate, it is sufficient for this analysis to point out that if caste applies to a hereditary non-corporate category, then *biraderi* can be considered the local manifestation of caste in that it is the minimal patrilineage. Blunt defined *biraderi*[5] as a fraternity, a group of caste brethren who live in a particular neighbourhood and act together for caste purposes, '*it is zaat (caste) in action*' (Blunt in L. Dumont 1980, 361). It is the *biraderi,* rather than the wider notion of *zaat,* which is the primary factor amongst the primordial loyalties that govern social organisation in Punjab villages. This is usually highlighted by the fact that Punjabis will refer to group members as being from '*sadee biraderi*' (our *biraderi*) rather than use the wider group of '*sadee zaat*' (our caste). *Zaat* is usually reverted to on occasions where there are not enough *biraderi* members present for support. For example, a member of a certain *biraderi* settling away from his natal village may find that he is unable to find any fellow members from his *biraderi*, but he is likely to find fellow *zaat* members. The 'mobility' of *zaat,* through its distributed nature, allows it to be used as a source of support for migrants and is something that has been particularly important in the case of Pakistani immigrants to foreign countries.[6] Locally, though, it is *biraderi* that is the primary group relation.

In relation to industry, De Neve (1999) and Nadvi (1990, 1999) both point out with reference to South Asia that when industry was based on traditional occupations, it tended to draw on the pool of specialised labour that was provided by *biraderis* monopolising that particular trade.

As the transfer of skill is based on the willingness of elders to teach youngsters on the job, skills are largely reproduced within circles of kin and caste relations. The lack of formal training makes it difficult for outsiders to enter the occupation and to acquire the necessary skills. Operators are aware of this and reluctant to train outsiders as they see them as potential competitors. They will only expend time and effort on those they know well. (G. De Neve 1999, 383).

Barriers to entry based on knowledge and expertise in football stitching were overcome by the simplification of the process and the introduction of softer synthetic material in football manufacture. The result was that a much wider group of casual, intermittent stitchers increasingly became the dominant stitcher profile, and as the level of skill required was not particularly high, the expertise spread rapidly through the district. In addition, since the market for lower quality balls is some four times that of match quality balls, the biggest expansion took place in the 'semi-skilled' stitcher workforce, which for reasons discussed later in the chapter, came to be dominated by women and children.

In the light of the above discussion, it is not surprising that during field interviews with stitchers I found, contrary to Nadvi's findings in other industries in Pakistan,[7] no evidence was found of any one *biraderi* dominating the football stitching labour force. The correlation with economic status was much stronger. Lefebvre (1999, 46) points out that entirely rich and entirely poor *biraderis* do not exist, but within each is found a continuum of households at different levels on the economic scale. As a result, I came across football stitchers from a wide range of *biraderis* from the highest ranked Sayyeds,[8] Mughals and Sheikhs to Jats and Arain as well as the lowest ranked artisan and service castes including Lohars, Nais and Fakirs. Almost every *zaat* was represented with no one *zaat* dominating. This cross-section of *biraderis* involved in football stitching has led to an interesting phenomenon. Football stitching is not a 'traditional' occupation. Instead it has come to represent a skill that is 'owned' by all Sialkotis regardless of *biraderi*. So, rather than the biraderi of *mochis* (cobblers) or *tarkhans* (carpenters) having the required skill for the specific industry, it is now the much wider group of Sialkotis having that skill collectively. It is considered an inherently Sialkoti skill due to its long history in the region and the success that the industry has achieved. From the inclusiveness of the *biraderi*, the claim on the skill of stitching widened to the inclusiveness of the 'Sialkoti'.

FROM CITY TO VILLAGE TO HOME

Thus, it was in the mid-1970s, following the developments described above, that the sports industry, now increasingly dominated by football manufacture, spread outside the urban environs of Sialkot city.

> First their husbands would travel to Sialkot city to stitch footballs. Slowly when demand began increasing the men began taking unfinished footballs home to be completed with the help of their families. Neighbours began to see that these families were eating good food daily and their houses were becoming pukka [brick rather than mud]. So they sent their wives to ask in the households what was happening. After a while more and more villagers started taking up stitching and brought material home to be stitched with the help of their families. When the workers were sent home the makers delivered material to the homes and even more than before the whole family stitched the footballs. That way the skill spread very quickly throughout the village. Certain villages, like Noorpura [no. 44], became known for the quality of their stitching. Often when a woman from a stitching family married a man from another village, she would move to her husband's village and teach her in-laws and neighbours. What started as an industry based in the city rapidly spread to every village in Sialkot as far out as 35kms from Sialkot city. (Naeem Javed).

The role of the sub-contractor or *maker*,[9] as he is known locally, was crucial in the decentralisation of the industry. *Makers* worked both as recruiters of labour and as conduits for passing on skill. Such was the increase in demand for footballs stitched in Sialkot that sub-contractors looked to widen the skill base in order to maintain a cheap labour supply. Footballs were given to an increasing number of homes starting with a *maker* distributing work to his own *biraderi* and family members. Stitching, after all, represented an additional source of income. In contrast, women, who became the dominant home-based stitchers, began to pass on stitching work to neighbours and friends. Had the home-based labour force been male-dominated it is more likely that the transfer of material would have occurred along family and *biraderi* lines. But the fact that marriage is patrilocal means that women move away from their own families and often strike up close friendships with their new neighbours, who in the light of the cultural and religious definition of 'acceptable' social spaces for women, are often those with whom social interaction is closest.

Apart from the factors examined above, other features inherent to the football industry made it suitable to the dispersed format. Seventy-five per cent of the work was done by hand, making it extremely labour intensive. Machinery was required only at the initial stage of cutting the panels, stamping logos and for quality control once the stitching process was completed. As a result, most work could be done at home. The seasonal nature of demand in the football trade—depending on the scheduling of large tournaments like the World or European Cups—results in work coming intermittently rather than on a regular basis. Additionally, being piece-rate based meant that unsupervised, slow workers were not overpaid. Moreover, the discontinuous, self-contained stitching process meant that the pace of work of one individual or family group did not affect the productivity of other workers. For employers, whenever demand increased, more workers could be added. When demand sagged, workers would be released without any obligations. For workers, the seasonal demand meant that they rarely stitched all year round. Most stitchers would stitch footballs in addition to other employment such as agricultural work. Stitching was used especially at times when the family required extra income, such as weddings or festivals like *Eid*,[10] when individuals buy new clothes and families distribute sweets and food to neighbours and relatives. Football stitching came to be seen as a convenient supplementary source of income that few families relied solely on, rather than a 'formal' industrial occupation. The way that Sialkotis came to perceive stitching is crucial, because the stitchers' own understanding contrasts markedly with the way that football stitching was viewed, and ultimately transformed, under the restructured unit system.

Naeem Javed had so far shown me around as a representative for Sublime Sports. But as we came to the end of the tour he increasingly began to voice his concerns as a 'Sialkoti'. He himself had worked his way up from being an occasional stitcher to being a *maker* for Sublime. His association with the company stretched over 15 years and, in recognition of his service, Naeem had been made foreman of the main stitching centre. His extensive contacts with stitchers, built up during his time as a stitcher and then sub-contractor, as well as his experience of stitching, meant that he was the ideal man to supervise the centre.

The emergence of employers and *makers* from within the group of workers[11]—many of today's industrialists in Sialkot worked their way up from being artisans—has, in fact, led to the formation of an uncharacteristically amicable employer–sub-contractor–worker relationship. 'Yeh log to mistri se Mianji ban gaye' ('these people went from being craftsmen to being gentlemen'), remarked Chaudhry Sher Mohammed, one of the few industrialists who had managed to break in from a different background. It was often pointed out by both workers and employers that one of the major reasons for the success of the sports industry was that the industrialists were familiar with every process involved in the production of goods. This not only improved quality control but also meant a very hands-on approach by employers, who would often spend time on the work floor passing on advice to their workers. The result has been a labour dynamic that promotes a relatively close and non-antagonistic employer-employee relationship. The fact that *makers*, stitchers, and owners all emerged from the same class of artisans has played down divisions that are often highly visible in other industries. In addition, the cottage industry nature of the sporting goods industry in Sialkot meant that the polarisation that tends to occur between owners and workers in a large factory set-up, did not take place. There is little sign of the antagonistic relationship described by Ong (1991) for example, in her description of the intimidating relations between the Korean supervisors of a multinational company and the local Indonesian workers. Nor is there the hostile arrogance that Punjabi Hindu employers show towards the caste of *Jatav* craftsmen involved in the Agra shoe industry of India (Knorringa 1996, 1999). *Makers* tend to be from the same *biraderis* as their stitchers. They live in similar houses and often occupy the same social spaces as their stitching labour force.

A similar dynamic works between stitchers and industrialists, and sub-contractors and industrialists. However, the difference in status and wealth is much greater than in the case with *makers* and stitchers. This means that while a relatively subdued hierarchy between industrialists and their employees (sub-contractors and through them football stitchers) may exist at the work place, this does not extend to social spaces or occasions. Intermarriage is ruled out, and while the industrialists may maintain houses in their native villages, and many make it a point to do so, further re-enforcing their local influence and identity as Sialkotis, these houses are usually ostentatious mansions compared to the modest two-room dwellings of their employees. Children of the industrialists are often educated in foreign universities, while those of the workers are lucky to receive any education at all. Despite these differences, the common feeling of belonging to Sialkot is a powerful bond between these three groups, and the ability to maintain the support of workers through timely reminders of shared roots and history is essential to the industrialist's strategy of maintaining a loyal, skilled and cheap labour force.

UNIVERSAL DISCOURSES, UNIVERSAL MODELS

As Naeem spoke increasingly freely, the remoteness of the imposed formal model from its employees started to become apparent. As mentioned, the structure of Sublime or Saga's main centres was inspired by the headquarters of their international partners and particularly by the Nike base in Oregon. But while Nike's headquarters, employees are steeped in the corporate culture of the company, that culture has no roots in Sialkot. The manicured sports fields, crèches and canteens may have been transplanted to Sialkot, but the corporate culture that led to the creation of a particularly aggressive and loyal group of Nike employees, who refer to themselves as 'Ekin's' (Nike spelt backwards!) in the United States, is not evident in Sialkot, where most employees are still trying to come to terms with the enforced changes.

Do you know that this whole structure has taken more than Rs. 2 million to construct? We used to have 108 village-based units and we have had to consolidate them into twelve larger ones as a result of the restructuring. Sublime has also had to put aside a further Rs. 75-100,000 annually for in-house monitoring as required by the programme. It used to cost us Rs. 20-25 to manufacture a ball, but now costs are up as high as Rs.50-55. Balls for which Pakistan is paying Rs. 31 to its workers, India is paying Rs. 9 for the same work. This cost is even less in China. It has meant a huge increase in costs for us and orders have gone down as a result. The people to suffer most are the stitchers because suddenly there is much less work around (Naeem).

When I voiced the opinion that 'formalising' the industry appeared to have led to better worker conditions and wages, Naeem revealed what he felt about the entire restructuring programme.

This whole thing is for show. The few centres that are showpieces for the companies have all these new facilities—canteens, subsidised shops, schools, crèches, recreational facilities and medical centres. But even Saga and Sublime continue to have all their footballs stitched by hand and the majority of their stitching is undertaken in smaller centres rather than in their showcase headquarters. It is too expensive to maintain a large permanent staff in an industry that is subject to seasonal shifts. So Sublime, like Saga, maintains a 'rolling' staff that is hired on demand. It is only the minority of permanent staff that are able to take advantage of the benefits offered by Sialkot's larger manufacturing companies. These employees will not only receive better wages than their more informal counterparts but they also receive additional benefits such as medical insurance, interest free loans and pensions. But these permanent employees are in a minority. The majority of stitchers still work on a daily basis. The reason these new facilities have been built is for the benefit of foreign buyers. When they come to Sialkot to see whether we have made progress in adhering to the conditions laid out by them they are shown these impressive headquarters with modern machinery and forward-looking policies. One look at this and they have no hesitation in putting in a big order. But we have given in to the demands of farners [foreigners] and the result will be detrimental to Sialkot. After World War II, the Japanese surrendered to the West, but the one thing that they did not surrender was their right to carry on their education the way they always had. See where they reached. We have allowed outsiders to change our tor tareekey [way of life]. The multi-nationals will squeeze us dry. They want to make Sialkot's manufacturers offer the lowest price possible. First they introduced the child labour issue. Now we have done that, they are talking about imposing labour standards and trade unions. What will they think of next to blackmail us? Our social conditions are not the same as in the West. But they take no notice of this.

Far from embracing the formalised system, there appears to be a feeling, amongst both industrialists and workers, that the system has been forced upon them. Just as many Sialkotis felt that the child labour issue had been imposed on them, so through the same process they felt that 'terms and conditions' not relevant to their social environment were being externally imposed, leading ultimately to what Escobar (1995) termed the 'total restructuring of underdeveloped societies'.

THE ONE AND ONLY WAY OF THINKING

As mentioned in chapter 1, it is often argued that development emerged out of colonialism, and that notions of progress and enlightenment were central to both discourses. Both also involved planned social and economic change that aimed at transforming the world in the image of the industrially advanced societies— *"the exploitation theory is... dead and the development theory has taken its place"* stated Bourdillon, the British Governor of Nigeria, addressing the Royal Empire Society in London in 1937 (quoted in Cowen and Shenton 1991, 165). These approaches, that envisaged developing countries passing through the same stages that developed countries passed through earlier, remained the guiding principles of development until the 1980s, when the continued 'underdevelopment' of the Third World led to a reappraisal. The 'inefficiency' of the externally imposed, expert-oriented, top-down forms of research and planning, seen as responsible for the failure of development, gave way to the concept of 'participatory development'. The ostensible aim of participatory approaches, of which Chambers (1983, 1992, 1993) was a leading advocate, was 'to increase the involvement of socially and economically marginalized people in decision making over their own lives' (Gujit and Shah 1998, 1). Participatory development, therefore, implies a more locally sensitive form of development, one that bypasses the problems associated with an imposition of external ideas and concepts. But while development institutions such as the World Bank[12] now put forward an image of a gender sensitive, bottom-up, participatory approach, this appears in several cases analysed by anthropologists[13] to be what Scott (1997, 313) terms the 'public transcript' of the development deal. According to the 'hidden transcript', the public face of development is strikingly similar to the old top-down approach. The formalisation of the industry through the child labour eradication project forms part of the public transcript. The route to development now involves the post-colonial strategy of adopting international standards, invariably drawn up along Western parameters and norms. What we therefore have, as Foucault argued, is a new regime of power exercised through disciplinary mechanisms and the stipulation of norms for human behaviour. Moreover, the ideological basis for this power seems even more firmly rooted than those of the colonial era, for while there was active opposition to colonial domination, it seems much more difficult to articulate a compelling argument against the apparently apolitical process of 'development'. This then is the process that Ramonet describes as 'the one and only way of thinking'.

> What is the one and only way of thinking? It is the translation into ideological terms that claim to be universal of economic interests, particularly those of international capital. It could be said that it was

formulated and defined from 1944 onwards, at Bretton Woods. Its principal sources are the great economic and financial institutions—the World Bank, the International Monetary Fund, the Organisation for Economic Cooperation and Development, the General Agreement on Tariffs and Trade, The European Commission, the Banque de France, and so on which in order to define their ideas through the world, finance various research centres, universities and foundations, which in turn disseminate the holy writ. (Ramonet 1997, 179).

Included in Ramonet's channels of transmission, and highlighted in chapter 1, are international treaties such as the Convention on the Rights of the Child, based on Western constructs of childhood, and recent social accountability clauses[14] which lay down conditions, again using Western values as normative standards, that must be complied with. Boyden (1997, 220-221) examines how the Convention on the Rights of the Child was used as a policing mechanism to bring governments and others to account. In the event of non-compliance, consumer boycotts and legal measures are threatened (e.g. The Harkin Bill). The 'globalisation' of standards is based on the assumption of a universal paradigm, of an economic, social, cultural and institutional norm applicable to all. But rather than 'embracing' the peoples of the world equally, the adoption of international standards condemns most to marginality or exclusion from social life. The export of a Western construct of childhood to the Third World as a universal norm has, for example, meant that many of the activities undertaken by children in these countries have been redefined as deviant. Ironically, it is these marginalized groups who are used to lend credibility and legitimacy to proposed interventions. Yet those on whose behalf the interventions are undertaken remain increasingly excluded, or as Amartya Sen[15] points out, are 'unfairly included', referring to the unequal nature of their inclusion. This will be examined in more detail in the section on the involvement of women in stitching units.

In the West, industrialisation and the growth of capitalism led to the break up of the home-based production system. Stephen Marglin points out in his examination of the organisation of work that, 'in the West work stands outside, if not actually opposed to life. The disembeddedness of work is doubtless related to a larger separation of the economic from its social, political and moral context' (Marglin 1990, 226). This form of production led to the formation of a new concept of 'work' and this, as Gramsci (1971, 279-348) emphasised with regard to Fordism in the 1930s, required new types of workers and ways of life. Just as education was taken out of the domain of the family by formal schooling, work was removed from the family and from the home by the emergence and subsequent dominance of the 'factory' system. 'Work' came to be associated with wage labour and with tasks that were highly specialised and undertaken on a full-time basis, at specific times and outside the home in an area designated specially for work. The restructuring programme was meant to allow the Sialkot football industry to follow suit. The cottage industry format was redefined as an 'abnormality', then subsequently changed and brought into line with the dominant formal model that is based on the strict separation of home and work.

It should also be remembered that the enforced formalisation of the industry goes against the dominant trend of industrialisation in developing countries, which has seen a move towards dependence on a more flexible workforce.[16] While the history of industrialisation in the West generally saw a linear progression at the end of which the majority of workers become 'formalised', the path towards industrial capitalism for much of the developing world has seen the expansion of the formal sector outpaced by growth in the labour force. Instead, much of the work force has been absorbed by what Hart (1973) first termed the 'informal sector'. The enforced formalisation therefore represents an about turn and ignores the local conditions that led to the formation of a cottage industry. But the logic of Hegemonic Universalism ensures that there is only one 'correct' way, and others are discounted and marginalized. The decentralised model must be replaced in favour of the dominant Western model if the area is to 'develop'. The result is a shift away from home-based work towards the formal structure epitomised by the showcase headquarters of Sublime and Saga.

But how has the implementation of an external model in the form of the industry's formalisation affected those involved in the industry? And has concretisation of a universal discourse into a universal model for implementation really led to the marginalisation of the majority of those the project was to benefit?

INCREASING FORMALISATION—STITCHING UNITS

Of the four hundred or so football manufacturing firms in Sialkot, approximately two hundred are registered with the Sialkot-based Pakistan Sports Goods Manufacturers Association. A further two hundred enterprises or more are not registered with the Association. According to Dr. Faiz Shah, who worked as Managing Director of Saga Sports, 60 per cent to 65 per cent of all football production from Sialkot was concentrated in the hands of 6-8 large companies, led by Saga Sports and Sublime. However, it is apparent from the numerous signs for sports manufacturers in Sialkot city, that there are hundreds of smaller companies struggling for a place in the export niche alongside the larger companies.

Sialkot's largest companies were part of the initial group that drew up the plans to restructure the industry. Their motivation, along with that of their international partners, was to avoid the sanctions that had crippled the carpet industry in Pakistan. These large firms had the financial means to undertake restructuring and the relative stability of long-term relations with their foreign buyers. Nevertheless, even the large manufacturers interviewed pointed to an increase in manufacturing costs and a substantial decline in profits. The manufacturers attributed the decline as entirely the result of the costs associated with opening and running large stitching centres and providing infrastructure that the home-based industry had long avoided. 'For now we larger firms are keeping our heads above water. But many smaller companies have already closed and many others will be pushed out of business by an industry-wide consolidation in the next few years' (Khwaja Zakaullah, Capital Sports).

Apart from resources, there is another reason that makes smaller companies and their 'employees' more vulnerable to the current consolidation. Smaller companies do not produce the *Vilayati* or even *Lahori* balls. Instead their trade is concentrated in non-branded, promotional or *Desi* balls. International firms are concerned with high quality and dependability and are therefore likely to remain committed to an existing relationship with local manufacturers with whom they have built long standing and trusted associations. In contrast, the *Desi* ball scenario produces no such bonds. The lower end of the market served by non-brands is where price competition is far more effective. Given samples of sufficient quality, the award of contract is primarily driven by price. Furthermore, the absence of brand backing means that these enterprises do not feel the additional pressure from their international partners for complying strictly with the programme's conditions. It is mainly at this end of the market that Sialkot has seen its share in the world market drop significantly.

It appears that, from the initial planning stage of the programme, it was the larger companies and their international partners whose interests would be dominant. This is not surprising considering that it was these groups that drafted the child labour eradication programme. The smaller companies were already being marginalized.

Medium and small sized firms have found it more difficult to absorb the increased financial and administrative demands imposed on firms as a result of the restructuring. Nevertheless, in order to join the programme, while keeping costs down, these medium and smaller sized firms constructed 'scaled down units'. Invariably these centres are located at some distance from Sialkot city so as to draw upon the labour force from the surrounding villages.

MEDIUM AND SMALL SIZED UNITS

One such medium sized centre is located near the village of Peero Shahi (No. 101), in Pasrur *tehsil*, approximately 20 kilometres from Sialkot city. At a distance of about half a kilometre from the village itself, and situated on the road leading from Peero Shahi towards the main road into Sialkot, is the Ali Trading stitching centre. Ali Trading is a medium sized enterprise manufacturing a range of footballs including *Vilayati* and *Lahori* footballs for their international partners Puma, and *Desi* balls for a variety of non-sporting clients. There are similarities with the Sublime stitching unit. A boundary wall keeps strangers out. On approaching the stitching centre I was met with large, locked gates and two uniformed, armed guards. Entry without identification and a valid reason was not allowed. This show of 'security' represented the increasing formality of the system. The overt message was that the centre was now governed by 'rules and regulations', which would be strictly enforced. In particular, no 'unauthorised' individuals (i.e. children) could enter the premises and no material could be smuggled in or out of the unit. Luckily, I was accompanied by Mohammed Aslam, my 'research assistant' from Bunyad. Aslam was a close friend of the man in charge of the unit. Having established our credentials, we were allowed in. Once inside the differences become more evident. There are no manicured lawns or sporting facilities within the unit. The actual area housing the stitchers is much smaller—resembling a large bungalow rather than a factory. The canteen is a small tea stall. There is no modern machinery, and work is done entirely by hand. Some stitchers sat outside in the warm winter sun, busily stitching panels together. Inside the constructed part of the unit—simply one large hall—about 100 stitchers sat on their custom-built low cut chairs, completing stitch after stitch. All of them came from the six or seven villages in the 5-10 kilometre surrounding radius. None were women. A stereo cassette player blared the latest Indian film songs. The structure is more informal than in the Sublime centre. Apart from the few supervisors in place, none of the stitchers are on a permanent contract with the company. Instead, workers turn up in the morning and take whatever work is available. 'These days there are fewer workers in because it is the harvesting season and many men prefer to go to the fields. The pay is better than stitching footballs,' stated Iftikhar Shah, Ali Trading's representative at the centre. Iftikhar Shah was not the sub-contractor for Ali Trading. He was there to ensure that there was no 'leakage' from the site—an issue examined in greater detail in the next chapter. The *maker* was not present at the time but had gone to Ali Trading's warehouse in Sialkot city to arrange for a delivery of material to the stitching centre. While we sat talking with Shah, a pick-up truck laden with panels arrived and unloaded its cargo. Once empty it was loaded up with completed footballs on their way to the central warehouse for rechecking and packing.

Despite being more common than the type of centre that Sublime constructed, this medium sized centre is still less widespread than the incongruous, minimalist structures found on the outskirts of villages or occasionally in the market areas throughout Sialkot. The relative number of large, medium and small units[17] reflects the structure of an industry that may be dominated by a few large firms but where a much larger number of small firms battle for a piece of the same niche.

About eight kilometres down the road from Peero Shahi is the village of Laleywali (No. 100). The sign on one side of the dirt track leading into Laleywali, said 'Lofty—Muhammad Afzaal Stitching Unit'. Muhammad Afzaal was the *maker* in charge of the stitching centre and, rather than being a particularly tall gentleman as the name might suggest, he was short and squat and worked for a company called 'Lofty Sports'. Lofty had just secured a large foreign order for footballs and, in response, established almost 700 stitching units throughout Sialkot. All their stitching units were based on the model of the one built in Laleywali. On the occasion I visited Muhammad Afzaal's stitching unit in Laleywali, he had just gone off to the neighbouring village to check on his other stitching unit. The Laleywali unit stood in stark contrast to Sublime's stitching centre or even the one in Peero Shahi. Gone were the boundary walls and intimidating guards. Measuring around 20m x 10m, it had brick walls and a thatched roof. There were holes in the walls for windows but no windows in the spaces. Three light bulbs hung from the ceiling, but as I had visited in the day none of them were on. There was electricity and, like the unit in Peero Shahi, a tape recorder played the latest hit songs from Indian films. Instead of the glossy pictures of sports stars, the walls were adorned with newspaper clippings of film actresses, mostly Indian, though Kate Winslet, the star of Titanic, was clearly a favourite. Also on the wall was scrawled the one line code of conduct 'bachey mana hain' (children not allowed). Apparently having this written in a prominent place in the unit was a requirement. In fact, everything in the unit fulfilled the very basic requirements placed on football manufacturers in the wake of the industry's enforced restructuring. Again this appeared to be a reflection of the emphasis on fulfilling requirements rather than concern over the working conditions of the stitchers. Stitching had to be undertaken in units, even if the unit comprised no more than four walls. Often the stitchers preferred to work outside the confines of the unit structure, which was hot in summer and cold in winter. The maker, Muhammad Afzaal paid Rs. 7000 to have this structure built. In the neighbouring village (Jassorran, No. 108) he had hired a shop in the market for Rs. 3000 a month to act as another stitching centre. His group of 10 adult male stitchers in Laleywali—all aged between 18 and 40 - received no extra benefits and were all part of a casual labour force paid by the piece.

Unlike the more formal, impersonal and intimidating atmosphere in the larger units, where on-site supervisors kept close tabs on workers, here there was a more relaxed environment. Talking to stitchers working within the larger centres was problematic. It was difficult enough gaining entry into the centres. To then interrogate workers inside would not be appreciated by stitchers or their supervisors. It was always easier to speak to those stitchers after they had finished work and were no longer within the confines of their workspace. In the smaller units, there was much less chance of outside surveillance and workers were all likely to be from the same village.

I began talking to Tariq Javed, one of the older stitchers in the unit. Tariq had been stitching longer than any of his colleagues and was much admired for the skill and speed of his work. He had stacked up three completed footballs next to his work place, and with a few hours to go, he would be able to finish at least one more. The others were mostly on their second ball of the day. Tariq had the stitcher's build—rangy with the noticeably enlarged middle finger—a result of pulling the thread taut for every stitch. The shoulder and chest are also put under considerable stress as each stitch requires the arms to move outward until completely extended. His tools consisted of a 'chair' with almost no legs, so that its seat nearly touched the ground. In between his bent knees he held a large pincer-like tool used to keep the panels being stitched firmly in place. A strong thread is used with a large needle to actually complete the stitch. Two other tools are used—a leather 'ring' placed on the middle finger of both hands to stop the thread from cutting into the finger; and a 'screwdriver' with a sharp point used to enlarge the holes in the separate panels through which the thread is to be passed. This basic equipment is standard in all the units, from the largest to the smallest. As I talked to Tariq he continued stitching. The romanticised notion of peasant production as espoused by E.P. Thompson (1968) and given example by Weiss (1991, 130) in her description of a sporting goods factory in Sialkot, 'The pace of work was relaxed, albeit slow, resembling that observed in rural industry elsewhere in Pakistan (as opposed to that of factories in industrialised nations')—was far from evident. I asked Tariq for his thoughts on the newly instituted unit system.

There are good and bad points to this system. When I started stitching, I would stitch at home and my wife and daughters would also help me. A maker would deliver material to our ghar [home] and we would stitch araam se [in comfort at home] and when stitching was completed, he would come and pick it up. Now we have to travel to this unit and work here. The rates are better but we are often not making any more money than we did in the past. You see under the 'gharayloo' [home-based] system I had help from my khaandaan [family] and therefore we were able to stitch more footballs than I do alone in the unit. Now I can make three maybe four footballs a day. We are currently paid Rs. 32 per ball, so I make about Rs. 120-130 per day here. At home, I was paid Rs. 25 per ball but with my family's help, I could make six footballs. The unit system hasn't really benefited us. Even stitchers who work in the larger units, like in Peero Shahi or Saga are not that much better off. I used to work at one of Saga's regional stitching centres but it would take me two hours to travel there and back in their bus. The wages were better but I was not a permanent employee and so I could not get any other benefits. Also I found that I would spend my extra wages on buying lunch at the canteen and then cigarettes and other small items from the subsidised shop. So in the end I preferred to work at this unit. It is more convenient and in the time I spent travelling I can stitch an extra football and make up the lesser wage.

Tariq's views on the unit system mirror similar views of weavers in industrialising England as described by Thompson in his analysis of the English working class. 'Weavers disliked handloom factories. They resented the discipline, the factory bell or hooter, the time keeping which overrode ill health, domestic arrangements, or the choice of more varied occupations' (Thompson 1968, 337). Stephen Marglin (1990, 267) also emphasises that formalisation, even with the promise of a higher wage often does not compensate for the onerousness and physical discomfort of factory work—a point highlighted by Tariq in his description of working in comfort at home.

But not all of Tariq's colleagues agreed with him. Some of the other stitchers, and particularly the younger members of the unit were more supportive of the new system. 'The pay is better, we aren't disturbed as we were at home and it gives us a chance to meet with our friends', said Waseem, an eighteen-year-old stitcher in the same unit. Waseem has two brothers and in the past all three would stitch footballs at home. But following the decline in home-based stitching his two brothers found alternative work and Waseem joined the unit. The elder brother now works in a surgical goods manufacturing workshop in Sialkot city. The younger one, aged 13, has found work at a local workshop stitching gloves. Waseem's family has therefore not suffered a decline in income.

As I carried out more interviews in similar units, the split between those in favour and those against the unit system began to take on a general pattern. Those who preferred the unit system tended to be single men or individuals with small, 'male dominated' families (families with more male members) or families who had few members capable of stitching. In their case the small number of family members or the small number capable of stitching did not provide the additional labour that could have substantially increased the number of footballs stitched per family. As a result the individual was able to stitch the same or more footballs in the unit rather than at home. In addition, if the family had a large number of boys who were no longer able to stitch at home, the boys could, if required, find other work outside the home as in Waseem's brother's case. With unit rates being higher than home-based rates by an average of Rs. 8-10, an overall rise in family income was possible. In contrast to Waseem, Tariq's overall income has declined by around 20 per cent. In these instances, the higher rates per ball in the unit have not compensated for the fewer number of footballs being stitched per family. My own data indicated that from an average of five balls per day per family an individual unit worker was stitching three.

Larger families, and particularly those with a high percentage of female members capable of stitching, tended to favour the home-based system. The large family size meant that there was sufficient family labour available to assist in stitching and considerably more footballs could be made with the help of the entire family rather than by an individual working at a unit. In addition, if the percentage of girls in the family was high then stitching provided an avenue for them to earn an income. The unit system, in contrast, meant that girls who were previously earning through stitching at home were now denied that income as, unlike boys, they were unable to find alternative employment. Therefore, in the case of larger families,[18] which are much more common in Sialkot, the unit system has often led to an overall decline in family income.

However, while considering 'family' choices on football stitching it is important to bear in mind that in the subcontinent, as Mamdani (1972, 132) pointed out, it is the family that is the unit of work. Therefore decision-making tends to be family rather than individual based. The extended kinship network creates social networks that are not primarily self-oriented, but are instead based on local solidarities of necessity, so that most action and behaviour in which an individual engages is in relation to and mediated by the various groups to which s/he belongs. In such an environment, where the family and not the individual is the unit of public social action, family members develop a strategy that is conducive to its well-being as a unit. This, as Sahlins (1988) points out, not only increases social cohesion but also assists in the economic survival of the family unit. Internally, the ideal type family in Punjab is patriarchal and patrilocal. There is a strict hierarchy within the family and each family member has a clearly defined role determined by age and sex. Male and female spheres are defined as separate, the household being the domain of the woman. Men are involved in the world beyond the household, so that there is a clear division of labour based on gender. The eldest male is the head of the family until he decides to hand over authority to a successor, usually his eldest son. Each junior male defers to his elder brother and father.

Clearly this is an ideal representation of the family in Punjab, and virtually every ethnographer writing about Pakistan has stressed the male dominated feature of households in all but a few exceptional circumstances.[19] There has in fact been little ethnographic research done on the internal domestic power relations in Pakistan, even though it is an area where recent changes in family structure, particularly through migration, return migration, Islamisation and drug abuse, have occurred. But, while acknowledging the existence of internal dynamics within the family, when it come to decision-making, it is the family group as a whole rather than individual choices that are forwarded. So for example as James, Jenks and Prout point out 'from the perspective of poor families, the harm that child labour may do to an individual child has to be weighed against the survival of the household as a whole' (James, Jenks and Prout, 1998, 109). Therefore, when I refer to the football stitching family's choices, it refers to the joint decision making of the family rather than the individual's choice.

Apart from affecting the structure of the industry, the stitching unit system has begun to change the way football stitching as an occupation is viewed, particularly for the larger stitching centres. Prior to the restructuring, football stitching was largely dependent on an informal work force. The majority of these workers never considered stitching as their main occupation. Male stitchers, like Tariq, often held down other jobs and would stitch 'after hours' with the assistance of family members or would stitch when there was no other better paid work available, e.g. in between agricultural seasons. Now, because they come to the unit in the morning and leave at around five, they are unable to undertake any other work. Either they miss a full day's stitching or a full day of other work. Combining both is difficult as footballs are not always available later on in the day at the unit. With family labour removed from the equation the burden of stitching falls solely on the shoulders of the individual. While the agricultural season will often see a drop in the number of football stitchers available, indicating the higher returns from agriculture, it also means that, unlike the past when both opportunities could have been combined, it is now a case of one or the other. Consistent with Gramsci's observation on Fordism, a new type of worker was being created for a new form of work.

THE *MAKER*

By the time I had finished talking with the stitchers in the Laleywali unit, the *maker*—Muhammad Afzaal, arrived back on his motorbike. Part of the reason that the unit structure was instituted, apart from eradicating child labour, was to cut out the middleman, thereby theoretically benefiting the worker through the possibility of a higher direct wage. Not only has this not happened, but in some cases the maker has thrived, as we shall see later in the chapter. Therefore, particularly in comparison to his stitchers, Muhammad Afzaal's support of the unit system is understandable. Afzaal, like Naeem Javed of Sublime, started his career as a stitcher. When the industry began decentralising, he found himself negotiating for footballs on behalf of fellow stitchers from the same village. This role pushed him into becoming a *maker*, ferrying material to and from the company 'headquarters'. He became the manufacturer's link with their labour, paying them wages and having work done on time. From being a village-level *maker*, Afzaal gradually increased his networks to neighbouring villages and now manages units in several of the surrounding villages. The restructuring did mean that his role changed somewhat. Whereas in the past he would transport material to a number of households from the central headquarters of the companies he worked for, now he simply receives the raw material—panels, string, gum—at the company headquarters based in Sialkot city and then delivers them to his stitching centres, where the balls are stitched by a group of stitchers whom he has arranged. Once completed, he tests the finished balls with a footpump, rejects those not up to the mark for re-stitching, and delivers the completed ones to headquarters. Afzaal says that he takes, on average, between Rs. 2 and Rs. 5 per ball, as his own cut. The basic system remains the same as the larger units, only the scale is different. Instead of a pick-up truck with footballs loaded into the luggage portion, Afzaal heads off to Sialkot with a sack full of footballs bulging out from either side of his motorbike. The maker's role has changed rather than decreased. In some of the larger firms, old sub-contractors, like Naeem Javed, have taken on the role of unit supervisors. Material is delivered from headquarters by truck, so these sub-contractors no longer have to deal with distribution. Instead, they deal solely with supervising labour and quality control within the large stitching centres.

So far we have dealt exclusively with male stitchers based in the various units. Amongst this group there is a gradation between those that stitch permanently in the established brand-backed centres, and those that continue to stitch in units on a more informal basis. However, it is important to keep in mind that, like the showpiece units, permanent stitchers form a small minority and it is only this minority that are able to make full use of the benefits offered by the larger companies. Often this is no more than 10 per cent of the capacity stitching labour force that a company can take on, and that also applies to the largest and most established companies. The percentage of permanent stitchers will be much smaller for the smaller companies. For the rest of the stitchers there is the increasing inflexibility of formalisation with few of its benefits. However, it is the effect that the restructuring has had on those groups that it was supposedly instituted to benefit that most clearly illustrates how the 'development' process has marginalized the already marginal. Removal of children from the labour force was to benefit them as well as women. Children would be able to attend school, and family income would be protected through women replacing children in the labour force. But shortcomings in the planning process meant that, contra the rhetoric of participatory development, there was a singular absence of input in terms of 'indigenous knowledge' from the 'target beneficiaries' of the project. The result was that the restructuring was based on assumptions defined by reference to Western knowledge systems. This led to an increasing marginalisation of both women and children both through their increasing exclusion from the formal system and through Amartya Sen's (2001) concept of 'unfair inclusion' within the formal system.

FEMALE STITCHERS—BOSERUP REVISITED

Even before the restructuring of the football industry, gender classification in terms of who stitched which type of football was evident. The implementation of the unit system polarised this distinction. At the outset, football stitching was concentrated amongst a small male population. It was only with the growth in demand and the introduction of softer material in the late 1970s that women and children became involved in stitching. But the identification of men as 'master stitchers' remained. To date, the prevailing view of stitchers and *makers* is that adult males stitch the best quality ball. However, this classification of men as the expert stitchers appears more a function of opportunities available to them rather than inherent ability. Men stitch *Vilayati* balls, because women rarely had the opportunity to stitch this type of ball. There are several explanations for this. Firstly, the *Vilayati* ball was almost always made in factories where women rarely worked. Even during the era of the home-based industry the small number of *Vilayati* balls stitched were usually completed in the central factories under close supervision. The higher the quality of the football the more likely it is to remain close to the company headquarters, as far more quality checks are needed. Also as *Vilayati* balls make up a small segment of the market (20 per cent) it is easier to rely on a small group of expert stitchers rather than expand the network to less skilled workers.

In contrast, *Desi* balls required decent quality at low cost, and consequently manufacturers were more willing to allow this grade of ball to be stitched at homes in villages some distance from their central factories. The lower skill level required meant that *Desi* balls could easily be stitched by part-time, home-based stitchers. While this stitcher subset included men who stitched around their main profession, home-based stitching was generally a family effort with women and children often dominating. In addition, the lower quality *Lahori* and *Desi* balls made up the largest segment of the market ensuring that particularly during periods of high demand, sub-contractors travelled further and further afield in an attempt to seek out this cheap and flexible work force. Secondly, because initially neither women nor children were involved in football stitching, experienced stitchers were almost always men. Thirdly, men were far more likely to be permanent, full-time stitchers, further enhancing their experience and skill. Women had their tasks divided between housework and child rearing, and therefore rarely had the time to become full-time stitchers. As a result, men stitched the highest quality *Vilayati* balls, and women and children stitched the *Lahori* and *Desi* balls. Where men did have a small advantage in stitching *Vilayati* balls was the fact that because the *Vilayati* ball is made of a tough PVC material, it requires considerable strength to complete the required tightness of stitch. But, as if in recognition of the fact that there was no inherent reason for women not stitching as well as men, a small minority of male stitchers grudgingly admitted that women were better stitchers than men because of their dedication to their work. But generally the view was that women did not stitch as well as men but were more accomplished than children.

In the case of child labour, this perspective is contrary to the view espoused in other child labour dominated industries, such as the carpet industry, where it is often stated that children's nimble fingers give them an inherent advantage in making the finest knots. In football stitching, children are not seen as the best-equipped stitchers. But as part of a family force they can perform certain time consuming tasks without affecting the overall quality of the end product. So the youngest children coat the thread with gum, the first and easiest task in the process. They then graduate to stitching a few panels until they are able to complete half a ball or *kholru*. Some children may not progress beyond this stage and the more accomplished stitchers in the family are left the job of completing the footballs by undertaking the more complex tasks of stitching the two halves together and finishing the final 'blind' stitch.

Re-defining 'Work' and Women's Involvement

Prior to the restructuring of the industry, a government (1996) estimate had put the total number of children involved in football stitching at approximately 7000 (17 per cent) out of a total number of 42,000 stitchers. However, this estimate was made on the assumption that workers stitched on a full time basis, all year round. This was certainly not the case for children and rarely the case for adults. Most workers clearly stated that football stitching was a 'seasonal job' for them, and that they would stitch during times of financial need, in between agricultural seasons, or during school holidays. Keeping this in mind, Save the Children produced a second, more realistic estimate of 60–65,000 people involved in football stitching with at least 15,000 (25 per cent) of these being children.[20] Similarly, women's involvement was severely underestimated, leading to a bypassing of this crucial set of stitchers. In fact, a later survey by Save the Children (1997) revealed that 58 per cent of stitchers were women. Anita Khwaja, who looks after the social programme instituted by her late husband's company (Anwar Khwaja Industries) explained how manufacturers had reached the fundamentally flawed assumption that most stitching was undertaken by men.

I had decided to maintain a list of all the employees in our company, including sub-contractors and who these sub-contractors gave work to. I contacted all our sub-contractors and found that they all had a list of the people they would regularly give work to. They also had details of how many balls had been given for stitching, when the balls were due back, whether any advances had been given etc. But when I followed these links in the field I found a very different situation. From the named person who was supposed to be undertaking the stitching, material was being further distributed to neighbours and those responsible for this redistribution were women. Everyone was under the impression that men were doing the stitching, but I found that almost 60 per cent of our actual stitchers were women and children. Where I had three names on paper, in the field I was dealing with 25 people, mainly women and children. It was only when I presented these findings to the Sialkot Chamber of Commerce that they realized the extent of the involvement of women and children. The project envisaged that women would replace children in the stitching labour force but how could women replace children when they were already working?

Most manufacturers were oblivious to the involvement of children or women in the industry. Their link was with their sub-contractor. Beyond that the chain of events was unclear. Yet it was these manufacturers who negotiated the programme to restructure the industry and consolidate it around stitching units. Boserup (1970) in her essay *Women's Role in Economic Development* argued that ethnocentric colonial policies had assumed that women were not involved in agricultural production and had thus bypassed female farmers in favour of men. In Sialkot, three decades later, in an era where development policy is meant to be increasingly gender sensitive, it was similarly assumed that most stitchers were men. This assumption meant that stitching units were devised for male stitchers. No account was taken of the presence of a female stitching force, let alone a female-dominated labour force. By the time it was recognised that women made substantial contributions to the stitching of footballs, many of the stitching centres had already been constructed.

In fact, the confusion over the estimates of football stitchers and the 'involvement' of women and children takes us back to the redefinition of the concept of 'work' and the propagation of this particular concept as an objective definition. As Thompson points out in his analysis of the changing work patterns of weavers in England during industrialisation, the 'definition' of 'work' changed dramatically when the factory replaced the home-based system.

Weaving had offered an employment to the whole family. The young children winding bobbins, older children watching for faults, picking over cloth, or helping to throw the shuttle in the broad-loom; adolescents working a second or third loom; the wife taking a turn in weaving in and among her domestic employments. The family was together. A whole pattern of family and community life had grown up this way. (E.P. Thompson 1968, 339).

The factory system redefined work as wage and factory-based, and controlled by the 'rules and regulations' of the factory environment, while home-based tasks were redefined as domestic tasks. But work, like childhood, as Wadel emphasises, is 'a socially constructed category. New types of activities are continuously included under the concept while others are excluded; and the way that we characterise work activities and distinguish them from non-work activities is continuously changing' (Wadel 1979, 365). Nevertheless, in much the same way as other Western constructs have become dominant as objective categories, so too has this particular notion of work .

Thompson's description has strong parallels with the Sialkot football industry prior to its restructuring. Football stitching was a supplementary, flexible, family-based source of income, usually occupying more than one household member to varying degrees of frequency and intensity, rather than a full-time, specialised occupation. For example, Tariq Javed, the stitcher at the unit in Laleywali, explained how, when football stitching was home-based, his family would stitch up to six footballs a day when working as a group. His two eldest daughters Fatima, 16, and Samia, 14, were both able to stitch complete footballs, but more often than not they would stitch the two *kholrus* (halves) and let Tariq finish stitching them together. Tariq's wife, Humaira, could also stitch a *kholru*, though less frequently than her daughters primarily because of the need to complete other household tasks, such as cleaning the house and cooking for the entire family. The three younger daughters, Afroze, 12, Sameena, 10 and Sameera, 7, were all 'helpers'. They, especially Afroze and Sameera, had graduated to stitching a few panels together, but more often would enlarge the holes along the sides of the panels, thread needles and apply gum to the thread used for stitching. The youngest child and the only boy, Zahir, aged 6, had not started stitching and would only thread needles and apply gum to the thread. Furthermore, stitching was rarely a continuous process for any of the family members. When better paid work was available Tariq would take that up, often returning home at the end of the day to complete footballs that had been partially stitched by other family members. Humaira worked around her domestic chores, with the girls also helping out around the house. At times when more money was required, such as during the *Eid* festivals, the family would take on extra stitching. The *maker*, though, would pay Tariq the wages for the entire family. Tariq would then give his daughters some of this income, which they would save for their dowries, or for *Eid* clothes, or occasionally for the purchase of hair clips, sweets and small toys. Thus, 'work' in this case was characterised by flexibility and the worker having a degree of control over its intensity and pace. It was also centred on the family and the home.

If however we use 'work' in the sense of a full-time, wage-based activity, it precludes the majority of football stitchers. Only Tariq in the above example would be a possibility, and that also because he receives the wage for work that is undertaken by his entire family. In fact, even Tariq is not a full-time stitcher as he would often take up other work and stitch simultaneously. This need to fit social forms into neat, bounded categories as defined by Western notions compounded 'inaccuracies' in the collection of information and contributed in particular to the underestimation of female involvement in football stitching.

WOMEN'S 'PREFERENCE' FOR THE HOME-BASED SYSTEM

When it was recognised that women made a substantial contribution to stitching footballs, the second incorrect assumption was made, that they could be persuaded to take up employment in formal units and thereby reduce the loss of income the family faced as a result of the decline in home-based work. Both assumptions were based on the dominant Western model for the formalisation of the workplace and took little account of factors that had in the first place led to a clustering of women in the home-based sector.

Kabeer (1994) indicates two dominant explanatory paradigms that are used to account for the clustering of women in certain occupations. The first revolves around the effect of cultural and religious factors on women, while the second focuses on economic choice. The economic choice model sees the process of decision-making within households 'as the allocation of resources such as members' labour time in accordance with the basic principle of rational behaviour, namely maximisation of the household's joint welfare function. The culturalist paradigm gives analytical weight to cultural construction of masculinity and femininity in explaining gender differences in labour supply behaviour' (N. Kabeer 1994, 166). Kabeer goes on to point out that Muslim women have attracted considerable attention within this paradigm because of Islamic ideologies in general, and the 'constraints' of *purdah* on women's mobility and visibility in particular. Both paradigms have their proponents. Samita Sen (1999) comes to the conclusion that the supply of the female labour force to the Bengal jute industry was more an outcome of the managers' desire for a casual, cheap labour force than social and cultural restrictions. De Haan (1999), writing on managers' and workers' strategies in the Calcutta jute industry disagrees, arguing that Sen underestimates the restrictions on women's mobility. I tend to agree with de Haan's analysis, which implies that, rather than being mutually exclusive, both paradigms can be evoked together. In fact, de Haan's argument is even more persuasive when applied to Sialkot.

Holmstrom (1984, 227) argues that women seem principally or exclusively to be assigned tasks that need no special knowledge or skill and which, though often monotonous, require precision and alertness. Therefore, women are favoured in the electronics industry for jobs that require tiny parts to be handled gently and carefully, and where fine wires have to be twisted and bound. Furthermore 'footloose' industries like the garment industry in Bangladesh (Kabeer 1994) or the shoe industry in Agra, India (Knorringa 1996, 1999), are highly labour intensive and therefore have to reduce their labour costs to be able to compete in international markets. In addition, they tend to be characterised by seasonal demand. These factors mean that employers are particularly keen to find a flexible, cheap, and unorganised labour force.

The football manufacturing industry has similar characteristics—the trade is labour intensive, seasonal and seeks a cheap and flexible workforce. Stitching 'though monotonous, requires precision and alertness'. But while women and children may fit this worker profile, managers did not specifically 'recruit' women or children because they met these criteria. Undoubtedly, the decentralisation of the 1970s was part of 'manager strategy' to bypass labour restrictions and gain access to the type of labour force that was most suitable to employers' needs. However, unlike the urban-based Bangladeshi garment industry or the

South-East Asian electronics assembling industry, female workers were almost entirely home-based, and as such could not be 'recruited'. Rather than be either economically driven or culturally/religiously determined, the pattern of women's employment appears to be the outcome of a combination of both. Employers sought a cheap, flexible labour force and the structure of the decentralised industry meant that such a work force was to be found through the family unit based at home. That women and children came to dominate this employer-friendly' home-based stitching system was an outcome of the cultural and religious factors that demarcate the home as the female domain. Male workers also stitched footballs at home, but whenever possible, would take up more lucrative work outside the home.

To these factors must be added another, even though it operates within the parameters set by the existing cultural and religious milieu. In keeping with the development discourse's focus on promoting Western norms, it is often assumed, without question, that women in the Third World would benefit from following the lifestyle of their 'liberated' sisters in the West. Furthermore, as Mohanty (1991, 56) argues, Western feminist discourse, like that of development, has been dominated by an ethnocentric universality that 'self-presents' Western women as educated and modern, as having control over their own bodies and sexualities, and the freedom to make their own decisions. In contrast, Third World women are represented as poor, uneducated, tradition-bound, domestic, family-oriented and universally oppressed. The representation of Western women becomes the model to be aspired to while the representation of Third World women consigns them and their norms and values, en masse, to being under-developed. It follows that in order to throw off the yoke of oppression, Third World women should aspire towards adopting the norms and values of the ideal model while discarding their own outdated traditions, which merely act as indicators of their under-development. Thus, for example, the wearing of veils by women or the gender-based division of labour is immediately assumed to be a sign of patriarchal dominance and oppression. Rather than be confined to the home, Third World women should be 'empowered' to take up 'employment' at a 'work place'. Just as men are able to take up employment outside the house, so should women have the same choice, rather than being bound to the home because of their 'traditional' domestic role. But in Sialkot, far from being preferred, work in restructured units was rejected by the majority of women. Instead it was home-based stitching that women saw as a convenient and safe form of supplementing household income. Ridd (1994), in her examination of Muslim women in Cape Town, underlines the 'preference' for home involvement and points out that the separation of male and female into different spheres (therefore the title of her chapter 'Separate but more than equal' lies at the heart of Western difficulties with Islam.

> It runs contrary to so much that the western feminists have struggled for. Although in the West we have tried to recognise the value of women's domestic work and the need to give women a choice between being a home-maker and having a career (and, indeed, a choice of both), our attention has focussed primarily on the problems for women of becoming integrated into the public world that has been so long dominated by men. It appears to be generally difficult for western feminists, even anthropologists, to look at Muslim societies in their own terms and to recognise the possibility that women can also enjoy autonomy and fulfilment within their own sphere. (R. Ridd 1994, 87).

Both male and female informants in Sialkot frequently emphasised the separation but equality of women and men in Islam. Each had their own separate spheres of dominance, and taken together man and wife complement each other ideally for the overall benefit of the family. Thus, whereas women will be dominant in the 'domestic' sphere, men are dominant outside the home. For this reason it is easier and more culturally acceptable for women to work at home, and for men to seek employment outside the home. Furthermore, when we speak of the 'restrictions' on women we must be careful that these, as Ridd emphasises, 'were restrictions that I, as an outsider, observed rather than anything that the Muslim women were themselves particularly concerned about' (R. Ridd 1994, 90).

Many of the female football stitchers that I interviewed showed little desire to take up work in the formal sector, often complaining that this would mean taking on the dual burden of house and wage work. Furthermore, there was little desire to adopt the 'liberation' of the West. Instead, it was common for football stitchers, and wider society, to identify the West as being a '*khula mahaul*' (an overly permissive environment) which they saw as leading to the West's moral corruption. They frequently point to accounts of unchecked sexual activity outside marriage, teenage pregnancies, drug and alcohol abuse, and frequent breakdown in marriage. In support of this view, Laura Nader argues that the increasing separation of work and home has caused serious social problems to families in the United States. 'Moving [for work] has its problems, and is undoubtedly related to an increased incidence of alcoholism, drug addiction, and child abuse, and to the fact that 76 per cent of all minor and major tranquilliser drugs are consumed by women in this country' (L. Nader 1980, 33).

But the formal model of work advocates the channelling of women's labour through national and international businesses, and increasing market determined productivity. The outcome is the attempt to persuade women to take on employment in an increasingly formalised Westernised format. Therefore, stitching was to be undertaken in large, centrally located units where fixed timings would be observed. This resulted in the exclusion of the majority of female stitchers from the formal unit system, primarily because formalisation did not take into account the local cultural and religious imperatives. For the majority of women, centralised stitching units were not viable alternatives to home-based stitching, and the resistance to women working in stitching units, even single sex stitching units, is a reflection of the mismatch between the Western formal model of employment and the work place, and the local socio-cultural environment. In order to better understand this resistance it is essential to examine the notion of *izzat* and its connection with women in Pakistan.

RESISTANCE TO FEMALE STITCHING UNITS—WOMEN AS THE EMBODIMENT OF IZZAT

The single sex style factories of Vietnam, Malaysia or even urban Bangladesh turned out to be incompatible with the cultural role of women in Sialkot. Not only did the unit system mean that women would have to work outside their homes, but the formalisation of work meant that they would have to maintain regular working hours at the centres. This was only considered feasible for women who had no children or had support in the form of other female family members to take care of daily household chores. But where there was little support, attendance at units could effectively result in the transfer of household chores to children, potentially removing them from school. 'Women are often dependent on children for performing their domestic roles as wives and mothers and for carrying on their subsidiary occupations in the cash economy' (E. Schildkrout 1981, 84). This interdependence means that changes in one affect the other.

The question of why women did not take up stitching in units was often met with a mocking response by female informants—an indication that it was not considered even a remote possibility. In Noorpura (No.44), a village close to Sialkot city, I met with the most vociferous opposition to the attempt to formalise the football stitching structure. A group of approximately twenty women had gathered at a non-formal school during one of my community group meetings. Far from 'docile' and 'oppressed' women as they are often stereotypically represented in the media and some academia,[21] this group was vocal and forthright in its views. While all the women wore dupattas (headscarves), these were draped loosely on their heads rather than tightly concealing the hair entirely in the fashion of the more conservative. Naseem, a middle-aged parent of a student in the school and a regular stitcher when work was available at home, took on the role of spokesperson. A group of about six or seven women actively joined in the discussion while the others, though more subdued, continued to voice their support, though less forcefully. Naseem angrily pointed out:

In the past there was so much work that we could pick and choose when we wanted to stitch. Also we used to ensure that the maker paid us an advance. Now we have no work and if there are children in our house the maker says it is too risky for him to give us any stitching. It's one thing to stop children from stitching but to stop their parents from earning their livelihood is a jurm [criminal act]. How are we meant to feed our families? How do we marry our daughters to izzatdaar [respectable] households?

There was widespread agreement with Naseem and the complaint was constantly reiterated. When I asked about the possibility of the women finding employment in a female stitching centre the response was quick and unambiguous. Naseem explained why the larger units were not options:

The big units are too far away for us older women to go to, and some male relative has to accompany us there and back. What about our housework? Who will do that and what do we do with our children in the meantime? I can't leave them alone for so long and I will not let some ghair [stranger] look after my child in the factory. Also it is difficult for us to go because my in-laws would never like it if I were to work outside the house, let alone outside the village. Home stitching was much better. It was so convenient for us. We could do it in the privacy of our house without anyone knowing.

And we cannot let our daughters go to work. They are our ghar ki izzat [family's honour] and we cannot take any chances with our izzat.

The concept of *izzat* or honour is an important one, and it lies at the heart of the dilemma that faces women, and particularly unmarried girls. In the Punjab, while the precedence of genealogy, age wealth, and gender are important in defining an individual's status, they do not necessarily guarantee authority or social precedence. *Izzat* can be earned but it can also be lost. One of the ways that individuals can earn *izzat*, as Abu-Lughod (1986, 86) points out in her analysis of honour and status in Bedouin society, is through aspiring to their society's moral ideals.

Thus a family has *izzat* when its men and women embody the ideals of Punjabi society. For men, this includes fulfilling the role of provider and protector for the family. Furthermore, a father must ensure that his daughters are married off 'appropriately' as this reflects on his *izzat* as well as the *izzat* of the wider group to which he belongs. A family also has *izzat* when its women are able to fulfil the role assigned to them by society. In Punjab, women must ideally be supportive and deferential to the male head of the household. More specifically, they must follow what Abu-Lughod (1986) identifies as the Muslim women's 'code of modesty'. This involves 'covering the hair, arms, legs and the outlines of the body as well as more personal gestures such as downcast eyes, humble but formal posture and restraint in eating, smoking, talking, laughing and joking' (Abu-Lughod 1986, 108).

Prior to the restructuring, girls in the age group 12-15 would stitch footballs primarily to save money for their dowries. Marriages represent the most expensive one-off event in the life of a family. A daughter's marriage has the added expense of a dowry, so that it is common for a family with two or three young daughters to consider how the daughters will be married off. This is important, not only because of the economic aspects, but also because daughters are both the core of *izzat* and also the primary elements for a man's ambitions to increase his and his family's *izzat*. If a father marries his daughter 'well', he has lived up to one of the most important tasks assigned to him by society. However, the failure to provide an appropriate dowry seriously affects the chances of finding a good match, thereby immediately reflecting on the status of the girl's family. Therefore girls saving for their dowries can be seen as saving for one of their own and their family's most important life events.

The sense of *izzat* is a status possessed collectively. *Biraderis* do not hold movable property in common nor do they share earnings, but the *izzat* (honour) or *sharam* (shame) of individual members affects the general standing of the *biraderis* within a village. A common Punjabi saying states *'one does not share the bread, but one shares the shame'*. Similarly, the daughter of one man of the *biraderi* is considered the daughter of all. The *izzat* of the *biraderi* is held collectively, with the women of the group seen as the embodiment of this *izzat*. It is for this reason that marriages are so important for the *biraderi's izzat*. *Biraderis* will often act as combined mutual aid societies and welfare agencies, frequently contributing collectively towards dowries and wedding expenses. This is particularly the case if the *biraderi* has done well but the individual who has arranged the wedding has not. In order to preserve the image of the *biraderi* and maintain its *izzat* it becomes necessary to subsidise the wedding.

Izzat is 'respected or ruined in social transactions, markedly those involving unmarried daughters' (K. Hall 1995, 253). As marriages are expected to take place between social equals, if a daughter is married to a 'bad family', the only interpretation by the community is that she was married to a family that was equal to her own. Furthermore, because *izzat* is seen as being collectively possessed, it means that any slight on the honour of the girl—malicious gossip, inappropriate public behaviour—can taint the reputation of the entire family and the wider *biraderi* and damage the girl's chances of attracting a suitable match.

Having braved the interview with Naseem and the other women, I proceeded to interview her daughter who attends the non-formal school where the community group meeting was held. Asiya is thirteen years old and when footballs were available for stitching at home, she was able to stitch two a day.

> My family would stitch footballs and after school I would also help out. This way I was able to save for my dowry or use the savings when the family needed it. Sometimes I would use my earnings for school fees. Now there are no footballs to stitch at home. My parents fight a lot, and they feel I am a burden on them. I can't go to stitching units. It is not possible. My parents have been threatening to take me out of school because they think that I am too old now and should be staying home. So far I have managed to convince them to let me stay on.

Asiya's story is familiar throughout Sialkot where parents are quick to take girls out of school once they reach puberty. The most common age for marriage is between the ages of 12 and 16[22], and during fieldwork one of the most widespread reasons given for female school dropouts, especially in the 12-15-age bracket, was early engagement or marriage. More often than not girls were stopped from studying by their parents. The position of girls as the embodiment of honour for the wider group means that extreme precautions are taken by families to ensure that women do nothing to bring *sharam* to their wider group. The importance of *izzat* to the family and particularly the men of the family, who are seen as the custodians of *izzat*, has also, in extreme cases, manifested itself through the incidence of honour killings. As Dasgupta (1993, 321) points out, the idea that men should be protectors of women may sound grand, but in the worst of circumstances the effects can be devastating. Honour killings usually involve male family members, most often brothers but also fathers and uncles, killing female relatives who are seen to have brought *sharam* upon their family. The most common instances of *sharam* are women marrying against their family's wishes. The 'loss' of *izzat* is experienced so deeply that in some cases certain members of the family may feel the only way to restore some semblance of honour is to kill the offending female relative. It rubs out the stain by rubbing out the cause of the stain. It matters not whether the woman is guilty or not of the charges levelled against her, or that she may be the victim, as in the case of a rape. The important thing is that a public shame is publicly redressed. It should be emphasised however, that honour killings represent an extreme response. Nevertheless, even in less extreme cases, girls above the age of 13 are often confined to their homes and social contact is limited to family members and close relatives. Thus, girls in this age group are often the most likely to drop out of school. For many, previous schooling was not possible and they therefore find it particularly difficult to adjust to a school environment. Parents point to poor school performance and use it as an added justification for removing the girls from school, leaving them without work or school. For Asiya and her friends even attendance at the local village school was problematic. Travelling some distance to a stitching unit would be out of the question.

The need to protect the *izzat* of the house (i.e. the women) 'restricts' female mobility in Sialkot. But, to a lesser extent, the *izzat* of the family is also affected if members, and particularly women, undertake work that is not considered *izzatdaar* (respectable). Naseem hinted that stitching at home meant that work could be done in private without others knowing what work was being undertaken. A number of women complained that going to work in stitching centres would mean that everyone in their village would be aware of their employment. Women are particularly reluctant to admit to 'working', primarily because for women to take on manual work is considered far more indicative of a family's economic hardship. In this strongly status-conscious society the employment of women, and particularly the employment of women outside the house as related by Naseem, represents the male head of household's failure to live up to his socially defined role as provider. This thereby implies a loss of *izzat* for the family. Home-based stitching was easier to conceal, and if the family had to work, at least with the work being home-based it could be justified to an extent as falling within the domain of household work, making it more acceptable for women to undertake.

Therefore football stitching is looked down upon because it shows that a family is struggling economically and that women in the family have to work as a result. But there is no moral condemnation of the profession, unlike the case of the Bangladeshi female garment workers. Kabeer explains that the garment workers are often described as 'shameless' women who 'walked boldly down the streets in groups, their heads uncovered, unaccompanied by male guardians' (Kabeer 1994, 173). Kabeer argues that the independence of these women, and their 'rejection' of religiously and culturally defined roles, leads to the garment workers being looked down upon by wider society. In contrast, the home-based football stitchers of Sialkot do not face the same disapproval. Football stitching is not denounced as representing a cultural or religious breach.

However, as soon as stitching moves outside the home it is no longer considered appropriate work for women and attitudes begin to resemble those in Bangladesh. There is some evidence of the moral condemnation of female work outside the house already in Sialkot. Some of the more 'conservative' families and particularly the religious *mullahs* (Muslim 'priests') that I spoke to stated that they felt that the large female stitching centres were promoting a Western way of life and encouraging women to neglect their household duties. No *izzatdaar* family would allow its women to work outside the home, leaving them vulnerable to the potentially corrupting influences of the outside world. The economic incentive of higher wages at centres, therefore, does not override social constraints in Sialkot. Cunningham (2000, 431) points out that similarly in the second half of the 19th century, despite increasing female wages, married women in Belgium, Wales and England did not take the place of children, reflecting possibly the value of their work in the home and more importantly the belief that a woman's place was in the home. In much the same way, women in Sialkot were generally unwilling to take up the limited opportunities provided by female stitching units.

It must also be pointed out that only the largest companies, probably no more than three or four, had the resources to build separate stitching centres for women, meaning that the number of female centres was extremely limited. The capacity of female stitching centres was never going to cover the number of women who had stitched footballs at home. At best it was a token gesture aimed at promoting the companies' image with foreign buyers, rather than a genuine attempt to benefit female stitchers.

At a fundamental level, it is questionable how 'formalisation' can even be justified as the preferred model. Some of the reasons why home-based work may be preferred over factory work have already been examined. Furthermore, experience from those areas where 'formalisation' has been enforced, shows that many of the problems that were supposed to be solved by formalisation remain in place along with a host of additional concerns. Recent reports on single sex work places in the export processing zones of countries such as Indonesia and Vietnam show that paid employment in a formal environment is no guarantee that workers will be treated fairly, or will be free from harassment, rape and injury. Indeed, often the opposite is more accurate. The factories of multi-national companies in South-East Asia, Nike being the most prominent, are consistently targeted by NGOs, anti-globalisation and labour activists for the excessive exploitation of workers, despite having set up the very structure that is now being advocated in Sialkot.[23] Simmons' (1997) feminist critique of development being driven by market determined productivity emphasises that women may not want to be part of the international economy, and that improving women's access to paid employment can in fact lead to further exploitation, poverty and social dislocation.

But it appears that so long as the 'conditions' imposed by the formalised model are met, the potential social upheavals caused by the imposed changes can be overlooked. The formalised, Western model advocates a particular 'development', and any deviations from this are increasingly marginalized even though there is strong evidence that the model may not be the most appropriate in the given social environment. It may have been impressive to international buyers keen on ensuring that local partners were seen to be making progress towards eradicating 'regressive' practices. It may mollify workers in Western countries who feel exposed to unfair competition, to follow a strict principle of eliminating children from work places. It may also reassure concerned consumers who feel their goods are tainted with child labour. But the unenthusiastic local response to the crèches and female stitching centres are testament to the inapplicability of these efforts and the lack of benefits to the supposed beneficiaries. The structures may look impressive but the effect is akin to a gourmet restaurant serving meat dishes to a vegetarian clientele.

For reasons that began with the incorrect assumption concerning the composition of the stitching labour force, women have been almost completely bypassed by the restructuring. This indicates the distance between the design and implementation of the project and the complex reality on the ground.

The outcome of the establishment of the stitching centre system was an estimated 37,000 female stitchers losing work, lending credence to Escobar's claim that development has not only rendered invisible women's contribution to the economy, as first argued by Boserup, but it has also had a detrimental effect on their economic position and status (Escobar 1995, 171).

FORMALISED INFORMALITY

The response from the Atlanta Agreement partners to the loss of home-based work for women was to allow a minor concession in the face of the wider restructuring. This involved the formation of *home-based female stitching centres*. As the name suggests, these refer to stitching centres being set up at home. The process involves three or four women getting together and registering the home-centre with the concerned manufacturer and the ILO. This allows both these bodies to monitor the centre. Not only was this system convenient for home-based stitchers, it was also more feasible for medium and small-sized manufacturers, who could not afford the investment that larger stitching centres required. Thus, the emergence of home-based female stitching centres was the result of a combination of religious and cultural obligations on women, and the economic requirements of particularly smaller firms.

My first experience of a home-based female stitching centre turned out to be a unique one. While visiting a school in Hundal (No. 34), a large village on the outskirts of Sialkot city, I was informed that a female sub-contractor provided material to a recently established home-based stitching centre. Because of the nature of the job sub-contractors are, almost without exception, male. I immediately inquired, therefore whether it would be possible to meet Bano, a rare exception. One of the parents at the school was happy to show me the stitching centre. As we wound our way through the village's narrow streets, I asked whether Bano would be willing to talk to me being a male interviewer. Much to my surprise, I received an almost mischievous reply, '*Bano to munda banke phirti hai*' (Bano roams around like a boy). I assumed from the tone and content of the response that Bano would talk to me and that she was simply trying to emulate her male counterparts. The reality turned out to be much closer to what I had been told.

On arrival at the stitching centre, my guide knocked on the door and introduced me. Bano had apparently just stepped out, but would be back in a few minutes. I could wait inside. Outside, a small sign had the name of the sponsoring manufacturer and a registered number. The stitching centre was simply a two-bedroom house. An outer wall enclosed a courtyard. To one side of the courtyard was a small covered area for cooking. In the courtyard itself, four women aged between 16 and 35 sat stitching footballs. I was ushered into one of the bedrooms that overlooked the courtyard. As I waited, one of the women came up to me, handed me a cup of tea and informed me that Shahbaz would be here soon. The fact that Shahbaz was to meet me made me assume that maybe Bano had decided not to be interviewed and was sending her brother instead. Disappointed, I waited for Shahbaz in the hope that maybe the two of them would come together. Minutes later a young man walked in, shook hands with me and introduced himself as Shahbaz, the son of the owner of the house. Shahbaz had boyish features, was of average height, spoke in a slightly husky voice and looked to be in his early twenties. I chatted with him for a few minutes hoping that Bano would appear. But it seemed that Shahbaz was keen on being my interviewee. A few of the other stitchers had also come into the room in anticipation of the conversation. Just as I was about to ask whether Bano would be coming the words of my guide hit me—Bano roams around like a boy—Bano literally did roam around like a boy. The young man sitting opposite me was, in fact, a young woman. Shahbaz was Bano! I had been further misled by the fact that

Bano/Shahbaz was wearing a *shalwar kameez* stitched in a distinctly masculine style. On top of that s/he wore a loose jacket—women hardly ever wear jackets, preferring to drape a shawl around themselves. Furthermore, s/he had shaken hands with me—something that women rarely do in Pakistan. Covering up my failure to recognise Bano, I asked her when she had decided to take on the male disguise.

> I used to be a stitcher a few years ago. Along with my sisters and a few friends we would stitch footballs at home. But over the last few years there has been a slump in trade and now footballs cannot be stitched at home. Since then some of the girls in the village have been asking me to try and arrange some stitching for them. They had been encouraging me to become a maker. So finally I decided to go to one of the firms that used to send material to our homes previously; Khalid Overseas. The owner was happy to make me a contact point for setting up a women's stitching centre. They have many makers working for them. I am just one of them. But by becoming a maker I can now supply work to some of the girls that are desperate for an income. I also try and get them good rates per ball. When I met some of the other makers they assumed that I was a *munda* [boy]. From then I decided that it would be easier for me to continue pretending to be a *munda*. They would never take a female maker seriously and they may misbehave as well. The owner is the only one who knows I am a girl but he doesn't tell anyone. It is more convenient for me this way. By being Shahbaz I can go and get material, I can use a motorbike and I can easily do this job.

Enterprising, resourceful and brave, Bano contradicted the stereotypical view of the passive South Asian woman. It may be a man's world but Bano had found a way of participating in it. She reminded me in some ways of Shaheen Atiq-ur-Rehman, Bunyad's inspirational founder. Both women contradicted dominant western and local stereotypes, challenging the Western perception of their passivity and the local view of women's 'traditional' domestic roles. Shaheen had gone further, by being accepted in a position of authority in what is considered a 'male' sphere of influence. Bano had managed to participate in a male-dominated field even though it was through 'deception'. When I had come to Bano's stitching centre she had been informed that someone had come to see her regarding footballs. Assuming that I was a supplier or someone from the company that she received footballs from, Bano decided to maintain her 'façade'. It was only having introduced myself and my work, and having realised that I knew her real identity, that

Bano began to speak openly about herself and her gender reversal role playing. Nevertheless, as if out of habit, Bano continued to 'behave' like a man. She walked with a slightly arrogant swagger and the voice remained low. But in a small concession to her 'feminine' side, when I asked about the effect of stitching on the hands she immediately thrust her own hands out and showed me the swelling around her middle finger. 'My hands are being ruined through stitching and my mother is always complaining that it is okay for men to have 'bad' hands but not for girls'.

On asking Bano what she thought of the unit system, she, like the majority of the other sub-contractors I interviewed, stated that the unit system was preferable to the old home-based system. 'Now *makers* don't have to go running to each and every house to give the material. It is also much easier for us to make sure that good work is being done and that it is done on time. The unit system is better for quality.'

Just before I took my leave from Bano I asked whether she was interested in increasing the number of female home-based stitching centres in Hundal. Her reply was illustrative of some of the continued problems that prevent women from organising effectively in Sialkot.

> I have been quite lucky because I knew some girls who wanted to work. Two of them are sisters and are known to my family. But for many other women in the village, they are worried that people will know that they are stitching and that will not be good for their family. Also it is so difficult to organise some of the women. They are constantly arguing over whose house the centre should be in or not. Some refuse to go to other's houses because of family differences.

Despite these misgivings, the number of home-based units apparently expanded rapidly in less than a year to a high of 962 home-based stitching centres where 4668 women[24] worked, indicating the demand for stitching by women who could only stitch at home. But as the number of centres increased so did concern that home-based stitching centres allowed easy involvement of children in the process of football manufacture. So while the ILO initially stated[25] that 'they had no problems monitoring these centres', within a year they had decided that home-based centres threatened the credibility of the entire project[26] and 'efforts would have to be made to decrease them and to realise more, somewhat larger centres in the villages'. Furthermore, without giving any further explanation, and contradicting the previous findings that home-based centres would be beneficial to female stitchers, it was decided in the same meeting that 'moving to the somewhat larger centres would benefit all the partners'. Subsequently, the number of home-based centres declined dramatically to just over 500, with approximately 2000 women attending these centres. The home-based centres therefore offered a limited option for women. They also represented a small concession, in the light of the wider programme, to the NGO voices that were highlighting the 'unintended consequences' of the restructuring on women.

Nevertheless, this 'formalised informality' constitutes a deviation from the dominant model and this has led to its marginalisation. In the past, because stitching was a family activity, *makers* paid piece rates depending on the quality of the ball, unlike the majority of 'child labour' scenarios where children are paid less for work by virtue of being children, or women paid less for being women. Wages were highest for the *Vilayati* balls and lower for the *Lahori* and *Desi* balls, a reflection of the greater skill and time required to stitch higher quality balls. *Makers* made payment per ball irrespective of who the ball was stitched by. The fact that the footballs were stitched collectively meant that discrimination based on gender or age was not possible. Now though, larger female stitching centres or home-based units meant that footballs were being exclusively stitched by women. As a result the rates of pay in home-based stitching centres dropped below those of male stitching centres. Formalisation brought with it, through Sen's concept of unfair inclusion, the increasing marginalisation of women within the formal sector.

From the Saga and Sublime headquarters through the Ali Trading medium sized unit and Lofty Sports' minimal unit to the home-based units, this chapter has examined a range of structures all with different degrees of 'formalisation' — from showpiece to basic. Just as development thinking is charged with the hegemony of Western culture and values, and relegates non-Western cultures to being 'traditional', so the formalisation of the work place, as part of this wider process, relegates all deviations to marginality. The resulting worker structure takes on the shape of a pyramid with permanent employees at the top representing a tiny minority. The lower down we get in the pyramid the more marginalized the workers and the greater their numbers. Permanent employees at the most formal units have the highest wages and access to a range of additional benefits. But they are also the smallest minority of workers. From there we move down to the larger group of temporary stitchers, who may still be offered better wages than in the smaller units, but who cannot access all the additional benefits. Further down the chain the medium and small-sized units offer marginally better wages but no benefits. The home-based units are the most marginalized, with wages being lower on the basis of the workers being women.

In this chapter, an examination of the changes resulting from the imposition of the unit system on Sialkot's football industry has shown that the formal restructuring has benefited the larger, more established firms. The outcome has been Sialkot's increasing reliance on higher quality balls that are almost entirely manufactured 'in-house' by the larger manufacturers. The large firms involved in the programme almost all joined the programme as soon as it was launched. Many of them had in fact been at the forefront of ensuring that a programme was put in place, to avert any threat of sanctions against the industry. These firms are also the ones that were backed by international brands and have managed to establish themselves on a sound financial footing. As a result, the adjustment to the stitching unit system has been less problematic and these large manufacturers have been able to offer their employees better wages and facilities. But these opportunities have been restricted to the few large manufacturers and the small subset of stitchers employed by them on a permanent basis. Formalisation has led to the securest jobs and remunerative opportunities being 'masculinised' (J. Parry 1999, xxiv) while the employment opportunities associated with a 'cheapening of labour and a renewed emphasis on its flexibility and docility' are feminised and found in the informal sector.

Many of the small and medium-sized firms joined later, and are still struggling to meet the conditions laid down by the programme. Most operate in the more competitive, price-driven, lower quality segment of the market. Profits and economies of scale tend to be much smaller in this sector and the smaller companies have found increased costs and foreign competition are beginning to squeeze them out of business. The response has been for several smaller firms, and some of the larger ones, to try and avoid the increasing costs, and to stay competitive through continued recourse to the home-based sector and the stitchers in this sector. It is these stitchers that constitute the base of the workers' pyramid described above.

This chapter has examined the process of marginalisation of the proposed beneficiaries of the project to eradicate child labour from football manufacturing, and the effects on these increasingly vulnerable groups of the 'unintended consequences' arising from the project's implementation. The marginalisation has taken place through the inclusion of small groups of individual workers at the expense of the exclusion of a much larger majority of workers, most of whom worked as part of a family unit. The majority of these excluded stitchers, in contrast to the individuals who may have benefited from the recent changes, are women and children, and it is this group that has borne the brunt of any adjustments. Furthermore, as women and children worked as part of a family group, it is the family as a whole that has suffered rather than simply the individual. The following chapter examines the effects of formalisation on family-based stitchers who have been increasingly excluded, as well as some of the strategies adopted by them and their families in order to minimise the project's 'unintended consequences'.

NOTES

1. Small Firms–those with an estimated annual production of less than 200,000 footballs. Medium Firms–estimated annual production 200,000 to 500,000 footballs. Large firms – estimated annual production of 500,000 footballs or more.

2. Z.A. Bhutto–President 1971-1973, Prime Minister–1973-1977.

3. For a political history of Pakistan see A. Jalal (1995), Talbot (1998).

4. For further information on the existence of caste in Muslim societies, see, I. Ahmed (1973), S. Ahmed (1971, 1974, 1977), F. Barth (1960), L. Dumont (1980), Alavi (1972), Lindholm (1986), A. Shaw (1988), P. Werbner (1989), Fuller (ed) (1996).

5. For a fuller discussion of caste and *biraderi* see Alavi (1972), A. Shaw (1988), M. Fischer (1991), P. Werbner (1989).

6. See A. Shaw (1988), Roger Ballard (1987), P. Werbner (1989).

7. Nadvi (1990, 1999) found that the textile industry in Faisalabad, one of Punjab's larger cities, was dominated by the *biraderi* of *Ansaris* or washermen. Similarly, he found that Sialkot's surgical manufacturing industry was dominated by the *biraderi* of *Lohars* or blacksmiths.

8. *Sayyeds* are considered the highest ranked of the 'Muslim' castes and trace their roots from the family of the Prophet Muhammad. *Mughals* (descendants of the Mughal rulers) and Sheikhs (of Arab descent) are also highly ranked because of their claim of being early Muslim converts who came to the subcontinent as conquerors from central Asia, Persia and Arabia. The *Jat* and *Arain* are landowning castes, not as highly ranked as the *Sayyeds, Sheikhs* or *Mughals*, mainly on account of being converts from Hinduism. The *Lohars* (blacksmiths) and *Nais* (Barbers) are low-ranked, non-landowning artisan and service castes. The *Fakir* (beggar) is amongst the lowest ranked caste. For details on Muslim castes, see, I. Ahmed

(1973), S. Ahmed (1971, 1974, 1977), F. Barth (1960), L. Dumont (1980), Alavi (1972), Lindholm (1986), A. Shaw (1988), P. Werbner (1989), Fuller (ed) (1996).

9. Maker–is derived from the English 'to make'.

10. There are three Eid festivals during the Muslim year; celebrating the end of the month of fasting *(Eid –ul–Fitr)*, the Prophet Muhammad's (PBUH) birth anniversary *(Eid-I-Milad-un-Nabi)* and the commemoration of Abraham's sacrifice of his son *(Eid-ul-Azha)*.

11. For an examination of this, see Weiss (1991).

12. Described by George and Sabelli (1994,1) as wielding significant influence in setting the agenda for the development mainstream and a primary producer of development knowledge.

13. see for example Ferguson 1990, Woost 1997, Hobart 1993.

14. For example, the SA (Social Accountability) 8000 according to its publicity leaflet 'provides a framework for ethical sourcing and production of goods made by companies of any size and in any location. It is based on the conventions of the ILO, the Universal Declaration of Human Rights and the U.N. Convention the Rights of the Child. Its aim is to guarantee that the lives of workers around the world are protected' (Council on Economic Priorities leaflet).

15. At a talk given in November, 2001, at the inaugural conference on 'Including the Excluded', arranged by South Asians for Human Rights.

16. See Knorringa (1996, 1999), Kapadia (1999), Breman (1999) and De Neve (1999).

17. Centres, particularly the smaller ones, are also commonly referred to as units.

18. Average family size is 7.3, Sialkot Census Data 1998, Government of Pakistan 2000.

19. See for example, S. Ahmed (1974), Khan and Bilquees (1976), Rauf (1987), Ahmed and Ahmed (1990), Donnan and Selier (ed) (1997).

21. Save The Children Social Monitoring Report, January 1999.

22. While Jeffry's (1979) examination of seclusion of a particular group of Muslim women in Delhi is not a stereotypical account as it examines a particular group, her description, when taken out of context and applied to Muslim women across the board, would represent the typical stereotype.

23. Sialkot Census Data 1998, Government of Pakistan 2000.

24. Examples of recent reports of labour exploitation by multi-nationals include the Oxfam Community Aid Abroad reports *We Are Not Machines* (March 2002) and *Sweating for Nike* (1996) and *Still Waiting to Do It* (May 2001) by Global Exchange. A more comprehensive list is given at the Oxfam Community Aid Abroad website www.CAA.org.au

25. Figures taken from minutes of ILO meeting, 1998-2000.

26. Minutes of partners' meeting, February 1999.

27. Minutes of partners' meeting, November 1999.

5

LOCAL REALITIES

The previous chapter examined how groups of individuals were affected by the child labour eradication project. These groups included employers both large and small, sub-contractors, and football stitchers. But while chapter 4 primarily studied the effects of formalisation on those stitchers *included* in the formalisation process, this chapter examines, in greater detail, how those home-based football stitchers *excluded* by the project have been marginalized by the restructuring process. This not only provides a description of the effects of the restructuring on those bypassed by the unit system, but also introduces some of the strategies used by these stitchers and their families to cope with the enforced changes. The source of this analysis will be a number of case studies based on families that I got to know well during fieldwork. Each of the case studies highlights the varying effects that the restructuring had on stitching families in Sialkot. As the case studies focus on home-based stitchers, the chapter also looks at the surviving home-based football-stitching sector. It is through this sector that these workers have continued to receive footballs for stitching at home. In conclusion the chapter adds a further reason for the economic and psychological marginalisation of football stitchers, revolving around the nature of their participation in the project and their position as the objects of development rather than active participants.

THE SURVIVING INFORMAL SECTOR

By mid 1999[1] the institution of the unit system had officially eradicated child labour from the football manufacturing industry. Mothers were to have replaced the labour of their children, and stitching was to be confined to registered stitching units. Neither happened, and throughout fieldwork I came across footballs that continued to be stitched at home. The now 'informal', 'unsanctioned' sector—informal and unsanctioned through not being part of the formal unit system—survived despite the restructuring of the industry.

On one occasion, I was visiting a non-formal school in Anjotar (No. 35), a village in Sialkot *tehsil*. The class of 20 students, 6 of whom were boys, were all aged between 8 and 14. The school itself constituted a single room in the teacher's house. On asking the children—none of whom were meant to be stitching footballs any longer—how many were stitching at home, four immediately claimed they were currently working. Two others had no footballs at the moment but had stitched footballs in the last two weeks. Of these six 'stitcher' children (one boy and five girls), the two older ones, Sumaira aged 14 and Rashid, the only boy currently stitching, aged 13, claimed to be able to stitch a complete football. Sumaira, being unusually talkative, explained how she had just received a batch of *sona* (excellent quality, literally golden) material and was going to go home and start on the stitching. Two of the other children, Salima and Nazia, said that they could stitch *kholrus*. The remaining two girls, the youngest of the stitchers, stated that they only helped their parents, referring to themselves as *madadgars* (helpers). On inquiring how many children stitched footballs two years ago (prior to the restructuring), twice as many children replied in the affirmative. They also claimed to have received work more frequently then. The pattern is similar elsewhere in Sialkot, though local variations, as we shall see in the case studies, do exist. On average, though, 1 in 4 children in the schools for 'ex-stitchers' revealed that they currently had some stitching work to do at home. This number, as in Anjotar, doubled if the children were asked whether they were stitching footballs two years ago.

These children, along with home-based women stitchers, form the majority of stitchers at the base of the worker pyramid described in chapter 4 i.e. those not covered by the Atlanta Agreement and its restructuring. Yet, despite not being part of the industry's restructuring, home-based stitchers have been disadvantaged, firstly through the large-scale exclusion of those who would stitch at home but are now unable to stitch at the units, and secondly, through the 'de-legitimisation' of home-based stitching.

But while the formalisation of the industry through the institution of the unit system has meant a decline in material being sent to homes, these stitchers continue to receive footballs at home primarily through two sources. Both concern mainly the smaller firms, a continuation of, or return to, the informal structure of the past and a reliance on a home-based labour force. The first avenue involves those firms that chose not to participate in the restructuring programme. In their case work continues unaffected by the restructuring. The second entails work being undertaken clandestinely, in the form of 'leakage' from registered units. Both avenues of work centre on the production of *Desi* and lower quality *Lahori* footballs.

The detailed description of the family's material conditions and daily routines through the following case studies provides a clearer understanding of the kind of adjustments that the families have had to make in response to the changes enforced by the industry's restructuring. Included in these adjustments is the continued recourse to home-based stitching. Furthermore, the evidence from the case studies provides the background for the next chapter, which argues that, in order to understand the determinants of children's involvement in stitching footballs, it is essential to go beyond the accepted discourse on the reasons for child labour and formulate a radically different theory.

LOCAL REALITIES

MOHAMMED ASHFAQ AND FAMILY

During a visit to a non-formal school in Noorpura (No.44), I was invited by one of my informants to join him and his family for dinner. Mohammad Ashfaq had been amongst my earliest informants, as had his daughter, Fatima, and wife, Safia. Ashfaq lives in Noorpura, a small village with a population of just over a thousand people. Situated close to Sialkot city it has been a centre for football stitching for several decades. Mohammad Ashfaq has lived there for all his 48 years. On a previous occasion, as I had sat with Ashfaq in the courtyard of his house while he stitched the two *kholrus* (halves) of his football, he informed me that football stitching had deep roots in Noorpura as the village had previously been known for its leatherwork. During colonial rule, Noorpura was apparently renowned for repairing saddles and the large British army contingent stationed in Sialkot city meant a steady demand for repair work. Football repair and then manufacturing extended from this point. Noorpura is also a particularly old village, and as you wind your way through the tight lanes and side streets, images of a bygone era spring forward. Some of the houses still have the names of the original Sikh and Hindu occupants. A disused Sikh temple remains part of the village's history. In contrast to the newer villages in Punjab, which that were built under the authority of the British at the end of the nineteenth century and were laid out in orderly squares, Noorpura, like most other villages of Sialkot, is an old settlement and this has led to a more haphazard layout in terms of dwellings.

Ashfaq and I made our way from the school, where I had interviewed a group of children, to his home nearby. Ashfaq's house was a *pukka* house, typical of houses in many parts of Sialkot. A *pukka* house refers to one constructed of kiln-baked bricks and mortar, and covered in a layer of cement and sometimes painted. In the past, *pukka* houses were seen as a sign of prosperity as the majority of houses were made of wood and bamboo, and coated with baked mud. Those houses were called *kutcha* houses, referring to the less sturdy material used. However, with bricks becoming inexpensive and widely available in Sialkot, the use of *pukka* material is no longer considered the marker of economic well being that it was.

Nevertheless, the proportion of *pukka* houses in Sialkot indicates the relative prosperity of the district in comparison to other parts of the Punjab, particularly the southern districts, where *pukka* houses remain far less common. The long presence of industry provided the populace with an additional source of income alongside agriculture. In addition, Sialkotis, well known for their love of travel, migrated in large numbers to the Middle-East[2] particularly in the 1980s, to take up available employment. During this period they sent home a steady flow of remittances which boosted the local economy.[3]

Ashfaq owns his house but has no land, apart from that on which the house is built. In fact, few of the football stitchers I interviewed had any land. The few that did seldom had more than two acres. This was typically used to grow seasonal vegetables for use by the household, as there was rarely enough to sell. Growing cash crops such as wheat, and particularly rice, requires larger parcels of land and a substantial investment in the form of buying the grain itself as well as pesticides and fertilizer. Few of the poorer households can afford these inputs and so land use is restricted to subsistence farming or for grazing livestock.

The small size or absence of landholdings amongst football stitchers, as with other groups, is an indication of their relative poverty. Historically, land in South Asia has provided security, identity and *izzat*. The fundamental division between the groups of castes was between the landowning zamindar *zaats* (castes) and the service and artisan *zaats* that did not own land. Thus, every *zaat* had a certain status or *izzat* associated with it. The landowning *zaats*, by virtue of their higher rank and ownership of land, have greater *izzat*. *Izzat*, therefore, was and still is linked to ownership of land, and the value and attachment to land, as mentioned previously, is such that it is only sold as a last resort. But despite their relative poverty, I came across only one football stitching family, out of over one hundred interviewed, that were renting accommodation. In the absence of land, a family's priority is to at least own their house. A further indication of the value attached to owning one's own land and/or house can be gauged from the priority that migrants give to improving their houses at home. Throughout the remittance boom in Pakistan, migrants invariably invested their earnings first and foremost not in the education of their children, but in their houses. Ballard (1987) studying Pakistani migrants to the Middle East observed that 'Few fail to buy more land, should it become available, and most important of all, to build themselves an elaborate new house. This partly reflects a concern for honour and status, and the wish to demonstrate how much success they have achieved overseas' (Ballard 1987, 22). This led to construction booms and a sudden spurt in the building of firstly *pukka* houses, and then double storey structures.

The migrants' order of priorities also challenges the theory most closely associated with the work of Nardinelli (1990), that as the incomes of lower-income families rise parents will increasingly put their children into schools. This assumes that poverty is the driving factor behind non-attendance in schools and a main determinant of child labour. It also presupposes that schooling is the households' main priority after household maintenance. Furthermore, it assumes that working class families' needs and expectations are constant and unchanging. The priority given to schooling may have been the case in Japan. Saito (1996) in his analysis of child labour in Japan in the early 1900s examines the influence of deep-rooted cultural factors on the tendency to favour education over work: 'despite their hard lot, peasant families placed great importance on education' (Saito 1996, 82). But this is not so in Sialkot. It is quite plausible that a rise in wages will be accompanied by an increase in demand for goods and services, which may be met by continuing to keep children in the labour market. Furthermore, a decline in wages may bring about a response by which households struggle to maintain a previous standard of living and, rather than curtail expenditure or accept a lower living standard, the family, including the children, collectively work harder. This is more likely to be the case where the household has experienced a degree of prosperity and is forced to adjust to a lower standard of living. Such a scenario may well have been the case in Sialkot, where both industry and remittances brought relative prosperity to the region in the past. In those days the stitching industry had to compete with migration, and wages, as a result, were comparatively high. However, since Ballard (1987) analysed the effects of remittances on migrant communities in Pakistan, the demand for migrant labour has dried up. More and more labourers have returned home and fewer find work overseas. But what the migration did lead to was a raised standard of living and a desire for consumer goods. The football boom allowed this lifestyle to be maintained. Now with football stitching becoming less accessible and migration increasingly difficult, families are finding it hard to adjust to more modest living standards.

Like most households in Sialkot, Ashfaq's family was a large one, consisting of his wife and eight children—six girls and two boys. When I asked him about the size of his family he was quick to say that children are Allah's gift, and the Quran says that one should have children and that He (Allah) would provide for them. But apart from the religious 'justification' provided by Ashfaq, culturally, too a large number of children are seen by Punjabis as bringing vitality and happiness to a house. Bearing children is highly valued in Punjabi society and generally it is as a mother that a woman receives the highest possible respect. Hence, the well known saying, 'heaven lies at the feet of the mother'. In fact, women unable to have children are often stigmatised and treated harshly by their husband's family. In Pakistan, it is a common and socially acceptable reason for a woman to be divorced if she cannot bear children. This can also be a reason for the husband to take a second wife.

Ashfaq's house was surrounded by a six-foot high wall, which afforded the family a degree of security and privacy. An iron door acted as the entrance to the compound. An adjacent wooden door opened into the 'guest room' or *baithak*. In Sialkot, as in most parts of rural Pakistan, the design of most houses is influenced by the principles of *purdah*—the separation of the sexes. Houses, ideally, will be divided into a *zenana* (women's area) and a *mardana* (men's area). In practice, few football stitchers have the resources to have a house large enough to be so divided. The purpose of the separate entrance to the *baithak* is to allow guests to enter directly into the room without having to trespass into the compound's more private areas. This means that guests can be entertained without the women of the household needing to come into contact with them. Food and drink will be prepared by women in the kitchen but will be taken through to the *baithak* by a male relative. The *baithak* could therefore be seen as a *mardana*.

While the basic principle of *purdah* specifies that women should ideally meet only close male relatives, fathers, brothers, uncles and nephews, in reality the observance of purdah varies enormously according to region, wealth, class, family, religious traditions and caste status. *Purdah* tends to be strictest amongst the Pathans of the North West Frontier Province and those groups who Fischer (1991) observes are approaching a 'critical point on the *izzat* scale'. The added religiosity, of which *purdah* is a symbol, is used to enhance *izzat* and increase the group's claim to a higher rank. Being able to place women in *purdah* also indicates that the family is wealthy enough to allow their women not to work. Poorer families can rarely afford the luxury of *purdah,* and women from these families often have to work in the fields alongside men. One of the advantages of football stitching, as mentioned in the previous chapter, was that it provided a discreet, home-based avenue of income for women. This was considered far more appropriate as 'women's work' than having to work outside the home, which immediately represents a more serious admission of economic privation. Age also affects *purdah,* with young girls under the age of 12 (pre-puberty) and old women (past child bearing) often not being restricted to the same extent as those falling between these ages.

In Sialkot, knocking on the door of a house would normally mean children answering if an adult male was not present. In the event that no one else is at home, a woman may wrap her veil across her face, revealing only her eyes, and engage in minimal conversation if faced by an unknown male. But generally women do not answer the door. While poverty may force women to take up work outside the home, wherever possible contact with unknown men is restricted. But I found amongst football stitching households that, though the majority of women minimised their movement outside the house, they rarely practiced a strict interpretation of *purdah*. Contact with adult males was not limited to only the prescribed male relatives but generally extended to neighbours and acquaintances. *Purdah*, therefore, tends to be relative—more strictly adhered to in certain circumstances and eased in others. Fischer (1991), for example, points out how women in the Greentown township of Lahore rarely observed *purdah* within the township, but when travelling on the bus out of the township, would go in their *burkas*.[4] Amongst football stitchers in Sialkot, *purdah* was exercised with strangers. All female informants, including teachers, parents of child stitchers and the girl stitchers themselves wore the *dupatta* (headscarf), but in the majority of cases, this was loosely placed on the head, with the hair visible. A few wore it as a *hijab* — tightly wrapped round, with only their faces showing. Only one teacher wore a *burka*, which revealed only her eyes. But even in this case, apart from the physical separation, her general communication and interaction with male visitors was unaffected.

In Ashfaq's home, neither Safia nor any of her daughters of which Fatima aged 14 was the oldest in the house observed *purdah* with me, and as a result I did not have to be confined to the separate *baithak*. On previous occasions that I had visited Ashfaq and his family, I would sit in the courtyard, usually on the *charpais*[5] that double up as 'sofas'. This time, though, Ashfaq insisted on making me sit in the *baithak*, primarily because the *baithak* is also the status room used to entertain 'special guests'. Having this room indicates that a family has the means to afford a room for the particular purpose of entertaining guests. Having guests over not only allows a family to display their own status through their hospitality, but it also raises the host family's *izzat* if the guest in question is considered to be of standing, summed up in Ashfaq's flattering remark (*khaaney pe aake aap ne hamari izzat barha di hai*) – your coming to dinner has raised our *izzat*.

The *baithak* itself is carefully decorated and kept in pristine condition. The furniture is often covered with a sheet to protect it from dust. Photographs of Mecca and *Ayats* (verses) from the Quran, sometimes carved ornately out of wood, are placed on the walls. The best crockery is displayed on shelves. Occasionally, the wealthier households will have refrigerators, televisions and cassette recorders in this room. The majority of these would have been brought across by family members or relatives returning from abroad. Possessions, particularly electrical goods purchased abroad, have become important status symbols used to enhance the family's standing in a village and, although I personally never came across any such instances, I was told on more than one occasion that it was quite common for these items not to be used 'conventionally'. Hence the story of the man who brought back a refrigerator and used it to keep his clothes in, or the man who returned with an air conditioner to a village that had no electricity. This trend is part of what has been dubbed the *Dubai Chalo* (let's go to Dubai) syndrome (Akbar S. Ahmed, 1986) which saw Pakistani migrants returning from the Middle East in the 1980s with their pockets full of money and a desire for a higher social status in society. The foreign goods were used as symbols for demanding enhanced *izzat*.

Ashfaq did not have a refrigerator or an air-conditioner, but the crockery was proudly displayed, as were the wall hangings of Mecca. He did have an old 14-inch black and white television, with a glass made of stainless steel used as a surprisingly good aerial. There was also an old cassette player. But neither was kept in the guest room, a possible indication that they were not considered worthy of displaying in the room. In fact, more than half the households involved in football stitching that I interviewed had televisions and tape recorders, and some had status-raising video recorders and refrigerators.

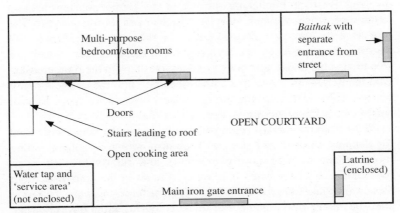

Mohammed Ashfaq's house.

As I had met Ashfaq and his family on several occasions, rather than make me wait outside while he opened up the guest room from inside, I was led into the main compound via the adjacent iron door. Once inside the main compound, the arrangement of the house becomes clear. A central courtyard dominates the layout and much of the household work is done here. On our arrival Safia, Ashfaq's wife, and their daughter Fatima were sweeping the yard. On one side were some pots and pans and a small stove. Cooking is done over an open fire using wood or cow dung pats for fuel rather than an electric or gas cooker, which are too expensive to buy and run. The cow dung pats, which women make from a mixture of dung, earth, straw and water, are left to dry in the sun, usually stuck to the side of the boundary wall. On the other side of the courtyard is an area where clothes are washed, beaten and then hung out to dry. A cold water tap, the only one in the house, is located in this 'service' area. Personal water connections are becoming increasingly common in Sialkot's villages, though in some of the more remote areas water is still obtained through communal hand pumps. The house also had a latrine, discreetly placed in the corner of the compound and separated from the rest of the courtyard by a small purpose built brick cubicle. Latrines are more common in the villages nearer urban centres than in the remoter rural villages. Where latrines are not present, villagers use the fields, and women are expected to go early in the morning (sometimes before dawn) or after dusk when there is less chance of encountering people. The courtyard may also be used to tether buffaloes and/or goats overnight, but Ashfaq's family did not own any livestock. Finally, on one side of the compound, steps lead up to the roof, where the men may sleep in the open during summer. The roof is also used for drying spices in the sun. In addition, the neighbouring house is often similarly built, meaning that women are able to visit the house next door by taking the steps to the roof, crossing onto the neighbour's roof and then descending into the adjacent house via the stairs in the neighbouring house. This allows them to visit neighbours without having to step outside their homes.

Apart from the *baithak,* the two other rooms in the house were used for sleeping quarters and storage. They also double as general sitting rooms when visiting family members and relatives come over, particularly in winter when it is too cold to sit in the courtyard. Both these rooms had little furniture except two or three *charpais* stacked to one side, along with a number of thick, colourful quilts for use during winter. All three rooms, including the *baithak,* had ceiling fans and as implied by this electricity was connected.

As we sat in the *baithak,* Safia began cooking the regional specialty—*sarson ka saag* and *makai ki roti*—a dish made from freshly picked mustard leaves, cooked in clarified butter and eaten traditionally with flat corn bread. The freshness of the ingredients and the open fire cooking gives the food a wonderful smoky flavour which cannot be replicated when cooked over an electric or gas hob. Ashfaq had wanted to prepare *karaahi murghi*—chicken in a rich tomato sauce—but I had dissuaded him, as chicken is expensive and only cooked on special occasions. The staple diet of lower income families in Punjab revolves more around vegetable and lentil dishes. So instead he had compromised by getting Safia to make *unday ka halwa* (egg halwa) another regional favourite. Eggs are also expensive items, but Ashfaq had insisted and dissuading him again would have been a slight on his hospitality.

Ashfaq says that he belongs to the *Awan* caste—originally one of the higher landowning castes in Punjab. But as mentioned in the previous chapter, football stitchers are found across the spectrum of caste groups in Sialkot. Caste affiliation does not appear to be a decisive factor in which families take up stitching. Any correlation between hereditary caste occupations and present day occupations has long since broken down.[6] Ashfaq's father's land was never large enough to be divided between his many children. So in the end the family land remained with Ashfaq's elder brother. With his 'share' of the inheritance, Ashfaq bought the house that he now owns.

Ashfaq has been stitching footballs for just over four years. Prior to this, he worked primarily as a daily wage labourer on the fields of local *zamindars* during the agricultural season, or as a manual labourer in Sialkot city. Most commonly, the manual labour meant working on a building site, painting and cementing walls or carrying and laying bricks. When football stitching began to spread through Noorpura it was his two eldest daughters who took up stitching, having learnt it from a neighbour about eight years before. Within two years of starting, Fatima and her elder sister Kulsoom were able to stitch an entire football and together could complete four footballs a day. In a reversal of the usual transference of skills, from parent to child, it was the daughters who taught their mother and then Ashfaq. At this point, home-based football stitching was the norm and work was plentiful. Increasingly Ashfaq began to stitch footballs rather than spend his time travelling to Sialkot city looking for work. Ashfaq told me that:

> In between the cropping seasons, I would stay at home and stitch footballs. We would get a steady supply of footballs. Safia would help whenever she got time from her household chores. Manual work is much harder on the body, and you have to travel to the city to find work because there is much less work available in the villages. Some days you find it, others you don't. Also I had to get a bus and that meant more expense. So when there were footballs to be stitched, I often stayed at home. With Fatima and Kulsoom also helping we were able to stitch as many as six or seven footballs a day. That provided about Rs. 4,000 a month. From that we were able to meet our household expenses and repay the advances from makers or the little

bit of credit one took from the shopkeeper. Kulsoom and Fatima were also able to save for their dowries.

The introduction of the unit system saw an immediate decline in home-based stitching in Noorpura. While some male stitchers took up work at the newly established centres, there were no female stitching units and the home-based centres became a limited option much later. The previous chapter examined how the unit system favoured some individuals—primarily single men—but tended to disadvantage the majority of stitching families and in particular, like Ashfaq's, large, predominantly 'female' households that could have provided additional labour at home but were marginalized by the unit system. Luckily for Ashfaq's family, within a few months of the restructuring, makers began to send footballs home for stitching again. Noorpura and surrounding villages such as Hundal (No. 34), Dheera Sandha (No. 33), Sidrana (No. 32) and Pathanwali (No. 43) are all located in Sialkot tehsil, close to Sialkot city where almost all the football manufacturers have their headquarters. In order to minimise transportation costs manufacturers have tended to concentrate their units in the villages surrounding Sialkot city. Material from these units has begun to find its way to houses through two avenues. Firstly, makers started delivering material surreptitiously to homes. Secondly, stitchers simply take unfinished footballs home at the end of a day at a unit. In larger stitching units, usually belonging to medium sized firms, the unfinished footballs may be smuggled out without the knowledge of management, completed at home and then smuggled back the following day. Occasionally, the *chowkidar* (guard) will work in collusion with stitchers, allowing them to take material out in exchange for a payment. Much of the leakage is in response to tight deadlines for large orders. Few companies pass up on large orders despite the possibility that they might not be able to produce the required volume in time. In an increasingly competitive environment, the company accepts first and then worries about fulfilling the requirements. With no fixed number of stitching units and a capacity of stitchers limited by the number able to squeeze into the units, the pressure to complete an order literally causes an overflow to leak to the much larger work force available in homes.

On other occasions, the *maker* may ensure that branded balls remain in the units, but that an order for *Desi* balls is sent to surrounding homes. This allows the *maker* the chance to maximise his unit space by allowing only the best stitchers to work on the *Lahori* balls. It also means that often stitchers are being turned away from units, as sub-contractors prefer to have a cheaper labour force available outside the units for *Desi* ball stitching, while maintaining a much smaller unit-based work force for the *Lahori* ball orders. The project, after all, concentrated on ensuring that branded balls were not 'tainted' by child labour. The same emphasis was not placed on the footballs of manufacturers not involved in the programme. Iftikhar Shah, the man in charge of ensuring that stitchers do not smuggle footballs out of the Ali Trading medium-sized unit in Peero Shahi said:

> The balls made for international brands are subject to much stricter checking because the brands put a lot of pressure on us to ensure that material does not leak out and reach homes. I have caught workers trying to take material out. But particularly in the units of smaller firms where monitoring is less strict, there is considerable leakage to surrounding villages.

Clearly, the involvement of children producing an Adidas or Nike football, endorsed by a high profile player, is a rumour that holds the potential of inflicting serious and long-term damage to the image of an international brand. In contrast, a non-branded football, used as a promotional or toy product, does not have the profile to cause similar damage. In Sialkot, large manufacturers who produce higher quality footballs have managed to meet the demands of the restructuring through the construction of stitching units and internal monitoring. This has allowed them to effectively eradicate child labour in the manufacture of their footballs. In contrast, smaller firms, whose production is concentrated on lower quality Desi balls, rarely have the backing of international brands or the resources to institute monitoring systems efficiently. Where monitoring is less intense, leakage tends to take place.

Leakage also takes place through unregistered units. These units belong to those manufacturers who had not registered all their units with the ILO monitoring programme. This means that the ILO does not monitor the units. Not providing the details of all stitching units by registered firms was a common strategy for avoiding external monitoring. Several voluntary partners of the Atlanta Agreement had not given the addresses of all their stitching centres.

Despite falling outside the purview of the restructuring, home-based stitchers have been affected through the formalisation of the industry, effectively 'de-legitimising' home-based stitching. With the child labour project sanctioning the unit system as the 'correct path', all other activities have been re-defined as deviant. This has allowed *makers* to exploit the situation at the expense of the home-based stitcher.

> These days even though we get some footballs at home the supply is not regular at all. In the past we used to get so many footballs that we could decide when to work and when not to work. Makers have become much more wary of giving any home-based work. They make all sorts of excuses, saying that employers have put pressure on them not to give footballs to homes. In the past we would only take stitching if the maker offered us a good advance. Now not only do they not give any advance, but also they only give us material if we agree to stitch at a lower rate, because they say it is a big risk for them to be bringing footballs to homes. So now instead of getting Rs. 22 per ball, they only offer Rs. 18 to us. Yet they make us feel like they are doing us a huge favour by giving us footballs to stitch. On top of that makers now reject many footballs and cut our wages because of that. My stitching has not become any worse. It is just a way for them to pay us less. But what choice do we have? We have to take whatever work we can get, Ashfaq's wife, Safia, told me.

The balance of power between *maker* and stitcher has tilted not so much in favour of the *maker,* but away from the home-based stitcher. The unit system was meant to reduce the power of the sub-contractor by cutting him out of the link altogether. Instead, *makers* have managed not only to maintain their positions, but also to exploit the 'black' market in football stitching to their own advantage. The fact that home-based stitching has been 'de-legitimised' by the unit system has resulted in sub-contractors offering lower rates of pay for home-stitched balls than they did two years ago. These *makers* now claim that the risk of allowing balls to go to homes is so great that it is only worthwhile if the wage is reduced. This reduced rate covers *all* footballs stitched at home, including the footballs of manufacturers *not* participating in the programme, and therefore not subject to its conditions. For example, Ashfaq, currently stitching an unbranded *Desi* ball provided to him at home by a *maker*, was not aware, like most stitchers, that only certain footballs could not be stitched outside units, and therefore the *makers* had no claim on demanding a lower wage rate for other footballs being stitched at home.

Thus, even those stitchers that have been bypassed by the unit system have not escaped its effects. There are now fewer footballs going to homes and the wages for those that do go home have fallen. For Ashfaq's household, the decline in income has meant a reduction in their ability to 'smooth' over the adverse effects of times when house expenditure may rise. For example, Ashfaq's eldest daughter, Kulsoom, recently got married and moved away. The wedding meant a considerable drain on the family's resources. Even though the girl had saved for her own dowry from her stitching earnings, there were still expenses associated with arranging a wedding feast and entertaining relatives and guests. Also with his eldest daughter moving away, the household lost an earning member. Furthermore, Safia's health has deteriorated in the last year. She suffers from a persistent cough and complains of 'weakness'. As a result, she is unable to carry out as much household work or stitching as she used to. She also needs expensive medicines. This has meant that Fatima, being the eldest child at home, has had to take on a much larger household workload, including football stitching and housework.

The decline in prices and the fewer balls reaching homes has meant a fall in income. However, the severity of this decline has been offset by material still reaching homes, albeit less frequently. Nevertheless, the reduction in home-based work has increased the family's insecurity. The response has been an increase in the intensity of work for many stitchers. Both Fatima and her father have had to work harder to make up for the decline in work and to cover for the periods of increased spending. Fatima told me:

> Now I wake up at 6am to clean the house and make breakfast for the family. That usually takes me three hours so that by 9 a.m. I am ready to start stitching some footballs. Four of my younger sisters help me as well. Most of them can't stitch yet, but they thread the needle and put wax on the thread for me. When my elder sister Kulsoom was here we could make four footballs between us. But now I can only stitch two a day and only if there is material. After lunch I go to school from 2 till 5. In the evening I help my mother prepare dinner. Then it's more stitching—for about three hours—while I watch TV. Sometimes Ammi [mother] also helps me.

With her younger sisters, Fatima is able to add around Rs. 1000 to the household's monthly earnings. Ashfaq also finds that he has to work harder now that there is less work at home. With the rates for football stitching falling, Ashfaq has returned to trying to find manual work in Sialkot city. This means leaving Noorpura by 6 a.m., travelling to Sialkot city and standing by *China Chowk*, one of the main traffic junctions in the city. Here, along with scores of other labourers, Ashfaq hopes to be 'picked up' by people requiring odd jobs to be undertaken. This may involve construction work, basic carpentry or even gardening. Unfortunately, Ashfaq, at 48, is often bypassed for younger workers and ends up with the lowest paying jobs. At the end of the day, he returns home usually at around 7 pm if he has found some work and, if material is available, helps in stitching footballs. For men, working longer hours and increasingly having to travel to Sialkot city, daily-wage work is the most common way of increasing their income. While Ashfaq's wife Safia does not do so, some women have also had to take up the far more stigmatising domestic work in the houses of the better-off families in their villages. Fatima used to stitch between five and six hours a day two years ago, but then she was used to taking breaks in between, often going off with her friends to play *staapoo*.[7] Now, when work is available, she finds it much more difficult to stop working once she has started. But with the money that she and her sisters make and her father's income, which varies between two and three thousand a month, the family have managed to maintain their standard of living, but at the expense of increased work intensity and greater insecurity.

Part of the reason that I have described Ashfaq's household in some detail is because it represents the most common profile for a football stitching family in Sialkot. There are, of course, families with varying experiences, some of which will be examined in the following case studies. But overall, with the exception of one family, all families involved in football stitching owned their own house. Few owned any land. The houses themselves were similar to Ashfaq's in layout and structure. Some may not have had the *baithak* or the latrine, but nearly all of them had electricity and many had personal water connections. Some families may not have had televisions but many had tape recorders and radios. Some even had video recorders and refrigerators. Overwhelmingly, football stitching families belonged to the lower income groups, rather than any particular caste, but while they may not have regularly been able to afford meat in their diet, they were still able to eat three meals a day. Football stitching may have helped add income to the household, but this was rarely enough to allow families to move to an altogether higher income level. How Ashfaq's family persisted in getting footballs at home also provides a description of one of the most common ways that stitchers continue to receive work. The other main avenue of home-based work is examined in the next case study. It is important to underline, though, that families like Ashfaq's do not represent the stereotypical, 'edge of existence' families that are often associated with child labour.

MOHAMMED RAMZAN AND FAMILY

Thirty-four-year-old Mohammed Ramzan, like Mohammed Ashfaq, has a large family with eight children, the youngest being eight months and the eldest being fourteen. Like Ashfaq and Safia, neither Ramzan nor his wife Bushra ever went to school and now only his two eldest daughters Samreen and Rabia attend the non-formal school for child stitchers. Neither attended government school previously.

Ramzan has been stitching footballs for ten years, and was able to stitch three to four balls a day. In the past there was enough material reaching home for him and his family to complete seven to eight footballs a day. Both his daughters, Samreen, 14 and Rabia, 10, would help in the stitching. His wife would also join in whenever she found time from her household chores. The other children, all younger than nine years were too young to help with stitching but would help with putting gum on the thread and threading the needles. The income from stitching meant the household could earn between Rs. 3000 to Rs. 4000 a month. This permitted the family to cover all their basic expenditure, as well as allow the girls some pocket money for clothes and personal items, and save for their dowries.

But unlike Ashfaq, Ramzan lives in Pasrur *tehsil*, in a village called Wajeedwali (No.94). Pasrur is the least industrialised or urbanised[8] of Sialkot's three *tehsils*. As a result, its population is more dependent on agriculture than Daska or Sialkot *tehsils*. During the football manufacturing boom, the availability of football stitching provided an important additional source of income for a large number of households. Dependency on football stitching was therefore likely to have been highest in Pasrur, where alternative sources of employment were far fewer than in the two other *tehsils*. Moreover, the unit system has hit Pasrur harder than the other *tehsils*. Villages in Pasrur are further away from Sialkot city than most villages in the other two *tehsils*. The result has been the establishment of a considerably smaller number of stitching units than in either Daska or Sialkot, and much less stitching work through stitching units or through leakage from these units.

In the absence of stitching units, manufacturers not registered with the ILO have maintained an informal sector that co-exists with the increasingly formal sector, but which has a quite distinct organisation. The ILO claims that production by registered firms accounts for almost 85 per cent of all exports. The remaining 15 per cent is exported to countries where importers are not concerned with the child labour issue. In fact, a review of export figures compiled by the Pakistan Federal Bureau of Statistics showing the export of goods by country, reveals that closer to 30 per cent of exports go to companies not concerned with child labour restrictions.[9] Manufacturers catering to these markets have continued to undertake business as usual—they are not compelled to join the programme and as a result are not bound by the restrictions and expensive restructuring that the unit system entails. Apart from the leakage from registered units, it is this unregistered component of the industry, made up of individual manufacturers, sub-contractors and agents dealing mainly in Desi ball production, that continue to send material to homes for stitching. In Pasrur, where there are few registered stitching units and consequently little leakage, most home-based stitching is the result of the work generated through these independent companies.

Much of the contracting in the independent informal sector goes on through agents or traders who organise deals either with sub-contractors or with small independent manufacturers. Agents receive orders but do not themselves have stitching capacity or labour. The agent organises a third party to undertake the stitching process but will usually arrange to buy the required raw materials from the open market, at least in the case of the sub-contractor.

Unlike a *maker* who distributes panels to homes, small independent manufacturers control an entire 'mini' production centre, known locally as a 'shed' as distinct from a 'unit'. All the machinery required to produce footballs is located within this shed, including panel cutting and laminating equipment as well as stamping machines. The only input not found in the shed are the stitchers. Stitching is done in homes in the surrounding villages.

Wajeedwali had received some footballs for stitching via two sub-contractors from a shed in Mundey Ke Beriyan (no. 93), a village some 5 kms away. I had again been lucky that one of my NGO 'research associates' was an old friend of Qayyum, the owner of the Mundey Ke Beriyan shed. Accompanied by Malik Nazir, I was able to visit the shed.

From the outside, the shed resembled a large one-story house. A high gate, locked from the inside, provided privacy. Having rung the bell, we were asked to wait outside while our arrival was announced. A minute later we were called in. It was around 10 p.m., but there was a buzz of activity inside. Qayyum greeted us warmly and then enthusiastically showed us around. Qayyum had himself started in the football business as a stitcher, working in one of the larger companies. From there he graduated to overseeing the production process of the company. Finally, five years ago, he began his own operation in Mundey Ke Beriyan.

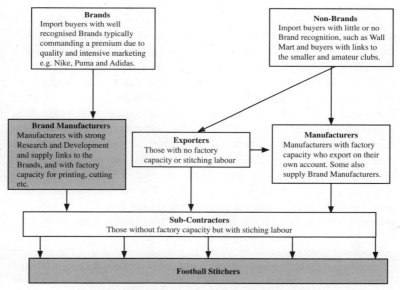

Football industry organisation in Pakistan
Shaded boxes denote those covered by the restructuring programme

At the time of my visit, Qayyum was in the midst of completing two orders—*Lahori* balls for export to Canada and lower quality *Desi* balls for export to England. Qayyum informed me that the majority of his orders were from private importers who sold through their own retail outlets abroad, and from importers in countries where child labour was not an issue. Neither of these was covered by the Atlanta Agreement, which involved only production for the main international brands. He also did a substantial amount of work through an agent for non-brand companies. Both his current orders had been arranged through an agent and were destined for amateur clubs. Qayyum stated that independent units like his own were largely dependent on orders for promotional balls. For example, MacDonald's and Coca-Cola often order large quantities of promotional footballs during World Cup years. These balls are used as 'tie- ins' in the World Cup marketing bonanza, being given away free with other purchases. Qayyum informed me that during the 1998 World Cup, MacDonald's placed an order for 1.2 million promotional footballs, all of which were made through independent manufacturers like himself. Many of the smaller firms, in fact, only come into 'being' when seasonal demand is high.

Unlike Ashfaq's house, which was built around a large courtyard, the shed's constructed area covered the entire compound in which it was located. There was little uncovered space. This allowed for a number of rooms in the house, each of which were used for separate purposes. The 'hall' was where completed footballs were checked and packed ready for export. In the 'guest bedroom' stood a stamping machine for embossing the required logos onto the panels before they are stitched together. Amongst the various stamps was one proclaiming 'Guaranteed Child Labour Free'. The 'storeroom' housed a crude-looking cutting machine. The 'master bedroom' doubled as Qayyum's office, sparsely decorated with a table, a few chairs and a phone-fax—his mode of receiving orders. The roof, incidentally, was used for drying the laminated sheets that are cut into panels. Qayyum informed me that all the machinery that I had seen was made locally.

> Sialkot's workers are very good at copying machinery. All of these machines used to be imported and the small owners could not afford them. Now workers here have learnt how to copy the machinery and it is produced locally and is so much cheaper.

Independent companies like Qayyum's, not participating in the programme, continue via their sub-contractors to send footballs out to homes for stitching. When I inquired over the possibility that his footballs were stitched by children, Qayyum replied frankly that this may be the case, but he was unaware of the exact situation as it was his sub-contractors that distributed panels to homes. However, he did say that children would frequently come to the shed and ask him for material for stitching for their families, and he would give them a few footballs to stitch. Occasionally he employed children to work in his shed as well, simply because they came looking for work. On the occasions that I visited Qayyum again, I did find boys aged between ten and fourteen working in his shed.

However, despite work sent out by Qayyum's makers, the small number of units in Wajeedwali and the fall in home-based stitching as a result of the restructuring has meant that the supply of footballs to homes in Wajeedwali has dropped dramatically. Furthermore, as in Noorpura, sub-contractors, even those not working for registered companies, have used the general de-legitimisation of the home-based system to offer lower rates for footballs stitched at home. Combined with the fewer alternative employment opportunities, this has meant a disproportionately severe effect on stitcher households in Pasrur. For Mohammed Ramzan's family this has caused serious problems.

The decline in the number of footballs available means that Ramzan only gets footballs for stitching occasionally—sometimes from one of Qayyum's sub-contractors. His daughters, Samreen and Rabia, were together able to stitch four balls a day whereas now they manage one, or at most two. Ramzan states that his household's income has fallen to half of what it was when home-based stitching was the norm.

Furthermore, unlike Ashfaq, Ramzan finds it difficult to contemplate work in Sialkot city, as the higher transport costs from his remote village would reduce whatever extra money he would make in the city as a daily-wage labourer. There is little alternative work in Wajeedwali for him to do, except work as a wage labourer during the agricultural season. He has no land or livestock of his own. His daughters now spend their time helping their mother with housework, sweeping the house, washing utensils and clothes and looking after younger siblings. That they have not been forced into other income-earning activities suggests that the family is not yet facing a position where they are compelled to make their children 'work' in a way that would be considered undesirable—i.e. outside the home. It is also an indication of the strength of the existing cultural and religious norms that strongly stigmatise women's work outside the home, and the specificity of football stitching as an activity involving children.

For Ramzan's family, the fall in income has meant cutting out all non-essential household expenditure. The family's staple diet consists of lentils and bread. The occasional chicken, meat and eggs that were affordable in the past are now beyond their means. In the past, Ramzan's family were able to store up essential items such as grains, pulses and flour. Now, increasingly, they are forced to buy these items on credit from local shopkeepers. Ramzan also pointed out that previously most families had a regular supply of milk from the few goats or buffaloes that they owned, but many have started selling the milk to supplement their income. Ramzan's daughters receive no pocket money, and celebrations over the *Eid* festival marking the end of the month of fasting (Ramadan) are muted, with Samreen and Rabia complaining that this year they would be unable to buy the new 'dress clothes' that are part of the *Eid* festivities. They also quietly say that their parents argue much more now, and that there is a growing tension at home as the family struggles to maintain their previous lifestyle. Ramzan states resignedly that he is no longer able to meet the needs of his children. 'When the children were allowed to stitch, they could make a little bit of money to look after their own needs. Now there is increased pressure on us.' So far Ramzan's pride has prevented him from taking loans, but unless there is an upturn in stitching activity this situation will soon change. It is fortunate that the family has so far not suffered any sudden misfortune, as their current situation makes them particularly vulnerable to unforeseen shocks.

Part of the reason that families like Ramzan's and Ashfaq's are facing increased insecurity is because one of their strategies aimed at tiding over times of heavy expenditure has been removed. As Camps I. Cura (1996, 17) points out in his examination of child labour in Colombia, even in times of prosperity, the contribution that women and children made to the family income could be critical. 'This was most obviously the case when families were affected by illness, death and other adversities.' In the informal sector there are no unemployment benefits, no health allowances or any other social benefits. Illnesses, festivals and life cycle rituals are recurrent occasions of heavy spending. Sudden job losses and failed harvests also constitute moments at which most families do not succeed in making ends meet. Often the only avenue for additional income is to take out a loan, but many poor households are particularly constrained in their ability to borrow (Dasgupta 1993, 240). Usually the only choice is to part with the only asset that they normally possess-land or housing-and this is only done when faced with an economic crisis, 'when the present moment dominates all thought' (Dasgupta 1993, 240). Football stitching not only augmented household income, but also allowed households to manage better the income risk they face, both through an additional form of income and from interest free loans or advances that stitchers would take from makers.

Very few stitcher families saved any money on a monthly basis and therefore rarely possessed liquid assets. What income came in was used almost immediately for purchasing essential household goods and the occasional non-essential items such as new clothes and expensive food. When extra income was needed, such as prior to festivals or for weddings, or in the event of treatment for illness or infirmity, families would usually increase income through taking on additional stitching, taking advances from sub-contractors, or by occasionally obtaining small loans and credit from shopkeepers. Two of these three strategies—taking on additional stitching and advances from sub-contractors have been greatly reduced, leading families to adopt new strategies. This includes continuing to find football stitching, curtailing household expenditure and increasing the intensity of work. An increased reliance on loans does not appear to be widespread, indicating that families are not yet facing the economic situation that makes them increasingly dependent on others.

For working class families in Sialkot, the employment of children was part of what the historian, John Modell (1979, 60), examining the significance of child labour for American working class families in the nineteenth and twentieth centuries, called a limited defensive mode of family cooperation—an attempt to pool risks in what was experienced as a very uncertain world. The risk argument goes some way towards explaining why families that may not belong to the poorest sections of society still encourage their children to work. Many football stitching households may own a house, television, radio and be able to afford three meals a day, but any unforeseen expense threatens the family almost immediately. The income from children's earnings is often used to offset sudden expenditure, thereby providing the family with some degree of social security. Furthermore, Bhalotra (2000) points out that child labour may be determined by the variability in income as much as its level. Football stitching, by virtue of its seasonal demand, has always provided an unstable stream of income, and this inherent instability has been exacerbated following the decline in home-based stitching. Similar evidence from rural India supports the view that child labour plays a significant role in the 'safety-net' strategy of poor households. Jacoby and Skoufias (1994) observed that when the variability of household income increased, measured by the difference in income from peak season to low season, children's school attendance declined in much the same way as children's attendance declined in Sialkot as soon as stitching was available. The uncertainty of employment may also explain the tendency of families not to save any money, for, as Thompson in his examination of the English working class argued, 'habitual uncertainty of employment, as all social investigators know, discourages forethought and gives rise to the familiar cycle of hardship alternated with the occasional spending spree while in work' (Thompson 1968, 292). This also implies that the safety-net strategy appears to work as a means of keeping options available to the family, rather than through 'saving for a rainy day'.

Ramzan's case highlights not only the range of effects that the decline in stitching had, but also how the plight of stitcher households is exacerbated in the more remote areas where there are fewer alternatives for work for both parents and children. There are also fewer stitching units and most home-based stitching is dependent on independent manufacturers.

Both Ashfaq and Ramzan's cases also indicate that the 'grinding poverty' that is represented as driving child labour in the Third World is not the driving force for football stitching. Invariably, though, it is the most vulnerable families that have suffered disproportionately from the restructuring imposed by the project. Ashfaq's family faced a decline in income, which was partly offset by the continued supply of footballs to homes, albeit at a lower rate and by family members having to work harder. Ramzan's family has suffered a larger decline in income and has also been less able to cover this decline with alternative sources. They have adjusted by reducing their household expenditure and through stitching whenever footballs are available. But while the household has adjusted, it has meant a lowering in their standard of living. However, in some cases even a small decline in household income has been difficult to absorb.

SHOAIB AKHTAR AND FAMILY

Shoaib Akhtar, aged 12, is the de facto head of his household. Shoaib and his family live in Amreekpura (No.61) in Daska *tehsil*. Daska is the second largest *tehsil* in Sialkot, with a total population of just over half a million. There are several large towns in the *tehsil* giving it a 22.7 per cent urban population. Much of this urban population is concentrated along Wazirabad Road, the main road that joins Daska *tehsil* with Sialkot city. Amreekpura is one of the smaller villages just off the main road.

Like both Ashfaq and Ramzan, Shoaib's family is large. He has two elder sisters and four younger brothers. Their house, like Ashfaq's is enclosed by a boundary wall. But there is no *baithak*—just two multi-purpose rooms used for storage and sleeping. There is also no latrine, but a separate water tap is connected, as is the electricity supply. Shoaib has a small tape recorder and there are ceiling fans in both rooms. His sisters sleep with their parents in one room. All four brothers share the other room. Two years ago, Shoaib, his two elder sisters Sumaira and Sameena, one younger brother, Zaheer, and his mother Hameeda would stitch up to ten footballs a day. His father, Ilyas, used to be a builder, but Shoaib informed me that four years ago an illness had left his father partially paralysed. Now unable to work, Ilyas has also begun to do *nasha* (take narcotics). This has not only meant the loss of the main earning member of the household, but the habit means an additional drain on the family's resources. Nevertheless, through football stitching the family were able to meet their basic needs. Unfortunately, with the advent of the unit system they suddenly found that there was no work available at home. Shoaib, because he was below the legal age for work at a unit, was unable to find work in the units that had sprung up in Daska. There were no female units, which meant that his sisters were also no longer able to stitch. Neither was Shoaib aware of independent manufacturers delivering footballs to Amreekpura. It may have been that the large number of registered units in Daska had meant fewer independent manufacturers setting up shop in an area where competition was stiff. In addition, unlike Noorpura, there was less leakage to the homes from the units, possibly implying that monitoring was stricter in this area. But in contrast to Pasrur, the greater urbanisation of Daska has meant more widespread commercial and industrial activity. Daska has a proliferation of small workshops associated with the surgical, carpet and leather industries. There are also diesel engine, centrifugal pumps, and associated spare parts industries specific to Daska. Additionally, there are growing numbers of brick kilns, and a barber's razors industry has taken root in the *tehsil*.

With the decline in home-based football stitching, households have tended to turn to several adjustment strategies, including increasing the intensity of work and curtailing household expenditure. But there is another avenue that some households have adopted in the face of declining incomes and fewer options. For families like Shoaib's, which have few alternatives, the choice has narrowed down to taking up whatever employment is available. The greater range of occupations outside the home in Daska has meant that a small percentage of children have found work in other sectors. This has also happened in other parts of Sialkot but was most noticeable in villages near the main road in Daska. These included Amreekpura [No. 61], Uggoki, [No. 114] Sambrial [No. 51], Begowala [No. 55], where there is a proliferation of brick kilns, surgical warehouses, and auto repair workshops. However, the decision to shift from football-stitching to other work is not one made lightly, primarily because of the specificity of football stitching. Children who stitch footballs may be working, but it is a specific form of work giving rise to a particular child-worker profile. Many parents do not consider other forms of work suitable substitutes. This is a crucial point and is one of the key themes examined in the next chapter in conjunction with the attempt to formulate a theory for the reasons children stitch footballs.

Shoaib Akhtar has found work in one of the surgical instruments manufacturing workshops on the main road to Daska. It means that he goes in to work at 7am and returns at 6pm.

> I started working at the surgical workshop when we stopped getting footballs at home. A friend of mine worked there and he got the job for me. Football stitching was much better. I could do it at home at my own pace. Now I go in early in the morning and spend all day working, usually filing instruments or then washing them in chemicals. The pay isn't much better than stitching because I am still a *shagird* [apprentice]. But we need the money at home. Abu [father] spends a lot of money on his *nasha*. I try and buy food items as soon as I get paid so that he doesn't take the money from me. My younger brothers can't work at the surgical workshop yet. They are too young. My sisters help Ammi [mother] with household work. They are also trying to get some household work in the houses of our neighbours so that we can get some income that way as well. It has become very difficult for us to make ends meet, now that there is no stitching available. Sometimes my uncle in Lahore sends us some money.

The position of Shoaib's family has meant that he has been forced to work in a surgical instruments manufacturing workshop, unlike the case in Ashfaq's or Ramzan's family where the children work when material for stitching is available. Furthermore, the decline in home-based stitching and his father's drug addiction have meant that his sisters and mother are looking for work as domestic help in the houses of those villagers who are better off.

But there are still more 'extreme' cases, all of which have been hit hardest by the project that was supposed to have benefited them. As the above case studies indicate, it is those families that are least able to cope that have suffered most from the formalisation of the industry. Invariably, these cases consisted of families that lost their major income earner through disability (as in Shoaib's father's case), or death. In Shoaib's family's example, some family members were still able to bring in an income, thereby allowing the family some semblance of independence. But they were becoming increasingly reliant on the generosity of neighbours and relatives. In other cases, families found that what little income they had managed to obtain had dried-up with the discontinuation of the home-based football trade. The women of the family were unable to find alternative work and in the absence of an adult male member there were few options open to the family, especially if the older children were girls. Wherever I came across families that had built up large debts, it was almost always the case that the family had lost its main income earner.[10] Alternatively, the family had suffered a major 'setback', usually through an expensive wedding, a protracted illness in the family, or the loss of livestock. For example, the largest single loans, equivalent to over a year's income for a football stitcher, were for the marriage of daughters. In the absence of football stitching they found their ability to cope with these periods of sudden expenditure greatly reduced.

In these cases, 'development' in the form of the removal of football stitching from the home has narrowed the options available to families rather than expanded them. The process has increased the vulnerability of the weaker groups in society, rendering them less able to cope with the external environment. Many families, like Ashfaq's or Ramzan's, have managed to adjust even though it has meant working harder than before, lowering their living standards and facing an increasingly insecure setting. For families such as Shoaib Akhtar's the response has been more drastic. A smaller number of families, already at risk through the loss of the male head of household, have been left with no immediate means of covering the loss caused by the decline in home-based football stitching. These families represent the more 'stereotypical' child-labour producing family. Nevertheless, while a stereotype may draw strength from 'extremes', that does not mean that these extremes do not exist, even though they may not be as common as implied by the stereotype.

MARGINALISATION THROUGH PARTICIPATION

Both chapter 4 and the families discussed in the current chapter have shown how the child labour project has in fact increased the vulnerability of the intended beneficiaries. The conclusion of this chapter adds a further reason for the marginalisation of football stitchers. This focuses on the nature of their participation in the project. Football stitchers are involved in the child labour intervention as the targets of the programme, as 'passive objects', to be acted upon and forced to adjust to enforced changes—rather than as active agents of change in the development process. This position of passivity in turn contributes to the stitchers' marginal position in the project, both because they are used to adjusting to conditions and because they have no voice in making decisions.

The child labour project in Sialkot was highlighted as a unique initiative that brought together a number of stakeholders, from industry to international development organisations to local NGOs and local 'beneficiaries', i.e. the football stitchers. This partnership would supposedly benefit all the participants, particularly keeping in mind that development had represented itself as a participatory process. Unfortunately, as a practice (in contrast to '*as a concept*'), 'participation' often overlooks the political constraints that are inherent in the process.

> Many participatory projects rest on the dubious assumption that simply identifying different 'stakeholders' and getting them round the table will result in a consensus being reached that is 'fair' to all. Such an assumption only works if all the actors involved are deemed to have equal bargaining power. (Hildyard et al., 2001, 69).

This is rarely the case, even if it is theoretically possible. Stakeholders, as Hildyard et. al. imply, do not all have the same bargaining power, and no amount of negotiation or facilitation is able to provide marginal groups with the bargaining clout they need to overcome the political, economic and structural dominance that more powerful groups hold. Only a much wider social and structural change would allow this imbalance to be redressed. However, the failure to take into account differences in bargaining power leads to 'participation' providing opportunities for powerful groups, and token participation for weaker partners in practice then. Participation, is frequently manipulated and made to fit the needs of the 'dominant' groups. In Sialkot, 'the call for local people to have a decisive say in the matters that affect their lives have been contained through the directed use of 'participatory' processes that are reworked to suit the ends of industry and other powerful groupings' (Hildyard et. al., 2001, 61).

The child labour eradication project was instituted at the behest of Sialkot's largest football manufacturers and their international partners, in response to the threat of consumer boycotts and legal sanctions. The removal of children working in the football manufacturing industry was essential if international companies wanted continued access to their Sialkoti suppliers. The Sialkoti manufacturers, in turn, were threatened by the loss of external markets. Thus, the impetus behind the envisaged restructuring of the football industry was the need to 'save the industry'. Not surprisingly, as pointed out in Chapter 4, the blueprint for the restructuring, which formed the basis of the project, came from plans drawn up by this group of industrialists. The entire planning and design of the project was done without the knowledge, consent or involvement of the supposed beneficiaries—the football stitchers of Sialkot. The project was finally unveiled at the 'Super Show', an annual sports trade fair held in the United States 'amidst a media blitz of high drama and expectations' (Robert Crawford 1999, INSEAD). This physical separation of the 'launch' from Sialkot is indicative of the distance of the designed project from the stitchers of Sialkot and the amount of input that these beneficiaries had in a project that was instituted to change the way they live their lives. 'Participation' on the part of the football stitchers only came about when they found themselves as the objects of the intervention. Moreover, the nature of their subsequent participation ensured that they remained the objects of development rather than active participants able to influence policy and ensure that their concerns were given due weight during project implementation.

The token nature of the stitchers' participation leading to them appearing, in Woost's words 'as an ideological apparition rather than a real presence' (Woost 1997, 231) has meant that it was the concerns of industry that dominated the way the project was implemented. For instance, the removal of children from football stitching does not necessarily mean that these children or their families would be better off. In fact, it can be argued that the partners involved in the programme were aware of the possibility of adverse affects on the beneficiaries— from past experience in Bangladesh and also from the fact that the international agencies, such as the ILO and Save the Children, were invited to join the programme to deal with 'disaster mitigation' and in order to give 'legitimacy to our efforts', as one of Sialkot's industrialists related to me. Bahaar Ali, Save the Children's programme manager for the Sialkot football project, informed me that SCFs main impetus for joining the Atlanta Agreement was to try and ensure that children and their families were protected from the worst effects of the project. This throws up the question of who the programme was instituted for—the children or the industry? The influence of the group representing the requirements of industry in the programme effectively meant that the social element in the project was relegated to 'minimising' the fall-out from the needs of industry. As a result, the football industry had to be restructured, even if it meant that the weakest groups would be made more vulnerable. The issue of child welfare was the humanitarian element through which the powerful interests in the project were able to satisfy their own requirements—the central concern being the eradication of child labour from the football industry and the transfer of all stitching from homes into units. What happened beyond that was considered secondary. If women and children were forced out of work in the football-stitching sector and left without an avenue for additional income, or had to move into more hazardous employment, this could still be seen, not as a failure of the project, but as a by-product, albeit an unfortunate one, of its success.

The participation of stitchers and their families, in fact, came in the form of Save the Children Fund undertaking a survey on football stitchers in Sialkot, in order to gauge their reaction to the proposed intervention. This 'participation' was important to the project—not because it influenced project design or policy, but because the 'participation' of the football stitchers provided the overall project with the legitimacy for the intervention.

Moreover, the nature of the stitchers' participation, as well as an indication of the relative importance attached to their needs, can be gauged from the fact that the SCF survey, through which the primary stakeholders were meant to influence project planning, was to be completed in four weeks. This was primarily because the requirements of Sialkot's industrialists and their international partners necessitated that project implementation be hastily undertaken so as to minimise the adverse affects of negative publicity on the multi-national sporting companies and to ensure that there was minimal disturbance to the production of footballs. Furthermore, the survey was actually undertaken while the project agreement was being finalised, meaning that the views of the stitchers were elicited *after* the project had already been finalised. By the time the results were available, the implementation of the unit system had already begun. The most apparent manifestation of bypassing the stitchers' views was the underestimation of women's involvement in stitching and the subsequent 'male bias' in the design of the stitching units. This, as we have seen, led to the exclusion of the majority of home-based female stitchers. Therefore, even this token input from the beneficiaries was not used to influence project design.

The claim that the next phase of the project may be influenced by SCFs findings was also tenuous. Once projects are drawn up with specific targets, budgets and life spans, they are difficult to rearrange after implementation has begun. In addition, changes in project implementation are often interpreted as resulting from a failure in project design. This can lead to a serious loss of credibility for the project and those involved in it. As Van Ufford (1993, 156) points out, institutions involved in projects are engaged both in their own survival and in trying to carry out tasks assigned to them. These two responses are potentially incompatible and in conflict, and in Sialkot, as described in Chapter 3, in the case of Bunyad and the ILO, survival took precedence over effectiveness.

A further outcome of the industry's need for 'rapid change' was that while 'Western Europe had several centuries in which to become accustomed to, and prepared for, change, so that the ideas of change, adaptability and mobility were gradually accepted as a way of life' (F. Fanon 1965, 41 in Weiss 1991, 5), Sialkot's stitchers were given eighteen months in which to remove children from the stitching labour force. An industry that had thrived through an informal, decentralised structure for over two decades was to be 'restructured' and formalised in less than two years. While this time-frame reduced disruption to manufacturers, it meant that the effects of the social change on workers were amplified as shown in the case studies presented in this chapter.

In the case of the effort to remove children from football stitching, the nature of the stitchers' participation was such that there was little possibility of their views being heard let alone influencing project policy. The demands of those driving the programme required quick and decisive action be taken. There was not enough time to ask what the 'target' population might or might not have desired. Far from being a transformative process in which local people were able to exert control over decision-making, participation therefore became a well-honed tool for engineering consent to projects and programmes whose framework had already been determined in advance—a means for top-down planning to be imposed from the bottom-up. This ensured that the weakest 'participants' (participants in terms of being the subjects of the project) remained the objects of the decisions and policies made by external bodies, but were not involved in the shaping of the intervention aimed at 'improving' their lives.

The result was that these 'beneficiaries' were singularly excluded from any input and, not surprisingly, remained divorced from the aims of the programme. Gardner and Lewis point out that people understand events and ideas on their own terms, and as long as 'development work' involves the 'imposition of ideas and knowledge rather than being a dialogue, people are unlikely to be able to gain greater control of it, or voluntarily participate in it' (Gardner and Lewis 1996, 100). The failure to involve the football stitchers in any meaningful way in the child labour project has meant that the weakest group's needs have been marginalized. It has also meant that the football stitchers see the imposed intervention as having been implemented by external organisations for reasons far removed from their own needs.

Both the previous chapter and the current one have shown how the 'development process' has decreased rather than increased the number of choices open to the football stitchers of Sialkot, thereby increasing their marginalisation and vulnerability to external factors. Through the case studies the current chapter has also highlighted some of the strategies adopted by football stitchers in order to cope with the externally imposed changes. The marginalisation of the stitchers has occurred at a psychological level in terms of their peripheral position vis-à-vis the decision-making and discourse driven processes. The unequal nature of their participation in the project—as objects of development rather than active agents of change—has also contributed to the beneficiaries, continued alienation from the project and within the project. Marginalisation has also occurred at an economic level with the decline in the incomes of many football-stitching families. However, this is not to say that were the views of football stitchers incorporated into the design and implementation of the project, it would subsequently have addressed all their concerns. But while the outcome of a development project is not simply the result of the marginalisation of 'indigenous knowledge',[11] the failure to incorporate local perceptions and knowledge into the design and implementation of the Sialkot project did reduce the chances that the concerns of the stitchers would be central to the project's aims. This in turn has contributed to the marginalisation of football stitchers from the very project that was meant to have benefited them.

NOTES

1. Following Bill Clinton's endorsement of the Sialkot football industry's success in removing children from the industry, See Chapter 1.
2. The majority of migrants came from Punjab and to a lesser extent NWFP. Sindh and Balochistan were largely bypassed by the migration phenomenon. For further details see Burki (1991), O. Noman (1991).
3. By 1984 remittances were totalling US$ 3.2 billion annually and constituted the largest single source of foreign exchange earnings in the economy (O. Noman 1991, 79).
4. Loose garment covering the entire body used specifically for the purpose of *purdah*.
5. Basic beds made of a wooden frame and strung with a rope meshing.
6. In fact, Quigley raises doubts over whether caste specific occupations were ever as rigid as earlier writings on the caste system had emphasised. 'It is not so much that everyone has (or ever had) a caste specific occupation in the first instance. Rather, everyone belongs to kin groups whose traditional function it is (or was) to provide certain functionaries for certain occasions. However, most members of most groups generally are (and always have been) in occupations such as agriculture and administration which do not themselves identify one's caste' (D. Quigley 1993, 91).
7. A traditional game akin to hopscotch.
8. 12.2 per cent urban, 1998 Pakistan Census.
9. There are a substantial number of footballs exported to South America, the Middle and Far East, and Eastern Europe as well as to countries such as South Africa and Turkey.
10. Over half the incidences of large debts were of families where the male head of household was either dead or in some way handicapped.
11. There is considerable anthropological analysis in this area. See for example edited volumes by Pottier (1993), or Hobart (1993).

6

TOWARDS A NEW DISCOURSE

The dominant discourse on child labour as examined in chapters 1 and 2 depicts a child that is forced to work long hours, for pitiful wages or sometimes no wages at all, usually in appalling conditions, for an unrelated and exploitative employer. Children are frequently abused, sometimes disabled, and are exposed to hazardous conditions. They are 'denied their childhood' and all the defining features of childhood, such as schooling. All this is seen as the result of grinding poverty, a poverty that compels the parents of the child to force their children to work so the family is able to eke out a living. This poverty is itself seen as the result of these underdeveloped societies being particularistic, unmotivated by profit and seeped in repressive traditions that have survived to the modern day. This contrasts with modern society at the other end of the evolutionary scale, which is secular, universalistic and profit-motivated. To move from one (bad) extreme towards the other (good) extreme, the underdeveloped societies are to pass through the process of development. But while development theory preaches increasing empowerment and independence to those that embrace it, it has in many cases led to further dependency through the narrowing of options, including (in the case of working children), the de-legitimisation and demonisation of all forms of child work. 'International agencies and highly industrialised countries now turn this yardstick into a tool to condemn as backward and undemocratic those countries with a high incidence of child labour' (Nieuwenhuys 1996, 246). Told repeatedly that child work is the response of an underdeveloped mentality, it is slowly removed or stigmatised as a life strategy.

WE ARE TOO POOR

The case studies of the last chapter identified that the majority of stitchers belong to the poorer sections of society, though they are rarely the poorest. But when football stitching families are asked why they send their children to work, they consistently respond with: 'We are too poor, we have no other choice but to send our children to work'? While this may be true for cases on the extreme, the statement needs to be challenged for most football stitching families including Ashfaq's and even Ramzan's. In this chapter I will attempt to show how the reality of football stitching contradicts the accepted discourse on the reasons for child labour, and how a radically different theory needs to be used for the determinants of children's involvement in stitching footballs.

The 'poverty' explanation is the easiest one to give from the informant's point of view, as it absolves parents and children from any agency in what is now a 'stigmatised' activity. It is also easy to accept as an explanation, as it reaffirms the dominant view of the Third World as poor, underdeveloped countries that are characterised by activities such as child labour. At the most fundamental level this poses the problem of 'relativity', which revolves around the definition of poverty.

What is poverty and how is it defined? While the answer to that question would involve a separate thesis altogether, even if we use a narrow definition of the term and assume it is linked to the material conditions of the families involved, Ashfaq's household, while poor, would not be classified as amongst the poorest. Ashfaq's family own their house, earn an income that is above the two dollars a day minimum standard set by the World Bank as their upper poverty line[1] for the country, and even with the decline in home-based stitching, are able to feed and clothe all the members of the family. Even Ramzan's family are able to do the same, though the adjustments to the decline have been more drastic.

Nevertheless, both Ashfaq and Ramzan, as well as almost all the other families that I interviewed, initially insisted that it was poverty that forced them to make their children work. It was only after winning a degree of trust with informants, and then probing further and gaining an understanding of their daily lifestyle and routines, that Ashfaq, Ramzan and the majority of football stitchers more or less reluctantly admitted that their households would be able to absorb the loss of income of their children without having to resort to measures such as taking large loans, which according to my research has not taken place except in the specific circumstances mentioned in chapter 5. Both the admission that families would be able to adjust, and the lack of recourse to loans, supports the view that poverty is not the primary reason for children taking up football stitching. Instead, the case studies appear to support the view that the income earned by children is more important as a 'safety net' or form of 'social security'. The loss of this social security may leave the family more vulnerable to external shocks, as pointed out in the case studies, but it does not necessarily leave the family in a position where they are suddenly forced to adopt strategies such as taking large loans or compelling their children or women to work. Admittedly, there are families—those at the extremes, like Shoaib Akhtar's—that have no choice but to send their children to work, be it football stitching or work in a surgical goods manufacturing unit or in a brick kiln. For them poverty is the primary factor behind the decision to work. But these represent a minority of particular cases. Unfortunately, for reasons examined in the second chapter, it is these cases that are most frequently used by the development discourse to form the dominant representation of child labour, including the stereotype of football stitchers.

In the absence of poverty as the primary driving factor for children stitching footballs, what then is the major determinant in the involvement of children in football stitching? My conclusion revolves around an apparently mundane and routine explanation, but which the ethnographic evidence points to as the crucial element in the reason for children taking up work as football stitchers. It was also the defining feature of football stitching in Sialkot. Furthermore, this explanation rejects much of the accepted wisdom on child labour, showing how misleading general stereotypes can be when applied indiscriminately across the board.

THE IMPORTANCE OF THE 'HOME'

It was Ashfaq's wife, Safia, who first brought the explanation to my notice, and possibly because I had been looking for a more profound justification for children's involvement in football stitching, it did not immediately register. The simplicity of the reason given by Safia is summed up in the brevity of her response to the question 'Why do children stitch footballs?' 'Our children become involved in football stitching because it is *gharayloo kaam*' –(work that is done at home). The crucial point revolves around football stitching being home-based.

It is from this fundamental point that this explanation gathers further strength. Safia emphasized:

> We do not like to send our children out (of the house) to work. With football stitching they can work at home under our supervision. The work is clean and not dangerous. Also it is easy to learn and the children can earn money for themselves and help in the running of the household. They feel proud at helping their parents. Also they start stitching because they see us (their parents) and their neighbours doing it day in and day out. A child always copies what it sees—that is why our children stitch footballs.

Various versions of this 'explanation' were constantly repeated by the parents of children who stitched footballs and like Safia in the quote above, they made a clear distinction between football stitching as a specific kind of work, and other forms of work. Safia's response has several important elements, all of which are interconnected. Firstly, football stitching was frequently described as *saaf*—clean and safe. Secondly, it was flexible in that it could be done around other activities such as household chores and even school. Thirdly, it was considered an easy skill to learn. Rather than the stereotype of all work being seen as detrimental to children, football stitching was perceived by parents as a positive form of work and one that had several advantageous features. This contrasted markedly with parents' views on other types of work and the effects on those who undertake it. As Safia explained:

> Children who work outside the home are not like our children. They work away from home and are not under the supervision of their parents. They pick up bad habits. All these boys that work in the surgical workshops... they are always using bad language, they come home filthy, they smoke cigarettes and get into drugs. Our children work at home. That way they learn a skill, keep themselves busy and earn an income to support themselves and their families.

The approval of football stitching as an acceptable form of work does not extend to other forms of work. And while the elements Safia highlights (easy, flexible, clean) characterise the type of activities involved in football stitching, the critical point is that football stitching is located in the home—it is *gharayloo kaam*. As soon as that same work is moved out of the home it is no longer viewed in the same way, as we have seen in the reluctance of women to take up stitching in female stitching units.

That football stitching was 'home-based' also meant that despite the nature of the work, which admittedly was a factor in parents' acceptance of the work as suitable for their children, football stitching was never viewed in the same way that work outside the home was. While waged employment is generally agreed to lead to objectionable exploitation of children, work undertaken under parental supervision is conceived of as part of the household's moral economy and an essential aspect of socialisation (Nieuwenhuys 1994, 9). In the subcontinent, before children began earning a wage, they would earn as part of the family, and primarily to learn a new skill. That was more important than the monetary side.

Nieuwenhuys attributes the 'romanticisation' of socialisation in the colonies to the anthropologist's misunderstanding of child—adult relations in terms of socialisation patterns that were based on learning by doing. She argues that these activities performed by children in the colonised societies, and studied by anthropologists, were not child labour in the sense given to it by European law, as they depicted how children were brought up in the company of women, who, in turn, they saw as housewives and mothers rather than workers. This led to confusion in the issues of socialisation and work. Furthermore, colonial authorities, fearful that the involvement of child workers in the industries of the colony would undermine industrialisation at home, were quick to pass legislation preventing children from working in industry.[2] In contrast to what had been defined 'child labour', housework was encouraged and lauded as a form of training and socialisation. This strengthened the patriarchal view of society, in which the home was marked out as women's proper domain, with home-making and child rearing their only legitimate concerns. As a corollary, domestic tasks, subsumed with definitions of femininity, were stripped of their labour context and denuded of their economic value for the household. Home-based work has retained this notion of not being 'waged employment', but socialisation. Even an ILO report (World of Work, 1993) stated 'We have no problems with the little girl who helps her mother with the housework or cooking, or the boy or girl who does unpaid work in small family businesses.' This also meant that in order to 'de-legitimise' the stitching of footballs by children, the activity had to be moved out of the house. The centrality of the home is again highlighted. Work done at home never had the legal or social sanction that other forms of work developed.

> For working class families, the usefulness of their children was supported by need and custom. When parents were questioned as to why their children left school early to get to work, it was often 'perplexing' for the mother to assign a reason for such an 'absolutely' natural proceeding—he's of an age to work, why shouldn't he? As one mother who employed her children in housework told an investigation, 'Everybody does it. Other people's children help. Why not ours?' (Zelizer 1985, 68).

In Sialkot there is a similarly perplexed response to questions of why children work. The acceptance of child work as a norm by society is important because it is then seen as socially acceptable and has no social sanction attached to it. This was strengthened by the fact that football stitching was home-based work and not factory work. The sanction was against factory work and not home-based work.

What we also have is the formation of a very specific child worker profile in the case of the home-based football stitcher, and like the nature of football stitching, this profile contrasts with that of children working in other sectors of work. Unlike children who work outside the home, football stitchers involve a much larger proportion of girls. Stitchers also tend to be younger than their counterparts and usually form part of a wider family work force. In contrast, the child working in the surgical instruments manufacturing industry or in a tea stall is far more likely to be the stereotypical child labourer—urban based, cocky and street smart. Talking to a teacher who taught both football stitchers and those working in the surgical industry I was told,

> ...the children from the surgical industry are usually older than football stitchers. They are all boys whereas stitchers are mostly girls. The surgical workers are much more difficult to teach and discipline. They are not interested in learning. They answer back and will skip classes just to smoke with their friends. They spend little time at home and are much more independent. Often they don't even give their earnings to their parents.

This group, which is exposed to a much greater range of environments and situations, is in sharp contrast to football stitchers who, because of their younger age, gender and home ties, are more protected and less independent. The child stitchers remain firmly part of the family group with, if anything, their earnings further strengthening the feeling of belonging to a group. The child worker working outside the family has his/her links with the family weakened. There is a much greater element of independence from the wider group.

The recognition of the specificity of football stitching was not simply the response of parents who wished to justify the involvement of their own children in stitching, and were therefore 'romanticising' football stitching as work while demonising other forms of work. The view on football stitching as suitable for children was espoused by a much wider section of society, including those whose children were not working as football stitchers and even people not connected directly with the trade. I am reminded of the occasion when during an interview, Pakistani child rights activist Fawad Usman Khan stated that:

> ...if it were up to me, I would take all child labourers out of the more hazardous professions and put them into the football industry—there are no chemicals, they are well paid, and the hours are flexible. The children can work at home in their spare time, mixing it with housework or after school. I am very worried that the children taken out will end up in more dangerous occupations. This is an easy sector compared to carpets or tanneries.

The influence of the 'home' on the nature of football stitching can also be gauged from the reluctance of parents to consider alternative avenues of work as substitutes for football stitching. Whereas, in the case of the Bangladesh garment industry, children removed from working in that industry almost immediately took up work in other professions, the drift to other sectors of work in Sialkot has been minimal. There are two possible explanations for this. Firstly, in the Bangladeshi case the availability of other work allowed the shift. Secondly, greater poverty in the Bangladeshi environment may have compelled child workers to take up the available alternative work. In Sialkot, both the fact that the economic pressure on families is not as great as may have been the case in Bangladesh, and that no other form of employment has emerged that can replace football stitching, has meant fewer children entering other occupations. However, this last statement needs to be further clarified to state that parents have found no form of employment that they see as a viable alternative to football stitching. Work such as filing surgical implements, carrying and baking bricks at brick kilns, working in automobile garages or tanning leather is clearly recognised as hazardous, and while Sialkot has an abundance of brick kilns, automobile workshops, and leather and surgical manufacturing units, few football stitchers have shifted to these occupations. These alternative occupations are based out of the home and parents rate them as dangerous work in unhygienic conditions—leather work requires the use of chemicals, automobiles involve machinery and moving parts, surgical goods manufacture involves chemicals, sharp cutting tools and inhalation of metallic dust, tea stalls and restaurants expose the child to abuse—physical and sexual—by customers, and brick kilns involve carrying extremely heavy loads and exposure to high temperatures. There is a clear distinction drawn between football stitching as home-based work and work undertaken elsewhere.

The result has been that only a small percentage of children have taken up new forms of work even in areas where other work was available. Almost all the girls I interviewed, and who used to stitch but do not do so now, are undertaking household chores ranging from cooking and cleaning to looking after younger siblings. The boys tend to be sent out of the house to purchase groceries or then spend their time looking after livestock, if the family has any. This points to the parents' reluctance to allow their children to work outside the home and their recognition of football stitching as a suitable form of work for their children. Those families that have had to send their children to other areas of work usually fall into the categories that need the extra income despite making other adjustments to their living standard. They may face additional drains on their income through loss of family members or protracted illnesses, as in the case of Shoaib Akhtar. Where there is a combination of alternative work and desperate need for income, there has been some enforced shift of work from football stitching to whatever other work is available, including surgical manufacturing and work in brick kilns. Most of these children work as wage earners (generally seen as particularly unprivileged), which opens up a completely different scenario of child labour. But the smallness of the drift to other occupations reinforces the centrality of the 'home-based' feature of football stitching, and supports the view that poverty is not the driving factor behind children taking up football stitching.

The widespread availability of work at home prior to the restructuring and the ease with which stitching could be learnt also had an effect, as Safia pointed out. From an early age children will copy their parents and elder siblings. If household members were involved in stitching footballs at home then inevitably children will also become involved in the process. The fact that football stitching involves a range of tasks, some of which can easily be undertaken by young children such as waxing threads, threading needles, also means that children can become part of the manufacturing process from an early age. The widespread availability of home-based football stitching and the relative simplicity of some of the tasks was critical to the level of involvement of children.

APPRENTICESHIP AND THE 'NATURAL PROFICIENCY' OF CHILDREN

The fact that children worked at home and often learnt how to stitch from their parents should not, however, be confused with the 'hereditary' occupational specialisation that was characteristic of the caste system. Much of the writing on child labour in the sub-continent[3] has highlighted the role of the traditional socialisation process, which is based on two interrelated 'beliefs' that apparently influence the early entry of children to the workforce. Both these beliefs are widespread in the discourse of child labour as determinants of children's involvement in work. The first involves the notion that apprenticeship needs to start at an early age in order that children learn the intricate skills of the profession. The second is the apparent 'natural' proficiency of children towards certain occupations.

> It is commonly recognised and emphasised that the human body is soft, flexible and pliable in childhood and can therefore learn with ease how to twist, bend, stretch or assume different postures as required by particular jobs. Coordination of limbs, balance of body, sense of timing and attuning of sense organs are relatively easier to learn at this stage. Skills are therefore best learned if learning is begun fairly early. It is not only a physical adjustment but also a mental adjustment that has to be achieved in learning skills. (Dube in Rodgers and Standing 1981, 188).

In the subcontinent, in the past, it was the norm not only for craftsmen but also for artists and dancers, for example, to start training from an early age. Traditionally, under the influence of the caste system, certain service and artisan castes were assigned a monopoly over certain trades. In order to maintain this monopoly skills would be passed on only within the particular caste group, usually from parent to child, but also from an *ustaad* (master) to a *shagird* (student). Both would be from the same caste. In this way the skill and occupational monopoly of a caste was reproduced. As a result, children began to learn a trade from an early age as part of this traditional socialisation process.

Today the hereditary occupational monopoly of castes has broken down and technology has made intricate tasks mundane, so that there is little need to start early to learn a skill that has been de-skilled. The original craft rarely exists now. This has meant that the *ustaad-shagird* relationship has undergone a complete transformation. A child may still be 'attached' to an *ustaad,* but for most children this practically means working without pay for up to two years, usually undertaking routine, unskilled tasks. The child may be provided meals and in time will begin to earn an income. But the fact that this particular socialisation process is still favoured by some parents points to the paucity of other options, including the viability of the 'other' form of socialization— schooling.

Football stitching, however, was never a 'traditional' occupation, but emerged as a form of work when the industry developed in the 1800s. Even then, while a small minority of families may have been involved in the football trade, for most, football stitching only emerged as a form of work with the expansion in trade in the 1970s. As a result, it was rare for football stitching to be seen as a major occupation. Most stitchers, like Ashfaq, tended to stitch in between other jobs or when there was an increase in the number of footballs being sent to homes for stitching. None of my informants, whether they were stitchers or not, proclaimed to be from a family that had stitched footballs for generations. Football stitching is a relatively new form of work. The skills required to stitch footballs are not exclusive to a particular caste but are accessible to a large population. Children do take up stitching because their parents stitch—but not because their parents and family have been stitching for generations—more because it is widely available, easy to learn and based at home. Children learn by imitation and no other occupation in Sialkot was as accessible as home-based football stitching.

The second reason that is often highlighted as a reason for children being put to work early is the belief that they have a natural proficiency towards certain professions. The 'nimble fingers' theory revolves around the oft-repeated claim by manufacturers, particularly in the carpet or match stick manufacturing trade, that the nimble fingers of children are essential in producing the tightest knots in a carpet, or are ideal for handling and sorting matchsticks. In fact in all these industries, children work alongside adults and are often consigned to the unskilled aspects of production. Furthermore, adults can and do perform the tasks assigned to children. In an ILO study on child labour in the hand-knotting of carpets, interviews among 2000 weavers showed that children were no more dexterous than adults and that the finest carpets were made by adults, not children. The Madras Institute of Development Studies (MIDS) comes to a similar conclusion on the match industry of Sivakasi based in the Indian State of Tamil Nadu (MIDS, 198, 53 in Burra 1995, 193-4).

While the 'nimble fingers' theory appears to be related to 'traditional' ideas about the need to start learning a skill from an early age, there is a definite promotion of this 'local' discourse, most often by employers and by those with related interests. It is also an example of a local representation of child labour that has been used to justify the continued use of children as an inexpensive supply of labour. The early involvement of children also ensures that these children are 'socialised' into accepting jobs that adults would refuse. Nevertheless, such has been the strength of its propagation, particularly in the carpet industry, that even the wider population offers it as an explanation for child employment.

However, while in certain sectors of work, such as carpet weaving, the involvement of children is often attributed to the 'traditional beliefs' of local people in the need to learn a skill early and the natural proficiency of children towards a particular trade, in the case of football stitching there appeared to be a singular absence of such 'traditional' beliefs. There was little use of the justification that stitching was a difficult skill to master and therefore required that children learn it early. Stitchers pointed out that children could be helping stitch a complete football within two to three months. Stitching a whole football independently would take longer to master, but most stitchers felt that football stitching was an easy skill to learn and there was no reason why individuals could not learn it later in life. Most adult stitchers themselves rarely stitched as children, primarily because, for most, stitching as a profession only became available fifteen to twenty years ago. As such, it was probably taken up when they had already reached adulthood. While a few stitchers in the age range 20-25 did point out that they stitched fewer footballs now than when they first started out, this was attributed to the mental and physical fatigue of stitching footballs day-in and day-out, rather than any particular skill they had when they were children.

Furthermore, the relative simplicity of learning football stitching meant that the need to hone a complex skill under the apprenticeship of an *ustaad* was not offered as a reason for children taking up football stitching. In place of the *ustaad,* children learnt at home under the tutelage of parents or elder siblings. Moreover, the fact that football stitching neither required children to learn from an *ustaad* nor an extended period of apprenticeship, meant that children could be earning an income within a few months of learning to stitch. This was an added incentive for parents to involve their children in stitching from an early age, and contrasts with skills that require long apprenticeships where children spend several months, and occasionally years, learning a trade, and are seldom paid during this period. Often such apprenticeships will be based outside the family. The absence of an *ustaad* also meant that master-craftsmen did not come looking for children as possible students. Instead football stitching remained entirely home-based. Thus the simplicity of the skill and the non-requirement of the *ustaad* were additional factors that contributed both to the early involvement of children in football stitching and in the process remaining home-based.

The natural proficiency argument was also not invoked, even by employers, possibly because in the existing sub-contracting system based on piece-rate wages, it did not matter who stitched the ball. Payment would be made per ball. Chapter 4 highlighted the fact that children are not considered the best stitchers of footballs and informants unequivocally placed children in the least skilled category. Ashfaq, who despite having learnt football stitching from his daughters, explained that children were not good at stitching and in most cases were only 'helpers'. This statement is borne out by my own findings, which, on average, found that only one or two children out of ten were able to stitch a complete football by themselves. These children were also almost always older than ten and usually closer to 14. The vast majority stitched only half a football, or then simply helped their parents or siblings in the process. Presently, Ashfaq is able to stitch two to three footballs a day. His daughter Fatima can stitch two complete footballs but it is more common, when they both have work, for Fatima to stitch the two halves of the football and let her father do the more complicated process of stitching the two halves together. In addition, unlike her father, Fatima did not stitch the higher quality Lahori balls, which required a tighter stitch. For the stitchers themselves there is no belief in the argument that children stitch footballs better because they have nimble fingers.

CHILDREN'S CHOICE: RECOGNISING AGENCY

The previous section has shown the significance and importance of the location and nature of football stitching as a determinant of children's involvement in the process. Furthermore it has shown the greater influence of these factors vis-à-vis the more accepted determinants that are part of the child labour discourse, those of poverty and tradition. It is also important to examine a further feature that I believe plays a crucial but again largely overlooked role in the decision to start stitching—the child's own preference.

Toren argues through her analysis of four ethnographic examples (Fiji, Manus, Abelan and Euro-American) that in these societies children's understanding of certain concepts are strikingly different to adult understandings of the same concepts, implying that children's cognitive processes are separate and different from those of adults. Toren therefore emphasises that children need to be recognised as a separate unit of analysis, as active rather than passive agents. 'Children have to live their lives in terms of their understandings, just as adults do; their ideas are grounded in their experience and thus equally valued' (C. Toren 1993, 463).

Equally, anthropologists such as Nieuwenhuys (1994, 1996) and Reynolds (1991), examining working children, have argued that children need to be moved to the centre of any analysis and their own decision-making capabilities recognised and respected. Chapter 5 argued that the position of football stitchers as the objects of development increased both their marginal position within the instituted development project and their marginalisation as a result of the project. Similarly, if children are seen as passive subjects of social structures and processes, their position as capable decision-making agents in their own lives is often overlooked.

In contrast, as James, Jenks and Prout (1998, 103) point out, recognising children as agents can allow one to ask how children's work takes place, and how it is negotiated and made more meaningful, with a commitment to a much fuller attention to children's own accounts and a respect for their competence in making decisions about their lives and futures. This opens up the possibility of including children's own preferences as an important determinant, not simply for taking up football stitching, but also in rejecting other options that may be open to them.

In Sialkot, children play a critical role in making decisions, albeit within certain predetermined boundaries. Moreover, the question of children's choice allows for the introduction of what is often considered the 'antithesis' to child work, but what in practice is frequently a cause of child labour, primarily through its rejection, by children and their parents, as a viable alternative to work, that of formal schooling. This reintroduces some of the themes examined in the first two chapters of the thesis, primarily the strength of dominant discourses and their ability to propagate themselves as the 'only path' through marginalizing other options.

Ashfaq's wife, Safia, pointed out that her daughters were proud to make a contribution towards the running of the household. In addition, Fatima and her sister decided by themselves to learn how to stitch from a neighbour. They then taught their parents. Mendelievich argues that even if the child him/herself 'decides' to work, the decision has already been taken for him/her 'through the attitude of his parents and through the influence of the entire social environment in which he lives' (Mendelievich 1979, 5-6).

Mendelievich again removes any agency on the part of children. But even while socio-cultural influences do 'constrain' social behaviour, there is room to manoeuvre within this framework. Fatima and her sister may eventually have been forced to work, by their parents, directly or indirectly through the influence of the existing social environment. But it is significant that they made that (predetermined) decision and perceived it as an individual choice. The evidence from the case studies, and the minimal shift to other occupations in the face of the decline in football stitching, indicates that households could do without the income brought in by children. These children could, therefore, attend schools. But the perception of a substantial number of children was that they had taken up work of their own accord and had not been pressurised by their parents. When I asked Fatima why she started stitching, her response indicated the influence of her own decision-making.

> I took up stitching of my own accord. My parents didn't force me. I used to see them working hard everyday, so I felt that I should also help my family. That is why I took up football stitching. Now I feel happy because

I am able to contribute to the welfare of my family and I can also save a bit of money for myself. Also I feel proud because my parents recognise my contribution and they always give me *shaabaashi* [encouragement]. I feel *zimmedar* [responsible] now.

Fatima's response was typical of many football stitching children that I interviewed. However, this response must be examined critically. Children may not have wanted to admit that they were forced into work or they may have overestimated their own agency in the matter. But the response of the children, as in Fatima's example, one of confidence and pride in their decision-making, indicates a degree of agency on their part. The same attitude is not displayed when children are forced into work, wherein the attitude is more of resignation and powerlessness indicating the inevitability of work. Often these children were also the ones that stated that they did not like stitching. Part of the feeling of pride comes not so much from the child stitchers' economic contribution, but from the contribution towards group cohesion. Nieuwenhuys points out that 'the domestic group that regulates children's activities does not stand on its own, and in a rural setting, in which most working children live, clustering of kin may play a significant role in providing the poor with a degree of security and solidarity' (Nieuwenhuys 1994, 199). Child work provides an additional income for the household but this contribution, no matter how small, increases group cohesion and family solidarity. As Greer points out in her observation on working children in developing countries, 'The children may be grubby...but they have a clear sense of the group they belong to' (G. Greer in Zelizer 1985, 219). Furthermore, parents in Sialkot clearly recognized and acknowledged the contribution children made to the family's welfare through their stitching. This recognition increased as children moved from being *madadgars*[4] (helpers) to being stitchers of a few panels to those able to stitch *kholrus* (half a football) or complete footballs. As pointed out in Fatima's quote, the encouragement and recognition offered by parents was important to the children's self esteem and feeling of being active contributors to the family's welfare.

For international agencies whose manifesto it is to fight child work and promote education, the recognition of children's decision-making capacity throws up the uncomfortable possibility that children may actually prefer work to school and that many children decide themselves not to go to school. As Boyden asserts 'for some, the idea that children might take an active part in decision making is still very novel; others may fear the consequences' (J. Boyden 1997, 222). In addition, children who work challenge the 'universal' definition that sees childhood as a time that is to be spent in school and not at work. It is possibly for these reasons that children's own preferences have rarely been examined as reasons for children working.

SCHOOL OR WORK?

The choice between school or work, and how this choice is reached, is a good example of how children exercise their decision-making agency. In contrast to work, schooling lies at the other end of the spectrum (the 'good' end). Education is the 'sacred cow' of development, an unquestionable instrument that brings progress across the board, a universal remedy applicable to all environments. Weiner, in one of the most influential books on child labour in the subcontinent, forcefully argues that 'compulsory primary education is the instrument by which the state effectively removes children from the labour force' (M. Weiner 1991, 3). In the last decade education has been aggressively promoted by international organisations as a panacea to the underdevelopment of the Third World. Such has been the strength of the dissemination of education as the 'one and only way' of progressing, of developing, that as discussed in chapter 2, all other paths have been almost completely 'disqualified'. The result is a reduction in the 'choices' open to people through the 'de-legitimisation' of alternatives, including work. The process by which this is achieved is highlighted in the quote of an elder of the Ethiopian Borana tribe, during an interview with two anthropologists:

> In my view, this is not education, I think of it as a device whereby the enemy (the state) is out to make people forget what they already know. The device whereby he destroys our age old wisdom, by making it impossible to pass it down to the younger generation. (G. Dahl and G. Megerssa 1997, 59)

The position of education as the 'universal remedy' has meant that its rejection is seen as an aberration and is attributed to entrenched, 'traditional' beliefs that give preference to socialisation through work, rather than socialisation through schooling. These same beliefs are seen to promote child labour. The poor of the Third World are viewed as not being able to recognise the intrinsic benefits offered by education. This is considered 'irrational' behaviour, motivated by the 'underdeveloped', unenlightened mindset that needs to be developed. If your child is working it is a sign of underdevelopment. If s/he is in school it is a sign of development. However, the research of authors such as Boyden and Schildkrout, both of whom have a practical knowledge of the everyday realities of children in the Third World, shows that the decision-making of parents and children when they consider that learning a trade early is the best way to prepare for future survival is far from irrational. In fact, it represents the most 'rational' response in the given environment. If we were to set aside preconceived notions of work and schooling and 'habitate the inner interpretive architecture of the resisting culture, which would be a prerequisite for a representation that does not depend so much on Western knowledge practices' (M. Strathern 1988 in Escobar 1995, 168) the reasons for the choices that are made by the child stitchers of Sialkot become much clearer. It also becomes more evident how education can often be part of the problem rather than the solution.

Schildkraut, drawing on her research with children in Islamic northern Nigeria, argues that in order to understand contemporary child labour, it is essential to examine in more detail 'the nature of the specific cultural and social contexts in which it occurs... child labour has to be evaluated in relation to the total life experience of the child, particularly... future occupational opportunities' (E. Schildkrout 1980, 481). Let us, therefore, consider the existing environment in Sialkot.

The expansion of industry in the region created a demand for industrial and construction workers who required little education, but who displayed a demonstrable vocational skill. From the outset this dampened the demand for education amongst the working class. Furthermore, the government schools aimed at the working classes were largely neglected through the elite-centred policies of the government. The result was the poor quality of education imparted by these institutions.

The fact that many football stitchers had at some stage attended school, but had dropped out, points to the low quality of education in government schools. However, it is, as we shall discuss later in this section, not only the quality of education that determines whether a child chooses school over work. Muhammad Ashfaq's two eldest daughters Fatima and Kulsoom had both attended government school briefly before dropping out. Fatima explained that:

Half the time we were in school the teacher would not be present. On other occasions she would make us do her housework for her, like sweeping the floor of her house. Also she would beat her students with a cane so that most of the students were too scared to learn anything.

Schools are often heavily congested, with children huddling into dark, cold rooms in winter and braving extreme heat in summer. It is common for electricity, running water, boundary walls and basic materials such as books and chalk to be missing. Buildings are often in such a state of disrepair that students invariably have classes in the open. If forced to sit inside because of inclement weather, they often sit on their haunches or if they are lucky on coarse matting called a *taat*. Teachers, many of whom have less than ten years education themselves, are frequently apathetic, unmotivated and often enforce discipline using corporal punishment. A survey by the World Bank (1995) revealed that many teachers performed as poorly as their students in administered tests. For the many children that are unable to adjust to this 'learning environment', the not uncommon humiliation in front of the entire class by teachers leads to feelings of inferiority and a lack of confidence in their own abilities. In such an environment it is not surprising that only 70 per cent of children enrol and of these almost half drop out before completing primary school. Thus, two out of every three children do not complete their primary education.[5] This high dropout rate provides a supportive framework for the prevalence of child labour. In many cases even the child that does complete its primary education can barely do more than write his or her own name.

The existing government education system, apart from its low quality, also suffers from a syllabus that has little relevance to the lives of its students. This contributes to the negative attitude of parents and children towards schooling, with many voicing a desire for education to be more vocation-oriented so that it could mirror the needs of the area.

Considering the discussion above, it is hardly surprising that, from the child's point of view, attendance at government schools is an experience at once tedious, frightening and pointless. There can be little doubt that the major cause of dropouts through primary education, and particularly during the first year, is the abysmally low standard of education and the misery which this involves for the students themselves. On several occasions during fieldwork, when I tracked down children who had dropped out of school in order to work, I was informed by their parents that the child had no *dilchaspi* (interest) in studying, or on some occasions, that the child persistently ran away from school. One mother even told me that she beat her son repeatedly to try and make him stay in school, but he refused. 'You talk to him now...I have given up', said the exasperated mother. Clearly the 'push' factor of poor quality schooling is an important reason for children deciding to drop out of school. Surveys undertaken by Save the Children Fund (1997) and the International Labour Organisation in the football manufacturing industry in Pakistan (1996) found that of those child stitchers who did attend government schools a substantial percentage did drop out due to uninteresting curricula, unsympathetic teachers and an uncomfortable school environment.

While the children's own experience of school is, in most cases, the most important reason for them opting out of school,[6] this attitude is strengthened by the lack of support they receive from their parents. This is often the result of parents themselves having had negative experiences with schooling. Adult literacy in Sialkot is comparatively high[7] but the overall statistics need to be kept in perspective. Firstly, male literacy[8] is considerably higher than female literacy. Secondly, for football stitchers, the situation is more acute. Of the household respondents that I interviewed, less than 1 in 5 fathers were educated to a primary school level. For mothers, the rate was even lower, with just over 1 in 10 having completed primary school education. As a result, parents, many of whom have themselves ended up in the semi-skilled football stitching vocation, are unlikely to espouse the benefits of education. Furthermore, the lack of awareness over what schooling entails for children, particularly amongst mothers, continues to be a major obstacle to improving student achievement. On several occasions when I asked why a certain student was not at school, the answer would invariably be because the parents had decided to keep the child home for some, usually not very important, reason. Few parents understood that missing two or three days a week would hinder their child's progress in school. In addition, almost all parents believe that educating a child extends simply to sending the child to school. The remaining onus is to be shouldered by the teacher. As a result there is virtually no support to students at home and there is little if any concession made for the child to do homework or revision. Along with the quality of teaching and the inadequate learning environment this usually leads to poor performance in school, which in turn promotes the view amongst parents that the child in question does not have the aptitude for education. This is more than enough of an excuse for the child to be removed from school and set to work. The result is a cycle that constantly reinforces the negative view and experience of schooling amongst parents.

However, the above discussion still assumes that, if the quality of education were better, children and parents would automatically prefer school to work. Undoubtedly, many would enjoy the school experience if the physical and learning environment improved, and there is evidence that this is the case in Sialkot where the non-formal schools are providing a positive change. In sharp contrast to government schools, where a gloomy atmosphere of coercion existed and students came across as depressed and subdued, the majority of children enrolled in the non-formal centres appeared cheerful, alert, and enjoying this schooling experience. It may also have been that the confidence and achievement that these child stitchers achieved from their work experience influenced their demeanour in school. Less intimidating teachers from the local community also did much to improve the working environment. But the relative 'success' of schools in this case should not mean education is seen as the exclusive option and all other activity is subsequently completely marginalized. Nieuwenhuys (1994) shows, through her ethnography in the Indian state of Kerala, that even amongst a community that values education highly, school and work are not considered mutually exclusive. Child workers frequently both work and attend school (see also La Fontaine 1978, Bekombo 1981, Reynolds 1991). In Sialkot, an SCF survey revealed that children often stitched footballs in order to help pay for the expenses accrued through school attendance. In some cases schooling may actually lead to an increase in child labour. My own research revealed that few child stitchers showed a preference for giving up their work entirely, and much of the attraction of the non-formal schools comes from the flexibility of their hours, which allows children to continue stitching if they want. Many child stitchers stated that they would like to combine both education and work, and the older children in particular were adamant that they did not want to lose the opportunity to stitch footballs. As White emphasizes 'alongside the causes that are better known and publicized—of children forced into labour by parents or unscrupulous labour recruiters—there are many children, all over the world, who simply decide they need to earn money' (White, 1995 in James, Jenks and Prout 1998, 120.

White's observation is an important one. The poor quality of education is frequently mentioned as a reason for children taking up work. However, it needs to be seen in combination with the active decision of children to choose an alternative to school. This requires the recognition of children's decision-making capabilities and their needs. Morrow (1994) has examined the affect of the new teenage consumer market on the incidence of children working in Britain. She points out that children from relatively affluent families often work in order to purchase luxuries not financed by parents. While the child stitchers of Sialkot may not be able to save money to buy 'luxuries' in the sense that Morrow discusses, many did save up to buy items that they would not have been able to afford otherwise. Children saved up to buy new clothes for *Eid*. Girls bought small cosmetic items. Boys spent money on confectionery and toys. On a smaller scale, a similar process to that described by Morrow is taking place in Sialkot. Furthermore, children seeing their peers able to buy these items feel the need to be able to do the same. Again this indicates that poverty is not the primary factor in the decision to start stitching. Thus in contrast to school, football stitching provided children with a degree of respect and recognition from their parents and peers, and some pocket money. School on the other hand offers few incentives. These are important motivations that need to be recognised as factors affecting children's decision to take up work.

> Therefore, unless the school can provide information that is at least as good as that which is available within the community—something that is unlikely with poorly trained teachers or inadequate curricula—rural families will have neither the social nor the economic incentive to consider sending their children to school. This is true especially in societies based on an ascriptive status hierarchy, where education makes no impact on social and economic circumstances. (Boyden 1997, 212).

The failure of education to bring about the practical benefits to a household that could subsequently challenge the existing order is a powerful disincentive against embracing it. Instead, there are several negative factors that continue to discourage school attendance. Unemployment amongst the educated youth in Sialkot is high,[9] with the result that many will be forced into occupations at which the uneducated are equally adept. In fact, of the adult stitchers interviewed, I found no correlation between higher levels of education and a higher income.

Stitcher incomes tended to vary between Rs. 2,000 and Rs. 4,500 per month irrespective of education levels. Both parents and children are also quick to seize on the more frequent work-related successes in contrast to the frustration that has come to be commonly associated with education. For example, while interviewing a group of stitchers in the village of Lalewali, I was told that one of the stitchers' sons had been educated till the 10th class (till the age of 18) but was still unable to find gainful employment. He now works as a stitcher at the unit of the son of another villager, who never went to school but took up stitching at an early age and then started up his own stitching unit. Most sub-contractors are uneducated or have minimal education but are seen as successful businessmen. In addition, many of the older industrialists were uneducated but became successful entrepreneurs. Education boasts few such positive role models, and status is increasingly equated with land and material wealth, rather than knowledge and education.

One of the other 'dangers' of education, as elaborated by parents of football stitchers and again connected to the issue of unemployment amongst the educated youth, is the feeling that it unrealistically increases the aspirations of children. Many parents stated that once educated, children tend to pass up employment opportunities that they no longer consider worthy of their new status as educated individuals, leading to them becoming voluntarily unemployed and subsequently unemployable for many jobs. In an apparent confirmation of this, almost all the children I interviewed stated that, if theoretically they were given the choice of completing their education without the constraints of poor quality and resources, they would not consider returning to stitching on completion of their schooling. Rodgers and Standing (1981, 33) go as far as to say that formal schooling may be seen as 'dysfunctional', in that it weakens rather than strengthens the child's ability to survive in an environment of poverty and high unemployment, implying that it is schooling that is the less rational response. Darling (1934) in his travels in British India, recounts a conversation with an Indian farmer during which the farmer ruefully describes the benefits of education on his son:

I have two sons. The elder went to school—he reads in the 8th class. The younger reads only in the mosque. He can do every kind of work; but the elder does not know how to twist the well rope to which water pots are fastened, nor to fit the wooden rings to it. The younger can lift any load:

the elder is too weak. Those who work when they are small can do any kind of work (Darling 1934, 68).

In similar vein, Grootaert and Kanbur (1995, 193) quote an African commentator saying that 'Education broadens your mind but it does not teach you how to survive.'

Despite these shortcomings, education is still usually forwarded as the only solution to a complex problem. But the position of education as a pillar in the development discourse, and its status as the binary opposite of child work, has meant that any positive benefits for children that may accrue from work have been disregarded. Yet, apart from the income that is brought in by children, which in some cases may be crucial to the maintenance of the household, the work activity as part of a group is often more important than the actual income – as in the promotion of group cohesion, increased self esteem and responsibility. In many cases learning a skill early may be the most 'rational' response to the existing environment. Similarly, Zelizer points out that Beatrice and John Whiting, in *Children of Six Cultures*, found that child work in farming communities taught children responsibility and gave them a sense of worth and involvement in the needs of others. She goes on to state that the authors noted that these children's jobs were 'not just make work but were directly related to the economy and welfare of the family' (Zelizer 1985, 220). Research by White and Tjandraningsih (1992) in Indonesia, Johnson, Hill and Ivan-Smith (1995) in Nepal and Szenton Blanc et. al., (1994) in Brazil all show that work can bring important social rewards for children. Certainly, many of the child stitchers I interviewed in Sialkot showed confidence, self-esteem, and a sense of responsibility and purpose that was absent from their non-working, school-going counterparts. Furthermore, Boyden highlights the fact that the beliefs of welfare practitioners about the activities and experiences suitable for child life may differ radically from those of parents and children, and that:

> From the point of view of the former, children present in public spaces... and absent from school or the home and children at work or living in the street all signify family or personal dysfunctioning. But the perception of parents and children may be that these are not pathological behaviour patterns. On the contrary, the development of precocious mechanisms for survival is seen by many as integral to normal socialization. (Boyden 1997, 213).

However, not only have the benefits of work been overlooked, but the power of the discourse of education has meant that apart from its 'dysfunctional' tendencies there are further negative effects that education can have, but which are rarely highlighted and are usually only associated with work. In addition, this has little to do with the usual observation that it is the poor quality of education rather than education per se which is to blame.

When a senior government employee proclaimed to me that work placed 'stress on children but so too did education', I dismissed it as a method of covering up the government's failure to tackle the child labour issue. I still believe that the quote in question was principally an attempt to justify government inaction on child labour and that it represented the views of policy makers. But it does allow the introduction of a less demonised view of work and a greater reluctance to acknowledge the universal acceptability of schooling.

The 'disappearance of childhood' is almost always associated with working from an early age and thereby being denied the right to an education—considered one of the defining features of childhood. But Norma Field (1995) examines the disappearance of childhood in Japan precisely through children's involvement in the socially defined tasks of education. The Japanese media have, for some two decades now, reported the rising incidence of student suicides committed by third-year high-school students under pressure of preparing for university entrance exams. There has also been a dramatic increase in the incidence of adult diseases among school-aged children.

A 1990 survey among school aged children nationwide showed that 63.2 per cent were suffering from high levels of blood cholesterol, 36.2 per cent from ulcers, 22.1 per cent from high blood pressure and 21.4 per cent from diabetes. School children also suffer from stress related baldness, eczema and chronic constipation. (Arita & Yamaoka 1992, 14; in Field 1995, 53).

Arita and Yamaoka go on to state that no child labour laws can be applied to protect children of fourth through sixth grade who attend crammer schools. These children endure a routine that appears at least as damaging as that of many working children,

Rushing home after school, grabbing dinners packed by their mothers, exchanging school books for cram school books, spending from 5 to 9 p.m. at the cram school (or going to more than one extra school if their mothers have chosen to have them specialise), perhaps staying on for private lessons until 11, and when entrance exams are around the corner, getting home after midnight to tackle school homework, topped off with a touch of video game playing before going to sleep around 2 a.m. (Arita & Yamaoka, ibid).

While the Convention on the Rights of the Child (CRC) proclaims the 'right of the child to rest and leisure, to engage in play and recreational activities appropriate to the age of the child and to participate freely in cultural life and the arts' (CRC article 31), no specific measures have been taken by the Japanese government. When Arita and Yamaoka discuss the increasing health hazards facing children and Field refers to children as prematurely aged, both mentally and physically, few would think that they were referring not to the victims of child labour but to the victims of education. Field goes further saying that the aim of education in Japan is 'neither merely to perfect small motor conduction nor to increase vocabulary per se, but to produce adults tolerant of joyless, repetitive tasks, in other words, disciplined workers' (Field 1995, 71). Education and work are not quite the opposite poles that they are made out to be. Sharp and Green (1975 in James, Jenks and Prout 1998, 119), in fact, distinguish between work, or what children do in the future, and 'work', or what children do at school, which looks just like work but cannot be given equivalence with it. But Japan's position as a 'developed' country and the position of schooling as a defining feature of 'childhood' means it is football stitching in Sialkot, rather than schooling in Japan, that is considered by the press, NGOs, international organisations, governments and the wider public as more detrimental to the children involved.

The aim of the argument on the benefits of work and the shortcoming of schooling has not been to promote one over the other, but to show that education should not be seen as the only path, the unquestioned alternative to work. As Braham and Braham succinctly sum up:

We shall not belay the point. Respect for the 'best interests of the child'? Yes. Respect for educative schooling? Yes. But the recognition, as well, that there may be such a disjunction between educative schooling—schooling that is in the best interest of the child—and the schooling that is on offer in child labour countries for poor children, that the assumption that all child labour is wrong, and only schooling, even if it is inadequately educative, is right, may be not only be a position that is wrong, it may even be punitive, by denying them the acquisition of some of their needed life skills, let alone needed personal and family income, and far from being in their best interests. (Braham and Braham 1999, 47).

On the face of it, recent statistics in Sialkot seemingly point to a change in the attitudes of parents and children in Sialkot in favour of school over work. This point is often highlighted by international agencies involved in the programme, who are keen to drive home their 'success'. My own data, when taken out of context, also supports this view, revealing that the percentage of children stitching footballs has fallen from over 60 per cent two years ago to just under 25 per cent at present. Furthermore, 6000 ex-stitchers had 'joined' the non-formal schools, apparently leading further credence to the claim that, if given the choice, children and their parents will always choose school over work. In fact, football stitchers had few options, and it is the shrinkage of choices open to them that has forced a change. This is hardly surprising given the time period involved. Past experience as related by Cunningham, with reference to compulsory schooling laws in Britain, indicates that 'the process of making people accept that regular attendance at schooling was normal may be seen as stretching out over some 30 years' (Cunningham 1996, 46). The decline in home-based work has left children with few alternatives. In the absence of options, many parents felt that, rather than spend their time idle, children would be better served by going to the non-formal schools, which provided free text books and stationery, and required no school fees or uniforms. In school at least it was felt that children would be kept away from bad habits and vagrancy. In fact, this widespread belief that if left unoccupied, children would fall prey to bad habits and vagrancy, was another reason that parents gave for putting their children to work.[10] Society is seen as dangerous, offering all kind of temptation, and children are viewed as particularly vulnerable to these. Being occupied through work or school is thought to prevent children from habits such as drug taking and smoking. But evidence of the lack of change in attitudes can be gauged from the responses of the child stitchers, and their desire to continue stitching footballs, even if they were also to go to school, and the fact that as soon as work was available children would stay at home and complete the stitching of footballs. The increasing instability of income due to the fall in home-based work also contributes to the tendency of children to miss school as soon as work is available, as it may be some time before any further work becomes available.

A further example of children's decision not to go to school has manifested itself in the emergence of a 'third option' available to children, apart from work and schooling (formal and non-formal). The *madrasa* or seminary is not a new phenomenon, but emerged in the eleventh century as the principal institution of higher Islamic learning.[11] However, it has grown in importance in the last three decades. The curriculum of *madrasas* has always stressed the purity of religious learning as being central to their role in society. This feature has remained largely unchanged since the birth of the institution[12] and *madrasas* have guarded their curriculum 'religiously'. Today many *madrasas* in Pakistan, even those that do teach some minimal non-religious subjects, rely on ancient sources. Jones (2002, 32), for example, points out that in some Pakistani *madrasas* medicine is taught through texts written in the eleventh century and geometry teachers use material written by Euclid in 300 BC.

Under General Zia's decade of state-sponsored Islamisation (1977–88), the influence of *madrasas* increased exponentially. The number of *madrasa* students expanded from 24,822 in 1979 to 218,939 in 1995 (Zaman 1999, 312). The most recent newspaper reports have put the current number of *madrasas* at between 7000 and 8000 with the number of students ranging between 600,000 and 700,000. Their expansion from the 1970s can be attributed to a number of factors, the most important of which were the growth of Islamic consciousness throughout the 1970s and generous funding to the seminaries from Saudi Arabia, Iran, and other Muslim states. In addition, the Soviet invasion of Afghanistan in 1979 led to both the United States and Pakistani government diverting funds to *madrasas* in an attempt to support an Afghan resistance that increasingly depended on recruiting students from these institutions.

The survival of the *madrasa* and its resurgence under the decade of Islamisation has meant that, what started as an alternative system for a small minority of conservative religious families, has been transformed into a countrywide parallel education system, catering to a substantial proportion of Pakistani children. But it is not simply state sponsorship that is the reason for the revival of these seminaries. Similar to Eickelman's finding in Morocco, once it became evident that the linkage between socio-economic opportunity and educational attainment had been weakened, popular enthusiasm for government education declined. Public disillusionment with the government system has clearly been a factor in students turning increasingly to religious education and Zaman (1999) points out that there is evidence that dropouts from government schools form an increasing proportion of students at *madrasas*. Many parents of government school dropouts feel that that the *madrasa* still provides an opportunity for some education. Furthermore, *madrasas* offer free meals, clothes and sometimes a small cash incentive for students. No fees are charged. These institutions also fulfil the parents' desire to ensure that children are kept off the streets and out of vagrancy. More importantly, as Metcalf (2002) points out, the *madrasa* through its routine missionary tours, gatherings in local mosques and homes and annual gatherings, clearly offers meaning and dignity to many who participate—something that government education is unable to do. Moreover, once 'graduated', some *madrasas* provide recruits to militant outfits, which, whatever their aims, offer a purpose and a way of winning respect within the community.[13] They also offer a small regular salary, which for some recruits can be a significant factor in their decision to become a *Jihadi* or holy warrior. There is also an additional consideration—if a *Jihadi* dies in a 'military operation', their family will be provided for.

In Sialkot, *madrasas* do not appear to be as influential as in other parts of the Punjab, particularly in southern regions of the province. Part of the reason may be southern Punjab's status as the heartland of sectarian violence. As a result, the *madrasas* of different sects have jockeyed for supremacy in these regions. Furthermore, Sialkot is known for the large number of *Sufi* shrines that are dotted throughout the province.[1] This is evidence of the strength of the 'popular' form of Islam that is largely opposed to the more revivalist Islam taught through *madrasas*. It may be for these reasons that while some of the boys stitching footballs that I interviewed, regularly said their prayers at the local mosque, none were attending *madrasas* in Sialkot. The other reason that none of my interviewees were enrolled in *madrasas* was because of the large proportion of female child stitchers. *Madrasas* largely, though not exclusively, cater to male students. Furthermore, there are a large number of non-formal and government schools in Sialkot, which despite their questionable quality, still act as competition to *madrasas*. Lastly, at least prior to the restructuring of the industry, the widespread availability of football stitching meant an option that parents viewed as suitable for their children.

Therefore, children also stitch quite simply because they actively choose to work, earn an income and recognition and respect from their family and friends, rather than spend their time in school where they are unable to receive these benefits. Moreover, while work may attract children, the poor quality of schooling has forced them further towards alternative choices such as work and the madrasa. But by indiscriminately promoting education, while also disqualifying work, it may appear that children are choosing one over the other, but in fact the number of choices is being reduced. If football stitching is removed as an option, some children may have no choices left to them. Others may attend schools offering meaningless and sub-standard education, or enter the parallel *madrasa* system.

Basu describes the literature on child labour as an *'illustration of abundance and anarchy'* (1998, 3). Nieuwenhuys also emphasises the conceptual confusion surrounding the issue, in which 'ill-grasped notions from diverse analytical fields are indiscriminately used' (Nieuwenhuys 1996, 241). In addition, recalling Ennew's quote from Chapter 1: 'Child labour is not just a topic for legislation, programming and research, it is also a public issue in which information is used, and often generated by mass media, as well as being part of the folk history of industrialised nations' (Ennew 1997), it is easy to see why child labour is so often a confused and confusing topic. For every statement there appears to be a counter statement, backed up by ethnographic and statistical data. Part of the problem lies with the inherent tendency of the development discourse to try and apply broad, ahistorical causes such as poverty, tradition and underdevelopment as the determinants of child labour. This penultimate chapter has tried to show that these generalities, particularly the issue of poverty and 'traditional beliefs' as driving factors, are not applicable to the activity of football stitching amongst children. Instead, determinants revolving around recognising children's agency in decision-making, and the importance of football stitching as a home-based activity, can be seen to better reflect the lived experiences of stitchers themselves.

Furthermore, the continued increasing vulnerability of football stitchers is examined through the promotion of education as part of the programme to remove children from the stitching labour force. The endorsement of schooling as the 'only' legitimate space for socialisation has meant that other forms of socialisation, including work, are being de-legitimised, leading to a situation where there is a danger of negating precious mechanisms of survival, and penalising or even criminalizing the ways that the poor bring up their children (Nieuwenhuys 1996, 242, Boyden 1997, 207). Yet, even without going into the detail that Mamdani (1972) did in arguing that Punjabi peasants, far from being 'irrational' in their rejection of birth control, showed economic rationality in having large families, it is clear that when parents and children choose work over education, they are not, in the given environment, making an 'irrational' decision. But the dominant discourse condemns virtually all non-Western forms of child work, equating them with negative stereotypes of child labour and the loss of childhood. This leads us back to the discussion on the strength of certain discourses of development.

NOTES

1. The poverty line is defined as the minimal acceptable level of income below which a person is considered poor. $1 a day is the poverty line for Pakistan and $2 a day is the 'upper' poverty line. Nationally 31 per cent of people in Pakistan in 1996 were below the $1 a day line (World Development Report 2001).
2. Nieuwenhuys (1994, 184) points out that nineteenth century economic thought in Britain was very much influenced by the belief that large-scale use of child labour was a necessary pre-condition for industrial development. Thus a firm stand against child labour in industry was part of a policy of discouraging the industrialisation of India so that competition for 'home' industries was minimised.
3. See for example Sahoo 1995, Tripathy 1989, M. Gupta and K. Voll (eds) 1987.
4. *Madadgar* means helper and refers to those children that undertake the simplest tasks—usually threading needles, putting gum on the thread. *Madadgars* do not stitch footballs.
5. Fatemi et al., 2000.
6. There are occasions when parents will decide, against the will of the child, that schooling will be bypassed. Often this occurs in the poorest families that cannot afford to lose the opportunity time that the child has to spend in school even if all other aspects of schooling are free. However, football stitchers generally do not fall into this class of the poorest groups. For girls, however, there is the additional concern of protecting *izzat* that affects their school attendance. Again, that choice is made by the parents. In these cases the decision-making capacity of the child is greatly reduced.
7. Overall literacy in Sialkot—58.9 per cent, Overall literacy in Pakistan 45.56 per cent (1998 Pakistan Census).
8. Male literacy—65.9 per cent, Female literacy—51.5 per cent (1998 Census of Pakistan, Sialkot Section).
9. 9.2 per cent employment rate amongst students in Sialkot, 1998 Census of Pakistan.
10. This is a view that echoes the concerns of parents in Britain and many parts of the now developed world during the seventeenth, eighteenth, nineteenth centuries. Cunningham (1996, 41) points out how in Britain it was believed that idleness would lead to disorder, and to children growing up without being habituated to the labour that would be their lot in life. Employment would prevent the much-feared idleness of children.

11. See G. Makdisi 1961, 1981, 1990 for a history of *madrasas*.
12. See Eickelman (1985) for a comprehensive description of religious education in *madrasas*. While Eickelman's study is based in Morocco there are striking similarities between his description of the nature and form of religious education imparted by Moroccan *madrasas* and the education imparted in Pakistani *madrasas*.
13. See for example Esposito (1991) or Roy (1994).
14. During fieldwork I visited three of the most famous of these shrines. The shrines and attached mosques of Imam Ali-ul-Haq, Maulvi Abdul Hakeem and Mian Barkhurdar are held in great reverence throughout the Punjab and there is a steady stream of 'devotees' visiting these sites at all times of the year from every part of the province.

7

CONCLUSION

The use of an anthropological approach to analysing the involvement of child stitchers in the football industry of Sialkot has, I believe, allowed for the emergence of a rich and largely untapped body of information. As mentioned at the start of the thesis, much previous research on working children has been analysed through an economic, quantitative-based lens. This has resulted in studies on working children being dominated by 'external' observations of their experiences. There is very little knowledge about the way children, who are themselves often the most severely affected by problems of life and survival, think about their situation. Thus, despite the importance of 'child labour' in the development discourse, the focus on quantitative analyses has meant that the diversity inherent in the experiences of working children has been minimised. A more qualitative, ethnographic methodology is better suited to capturing the complexity of working children's lifeworlds 'in their own voices', thereby also placing children at the centre of the analysis. This thesis therefore fills gaps identified in the literature on child labour, while contributing a fresh perspective on the lives of working children.

Furthermore, apart from focussing on research involving children, this thesis also involved a thorough ethnography of the development process taking a particular project as a case study. This involved deconstructing the discourse of development, the way this discourse was propagated, including the agencies and techniques used in this process, and the concrete manifestation of this discourse in the form of a particular 'development project'. Thus the research looked to examine 'the whole process of making and implementing policy, the hidden as well as the public, the unintended as well as the blueprint' (E. Goody, Forthcoming, Cambridge Anthropology, Vol 23,1).

More specifically, in Sialkot it appears that the restructuring of the football manufacturing industry has been an example of the ideologies and policies of development, despite genuine humanitarian concerns, extending the universal principles and discourses that are central to development theory. The strength and 'legitimacy' of these discourses was reinforced through the international development agencies and the international treaties that increasingly define universal norms and values. The international treaties and development agencies therefore contribute to the formation of these discourses and universal standards while also acting as channels for their dissemination. Moreover as Gardner and Lewis (1996, 73) argue, these universal principles of progress often involve ethnocentric assumptions about what constitutes desirable social change. Local discourses are commonly marginalized by dominant ones. In a similar but more concrete sense, projects that are implemented on the basis of dominant discourses also work through marginalizing indigenous strategies of survival.

In Sialkot this meant that Western notions of childhood (protected and confined to school) and work (separated from home, individual wage-based) were externally imposed and resulted in the local notion of domestic-based, family production being marginalized. This led to the 'development' orthodoxy viewing, and categorising, children working as football stitchers as an aberration to the ideal of childhood. In contrast, the local discourse viewed football stitching as a respectable, positive, child-friendly activity. But being the dominant discourse meant that a project to remove children from stitching footballs was instituted. The focus of the project was to correct deviations from the norm—children were to be restored to school rather than work; and work was to be moved out of the house to a prescribed 'workplace'. Thus, dominant discourses of work, childhood and development were able to present realities, transform them, and then re-present them in the form envisaged under the universalising notions propagated through development. But the fact that the intervention was based on non-local discourses and interests meant little local commitment or participation. This is not to imply that had the beneficiaries been involved in implementing policy the project would have been successful. Instead, the point being made is that, while their genuine participation in design and implementation may not have guaranteed success, their exclusion or unfair inclusion did reduce the chances of the beneficiaries having a positive effect on a project targeted at their welfare. The lack of local involvement also ensured that the 'beneficiaries' of the project were firmly cast as passive objects of development and remained on the edges of the development initiative, unable to influence the project or the way it affected their lives.

Yet the project has been defined a 'success', as illustrated by Clinton's quote at the beginning of the thesis. Undoubtedly, if the project's achievement is measured through how well it fulfilled conditions laid out in the original design, then the project can be deemed a success. The central requirement was to eradicate child labour from the football manufacturing industry and the transfer of stitching from homes to units. This was 'officially' accomplished, even though children may have moved to other occupations and many women were left without an acceptable avenue for additional income.

Unquestionably, home-based stitching has declined and fewer children are stitching footballs as a result of the project. But this narrow definition of success revolved around compliance rather than the welfare of the beneficiaries. Nevertheless, this definition sufficed for the local industrialists and their international buyers, who could continue with business. It also sufficed for the ILO, who according to the ILO official in charge of the initiative, could not afford to fail, as this was the first programme in which the ILO was getting its hands dirty in the details of implementation. In addition, labour and human rights groups in the United States felt vindicated. The project had accomplished almost all that was expected of it when it was designed. The plight of the stitchers themselves appear to have been of secondary importance, as indicated in the remark of an official of the International Football Association (FIFA) who stated on the eve of the 1998 World Cup: 'Our main preoccupation is with the World Cup. We can't scour the world looking for children stitching footballs' (Quoted on BBC Website in the article entitled 'Football Child Labour Lives On', 16 April 1998). It was this narrow definition of 'success' that was projected, rather than whether the best interests of the child or its family had been addressed.

But the imposed project has left the supposed beneficiaries more vulnerable to external forces than they were prior to the start of the intervention. There has been little positive change in the lives of the football stitchers as a result of the project, and while the international development community celebrates the project's success, there is bewilderment on the part of the stitchers at the mention of this success. When I asked Ashfaq what he felt was the biggest change in his life as a result of the project, he stated dejectedly:

Football stitching helped stave off poverty for my family. You know prices of everyday items—pulses, grains, cooking oil—are going up everyday. Now football stitching at homes has declined. We used to use our hands in honest labour—now we will be left opening our hands, palms up, asking for help from donors.

BIBLIOGRAPHY

Abu-Lughod, L. *Veiled Sentiments: Honour and Poetry in a Bedouin Society*. University of California Press: Berkley & Los Angeles, London, 1986.

Addleton, J. S. *Undermining the Centre: The Gulf Migration and Pakistan*. Oxford University Press: Karachi, 1992.

Ahmad, I. *Caste and Social Stratification Among the Muslims*. Manohar: New Delhi, 1973.

Ahmad, N. and Ahmad, S. 'A Day in the Life of Masi Jheelo'. In L. Dube and R. Palriwala (eds) *Structures and Strategies*. Sage Publications: New Delhi, 1990.

Ahmad, S. 'Social Stratification in a Punjabi Village'. *Contributions to Indian Sociology* 4: 105-25, 1971.

Ahmad, S. 'A Village in Pakistani Punjab'. In C. Maloney (ed) *South Asia: Seven Community Profiles*. Holt, Rinehart and Winston: New York, 1974.

Ahmad, S. *Class and Power in a Punjabi Village*. Monthly Review Press: New York, London, 1977.

Ahmed, A. S. March 'Death in Islam: The Hawkes Bay Case'. *Man*. New Series. 21, 1. Royal Anthropological Institute, 1986.

Ahmed, A. S. *Pakistan: The Social Sciences' Perspective*. Oxford University Press: Karachi, 1990.

Alavi, H. 'Kinship in West Punjabi Villages'. In *Contributions to Indian Sociology* 6: 1-27, 1972.

Alavi, H.(ed) *Capitalism and Colonial Production*. Croom Helm: London, 1982.

Alavi, H. 'Introduction to Sociology of the Developing Societies'. In Teodor Shanin (ed) *'Peasant and Peasant Societies'*. Penguin, 1988.

Alavi, H. 'Formation of the Social Structure of South Asia under the Impact of Colonialism'. In Hamza Alavi and John Harriss (eds) *Sociology of Developing Societies*. Macmillan, 1989.

Alavi, H. 'Nationhood and the Nationalities in Pakistan'. In H. Donnan and P. Werbner (eds) *Economy & Culture in Pakistan: Migrants and Cities in a Muslim Society*. Macmillan: London, 1991.

Alvares, C. 'Science'. In W. Sachs (ed) *The Development Dictionary: A Guide to Knowledge as Power*. Zed Books: London, 1992.

Anker, R., Barge, S., Rajagopal, S., and Joseph, M.P. (eds). *Economics of Child Labour in Hazardous Industries of India*, Hindustan Publisher: New Delhi, 1998.

Anti-Slavery International, *Helping Business to Help Stop Child Labour*. Report, undated.

Aries, P. *Centuries of Childhood*. Vintage Books: New York, 1962.

Aziz, M. *'The Magnitude and Multitude of Child Labour'*. *Pakistan Economic Review*, 1998.

Ballard, R. 'The Political Economy of Migration: Pakistan, Britain and the Middle East'. In J. Eades (ed) *Migrants, Workers and the Social Order*. Tavistock Publications, 1987.

Banuri, T. 'Development and the Politics of Knowledge: A Critical Interpretation of the Social Role of Modernization'. In S. Marglin and A. Marglin (eds) *Dominating Knowledge*. Oxford University Press, 1990.

Barth, F. 'The System of Social Stratification in Swat, North Pakistan'. In E.R. Leach (ed) *Aspects of Caste in India, Ceylon and North-West Pakistan*. Cambridge University Press: Cambridge, 1960.

Basu, K. and Van, P.H. 'The Economics of Child Labour'. *The American Economic Review:* Volume 88, Issue 3. (June 1998).

Basu, K. *Child Labour: Cause, Consequence and Cure* with remarks on International Labour Standards, *Journal of Economic Literature*, Vol. XXXVII, September 1999.

Bekombo, M. 'The Child in Africa: Socialisation, Education and work'. In G. Rogers and G. Standing, (eds) *Child Work, Poverty and Underdevelopment*. International Labour Office: Geneva, 1981.

Benaria, L. *Women and Development*. Praeger, 1982.

Benedict, R. *Patterns of Culture*. Routledge and Kegan Paul: London, 1935.

Berlau, J. *The Paradox of Childhood Reform*. Insight: 24 November, 1997.

Berthoud, G. 'Modernity and Development'. *European Journal of Development Research* 2,1: 22-35, 1990.

Beteille, A. 'Caste in Contemporary India'. In C.J. Fuller (ed) *Caste Today*. Oxford University Press: Delhi, 1996.

Bhalotra, S. *Is Child Work Necessary?* Working Paper, Department of Applied Economics, University of Cambridge: UK, 2000.

Bloc, M. L. B. *Feudal Society*. Translated from French by L.A. Manyon. Routledge and Kegan Paul: London, 1962.

Boserup, E. *Women's Role in Economic Development*. Allen and Unwin: London, 1970.

Boyden, J. with Holden, P. *Children of the Cities*. Zed Books: London, 1991.

Boyden, J. *The Relationship Between Education and Child Work*. UNICEF International Child Development Centre: Florence, 1994.

Boyden, J. 'Childhood and Policy Makers: A Comparative Perspective on the Globalisation of Childhood'. In Alison James and Alan Prout (eds) *Constructing and Reconstructing Childhood*. Falmer Press, 1997.

Boyden, J. and Levison, D. *Children as Social and Economic Actors in the Development Process*. Working Paper 2000:1. Expert Group on Development Issues, Ministry of Foreign Affairs, Stockholm, Sweden, 2000.

Braham, M. and Braham, M. *Indicators of Child Labour: A Report to the International Programme on the Elimination of Child Labour*. International Labour Office: Geneva Field Research, April 1999.

Breman, J. 'The study of industrial labour in post-colonial India—The formal sector: An introductory review'. In Jonathan P. Parry, Jan Breman and Karin Kapadia (eds) *The Worlds of Indian Industrial Labour*. Sage Publications: New Delhi, 1999.

Brock, K., Cornwall, A. and Gaventa, J. *Power, Knowledge and Political Spaces in the Framing of Poverty Policy*. Institute for Development Studies, University of Sussex, 2001.

Burgess, R.G. (ed) *Field Research: A Sourcebook and Field Manual*. George Allen & Unwin: London, 1982.

_____. *In the Field*. Routledge: London, 1995.

Burki, S.J. *Pakistan: The Continuing Search for Nationhood*. Westview Press: Boulder, 1991.

Burra, N. *Born to Work*. Oxford University Press, 1995.

Business Ethics. Vol. 10, 16 Nov/Dec 1996.

Buvinic, L. M., McGreevey, M. and William, P. (eds) *Women and Poverty in the Third World*. Johns Hopkins University Press, 1983.

Camps I Cura, E. 'Family Strategies and Children's work Patterns: Some Insights from Industrialising Catalonia, 1850-1920'. In H. Cunningham and P. Viazzo (eds) *Child Labour in Historical Perspective*, UNICEF, 1996.

Chambers, R. *Rural Development : Putting the Last First*. Longman Press: London, 1983.

_____. *Rural Appraisal: Rapid, Relaxed and Participatory*. IDS Discussion Paper 311. Institute of Development Studies, University of Sussex, 1992.

_____. *Challenging the Professions: Frontiers for Rural Development*. Intermediate Technology Publications: London, 1993.

Cohen, B. S. *Social Anthropology of a Civilization*. Prentice Hall Inc., 1971.

Cohen, R. and Britan, G. M. *Hierarchy and Society: Anthropological Perspectives on Bureaucracy*. Institute for the Study of Human Issues: Philadelphia, 1980.

Cowen, M and Shenton R. *The Origin and Course of Fabian Colonialism in Africa*. Journal of Historical Sociology 4,2: 143-174, 1991.

Cowen, M. and Shenton, R. 'The invention of development'. In Jonathon Crush (ed) *Power of Development*. Routledge: London, New York, 1995.

Cowen, M. and Shenton, R. *Doctrines of Development*. Routledge: London, 1996.

Crawford, R. 'One Step Forward, Two Steps Back'. *Financial Times*.

_____. *Soccer Balls Made for Children by Children: Child Labour in Pakistan*. INSEAD: Fontainbleau, France, 1999.

Crush, J. (ed) *Power of Development*. Routeldge: London, New York, 1995.

Crush, J. 'Imagining Development'. In J. Crush (ed) *Power of Development*. Routledge: London, New York, 1995.

Cummins, E. *The Pakistan Football Stitching Industry*. Unpublished Paper prepared for the Dept. for International Development (DFID): UK, 2000.

Cunningham, H. and Viazzo, P. P. (eds) *Child Labour in Historical Perspective*. UNICEF, 1996.

Cunningham, H. 'Combating Child Labour: The British Experience'. *Child Labour in Historical Perspective*.

Cunningham, H. *The Decline of Child Labour*. Economic History Review LIII, 3. Blackwell Publishers: Oxford, 2000.

Dahl, G. and Megerssa, G. 'The Spiral of the Ram's Horn: Boran Concepts of Development'. In M. Rahnema and V. Bawtree (eds) *The Post-Development Reader*. Zed Books: London, New Jersey. University Press Ltd: Dhaka. Fernwood Publishing: Nova Scotia, 1997.

Darling, M. *Wisdom and Waste*. Oxford University Press, 1934.

Dasgupta, P. *An Inquiry into Well-Being and Destitution*. Clarendon Press, 1993.

Dawn, Karachi, Pakistan. 12 February 1998.

De Haan, A. 'The badli system in industrial labour recruitment: Managers and workers strategies in Calcutta's jute industry'. In Jonathan P. Parry, Jan Breman and Karin Kapadia (eds) *The Worlds of Indian Industrial Labour.* Sage Publications: New Delhi, 1999.

De Neve, G. 'Asking for and giving baki: Neo bondage or the interplay of bondage and resistance in the Tamilnadu power-loom industry'. In Jonathan P. Parry, Jan Breman and Karin Kapadia (eds) *The Worlds of Indian Industrial Labour.* Sage Publications: New Delhi, 1999.

De Vylder, Stefan. *Development Strategies, Macroeconomic Policies and the Rights of the Child.* A Discussion Paper for Radda Barnen, Art no. 96-1058. Radda Barnen: Stockholm, 1996.

Devereux, S. and Hoddinott, J. (eds) *Fieldwork in Developing Countries.* Harvester Wheatsheaf: UK, 1992.

Donnan, H. and Werbner, P. (eds) *Economy & Culture in Pakistan: Migrants and Cities in a Muslim Society.* Macmillan: London, 1991.

Donnan, H. 'Family and Households in Pakistan'. In Hastings Donnan and Frits Selier (eds), *Family and Gender in Pakistan.* Hindustan Publishing Corporation: New Delhi, 1997.

——————. 'Return Migration and Female Headed Households in Rural Punjab'. In *Family and Gender in Pakistan,* 1997.

Donnan, H. and Selier, F. (eds) *Family and Gender in Pakistan.* Hindustan Publishing Corporation: New Delhi, 1997.

Dorman, P. '*Child Labour in the Developed Economies*'. ILO/IPEC Working Paper: Geneva, 2001.

Dumont, L. *Homo Hierarchicus.* University of Chicago Press, 1980.

Eades, J. *Migrants, Workers and the Social Order.* Tavistock Publications, 1987.

Eglar, Z. S. *A Punjabi Village in Pakistan.* Columbia University Press: New York, 1960.

Eickelman, D.F. *Knowledge and Power in Morocco: The Education of a Twentieth-Century Notable.* Princeton University Press: New Jersey, 1985.

El-Solh, C. F. and Mabro, J. (eds) *Muslim Women's Choices: Religious Belief and Social Reality.* Berg Publishers: Oxford, 1994.

Ennew, J. *The sexual experience of children.* Polity Press in assoc. with Basil Blackwell: Oxford, 1986.

Ennew, J. and Milne, B. *The next generation: Lives of third world children.* Zed Books: London, 1989.

Ennew, J. October *Measuring and monitoring child work & child labour.* International Conference on Child Labour, Oslo, Norway, 1997.

Epstein, S. T. *A Manual for culturally adapted market research.* RWAL Publications: England, 1988.

Escobar, A. 'Anthropology and the Development Encounter'. *American Ethnologist.* 18,4:658-82, 1991.

——————. *Encountering Development: The Making and Unmaking of the Third World.* Princeton University Press: New Jersey, 1995.

Escobar, A. 'Imagining a post-development era'. In Jonathon Crush (ed) *Power of Development.* Routledge: London, New York, 1995a.

Esposito, John L. *Islam and Politics,* (3rd ed) Syracuse University Press: New York, 1991.

Fatemi, S., Gilani, M.M., Jillani, Z., Khan, A. and Sambreen, R. *The State of Pakistan's Children 1999*. SPARC: Islamabad, 2000.

Fayyazuddin, S., Jilani, A. and Jilani, Z. *The State of Pakistan's Children 1997*. SPARC (Society for the Protection of the Rights of the Child): Islamabad, 1998.

Ferguson, J. *The Anti-Politics Machine: Development, Depoliticisation and Bureaucratic Power in Lesotho*. Cambridge University Press: Cambridge, 1990.

Ferguson, J. 'Development and Bureaucratic Power in Lesotho'. In M. Rahnema and V. Bawtree (eds) *The Post-Development Reader*. Zed Books: London, New Jersey. University Press Ltd: Dhaka. Fernwood Publishing: Nova Scotia, 1997.

Field, N. 'The Child as Labourer and Consumer: The Disappearance of Childhood in Contemporary Japan' In Sharon Stephens (ed) *Children and the Politics of Culture*. Princeton University Press: New Jersey, 1995.

Fischer, M. D. 'Marriage and Power: Tradition and Transition in an Urban Punjabi Community'. In. Hastings Donnan (ed) *Economy and Culture in Pakistan*. Macmillan, 1991.

Foucault, M. 'The Order of Discourse'. In M. Shapiro (ed) 1984 *'Language and Politics'* Basil Blackwell: Oxford, 1971.

Foucault, M. *Discipline and Punish*. Penguin: Harmondsworth, 1977.

Foucault, M. *The History of Sexuality, Volume One: An Introduction*. Translated by Robert Hurley. Penguin: London, 1977.

Freeman, M.D.A. *The Rights and Wrongs of Children*. Francis Pinter Publishers: London, 1983.

Fuller, C. 'British India or Traditional India?: Land Caste and Power'. In Hamza Alavi and John Harriss (eds) *Sociology of Developing Societies*. Macmillan, 1989.

Fuller, C.J. (ed) *Caste Today*. Oxford University Press: Delhi, 1996.

Fyfe, A. *Child Labour*. Polity Press, 1989.

Gans, H. J. 'The Participant Observer as a Human Being: Observations on the personal aspects of fieldwork'. In Robert G. Burgess (ed) *Field Research: A Sourcebook and Field Manual*. George Allen & Unwin: London, 1982.

Gardezi H. *A Re-examination of the Socio-political History of Pakistan*. Edwin Meller Press, 1991.

Gardner, K. and Lewis, D. *Anthropology, Development and the Postmodern Challenge*. Pluto Press: London, 1996.

Gardner, K. 'Mixed Messages: Contested "Development" and the Plantation Rehabilitation Project'. In R.D. Grillo and R.L. Stirrat (eds) *Discourses of Development*. Berg: Oxford, 1997.

Geertz, C. *Islam Observed: Religious Development in Morocco and Indonesia*. Yale University Press: New Haven, 1968.

_____. *'The Interpretation of Cultures'*. Basic Books: New York, 1973.

George, S. and Sabelli, F. *Faith and credit: the World Bank's secular empire*. Penguin: London, 1994.

Gilsenan, M. *Lords of the Lebanese Marches: Violence and Narrative in an Arab Society*. I.B. Tauris: London, New York, 1996.

Glauser, B. 'Street Children: Deconstructing a Construct'. In Alison James and Alan Prout (eds) *Constructing and Reconstructing Childhood*. Falmer Press: London, Washington DC, 1997.

Goody, E. 'The Roles of Knowledge and Policy in Contributions of Research and Education to Development: Observations on Social Anthropological Research for the 21ˢᵗ Century'. *Cambridge Anthropology*, Vol. 23, 1: Cambridge, 2002.

Govt of Pakistan. *Pakistan Census*. Statistics Division, Govt of Pakistan: Islamabad, 1970.

Govt of Pakistan. *Pakistan Economic Review*. Dept of Economic Affairs, Govt of Pakistan: Islamabad, 1996.

Govt of Pakistan. *District Census Report of Sialkot Population*. 2000 Census Organisation, Statistics Division, Govt of Pakistan: Islamabad, 1998.

Gramsci, A. *Selections from the Prison Notebooks of Antonio Gramsci*. International Publishers: New York, 1971.

Grillo, R. D. 'Discourses of Development: The View from Anthropology'. In R.D. Grillo and R.L. Stirrat (eds) *Discourses of Development*. Berg: Oxford, 1997.

Grootaert, C. and Kanbur, R. *Child Labour: A Review*. Background Paper for World Development Report 1995. World Bank, Washington DC, 1995.

Gujit, I. and Shah, M. *The Myth of Community: Gender Issues in Participatory Development*. IT Publications: London, 1998.

Gupta, M. and Voll, K. (eds) *Child Labour in India*. Atma Ram & Sons: New Delhi, 1987.

Hailey, J. 'Beyond the Formulaic: Process and Practice in South Asian NGOs'. In Bill Cooke and Uma Kothari (eds) *Participation: The New Tyranny?* Zed Books: London, New York, 2001.

Hajer, M. *The Politics of Environmental Discourse: Ecological Modernization and Policy Process*. Clarendon: Oxford, 1995.

Hall, K. 'There's a Time to Act English and a Time to Act Indian: The Politics of Identity among British-Sikh Teenagers'. In Sharon Stephens (ed) *Children and the Politics of Culture*. Princeton University Press: New Jersey, 1995.

Hall, S. 'The West and the Rest: Discourse and Power'. In Stuart Hall and Bram Gieben (eds) *Formations of Modernity* Polity Press: Cambridge, 1992.

Hall, S. and Gieben, B. (eds) '*Formations of Modernity*' Polity Press: Cambridge, 1992.

Haq, Mahbub ul *Human Development in South Asia*. Oxford University Press: Karachi, 1997.

——————. *Human Development in South Asia: Education Report*. Oxford University Press: Karachi, 1998.

——————. *Human Development in South Asia: Governance Report*. Oxford University Press: Karachi, 1999.

Hart, K. 'Informal income opportunities and urban employment in Ghana'. *Journal of Modern African Studies* (reprinted in several publications), 1973.

Henderson, D. R. *The Case for Sweatshops*. Fortune, 28 October 1996.

Hildyard, N., Hegde, P., Wolvekamp, P. and Reddy, S. 'Pluralism, Participation and Power: Joint Forest Management in India'. In Bill Cooke and Uma Kothari (eds) *Participation: The New Tyranny?* Zed Books: London, New York, 2001.

Hobart, M. 'Introduction: The growth of ignorance'. In M. Hobart (ed) *An Anthropological Critique of Development: The growth of ignorance*. Routledge: London, 1993.

Holmstrom, M. *Industry and Inequality: The social anthropology of Indian labour*. Cambridge University Press: Cambridge, 1984.

Hussellbee, D. 'How close is too close? International NGOs as Development Partners with the Corporate Sector'. Paper presented at Conference of Business for Social Responsibility, Los Angeles, 1998.

ILO, *World Labour Report 1993*. International Labour Office: Geneva, 1993.

_____. *Child Labour: How The Challenge is Being Met*. International Labour Review, International Labour Office: Geneva, 1997.

ILO-IPEC in collaboration with Govt of Pakistan. *Child Labour in the Football Manufacturing Industry*, 1996.

_____. *Elimination of child labour in the soccer ball industry in Sialkot: Report on Internal Mid-term Review*. International Labour Office, Geneva, November 1998.

Jacoby, H. and Skoufias, E. *Risk, financial markets and human capital in a developing country*. (mimeo). World Bank Policy Research Department, Washington DC: The World Bank, 1994.

Jalal, A. *Democracy and Authoritarianism in South Asia*. Cambridge University Press: Cambridge, 1995.

James, A., Jenks C. and Prout A. *Theorising Childhood*. Polity Press: Cambridge, 1998.

James, A. and Prout, A. (eds) *Constructing and Reconstructing Childhood*. Falmer Press: United Kingdom, 1998.

James, A. and Prout, A. 'A New Paradigm for the Sociology of Childhood? Provenance, Promise and Problems'. In A. James and A. Prout (eds) *Constructing and Reconstructing Childhood*. Falmer Press: United Kingdom, 1998.

Jilani, A. *Child Labour: The Legal Aspects*. SPARC (Society for the Protection of the Rights of the Child): Islamabad, 1997.

Johnson, V., Hill, J. and Ivan-Smith, E. *Listening to Smaller Voices: Children in an Environment of Change*. Action Aid: London, 1995.

Jones, O.B. *Pakistan: Eye of the Storm*. Yale University Press: New Haven, London, 2002.

Joseph, J. D. *Our Purchases keep Children in Chains*. Knight Ridder Tribune: 28 May 1996.

Kabeer, N. 'Women's Labour in the Bangladesh Garment Industry: Choices and Constraints'. In Camillia Fawzi El-Solh and Judy Mabro (eds) *Muslim Women's Choices: Religious Belief and Social Reality*. Berg Publishers: Oxford, 1994.

Kapadia, K. 'Gender ideologies and the formation of rural industrial classes in South India today'. In Jonathan P. Parry, Jan Breman and Karin Kapadia (eds) *The Worlds of Indian Industrial Labour*. Sage Publications: New Delhi, 1999.

Kessinger, T. G. *Vilyatpur, 1848-1968; Social and Economic Change in a North Indian Village*. University of California: Berkeley, 1974.

Key, E. *The Century of the Child*. G.P. Putnam's Sons: New York, London, 1909.

Khan, A. H. *Orangi Pilot Project: Reminiscences and Reflections*. Oxford University Press: Karachi, 1996.

Khan, A. N. *Sialkot: An ancient city of Pakistan*. The Punjabi Adabi Academy: Lahore, 1964.

Khan, S.A. and Bilquees, F. *The Environment, Attitudes and Activities of Rural Women: A Case study of a village in Punjab*. Pakistan Development Review 15 (3) 237-71, 1976.

Knorringa, P. *Economics of Collaboration: Indian Shoemakers between Market and Hierarchy*. Sage Publications: New Delhi, 1996.

Knorringa, P. 'Artisan labour in the Agra footwear industry: Continued informality and changing threats'. In Jonathan P. Parry, Jan Breman and Karin Kapadia (eds) *The Worlds of Indian Industrial Labour*. Sage Publications: New Delhi, 1999.

Knuttson, K. E. *Children: Noble Causes or Worthy Citizens*. UNICEF, 1997.

Kothari, R. *Rethinking Development: In Search of Humane Alternatives*. Ajanta: Delhi, 1988.

Kothari, U. 'Power, Knowledge and Social Control in Participatory Development'. In Bill Cooke and Uma Kothari (eds) *Participation: The New Tyranny?* Zed Books: London, New York, 2001.

La Fontaine, J. S. *Sex and Age as Principles of Social Differentiation*. London Academic, 1978.

La Fontaine, J. S. 'Social Anthropology and Children'. In Martin Richards and Paul Light (eds) *Children of social worlds: Development in a social context*. Polity Press: Cambridge, 1986.

Lefebvre, A. *Kinship, Honour and Money in Rural Pakistan*. Curzon, 1999.

Lee-Wright, P. *Child Slaves*. Earthscan Publications: London, 1990.

Lindholm, C. 'Caste in India and the Problems of Deviant Systems: A Critique of Recent Theory'. *Contributions to Indian Sociology* 20: 61-96, 1986.

Lukes, S. *Power: A radical view*. Macmillan: Basingstoke, 1974.

Lyon, W. and Fischer, M. 'Household Structures and Household Income in Lahore'. In Hastings Donnan and Frits Selier (eds) *Family and Gender in Pakistan*. Hindustan Publishing Corporation: New Delhi, 1997.

Makdisi, G. 'Muslim Institutions of Learning in Eleventh-Century Baghdad'. *Bulletin of the School of Oriental and African Studies*, 24.1, 1-56, 1961.

_____. *The Rise of Colleges Institutions of Learning in Islam and the West*. Edinburgh University Press: Edinburgh, 1981.

_____. *The Rise of Humanism in classical Islam and the Christian West*. Edinburgh University Press: Edinburgh, 1990.

Mamdani, M. *The Myth of Population Control*. Monthly Review Press, 1972.

Manzo, K. 'Black Consciousness and the Quest for a Counter-Modernist Development'. In Jonathon Crush (ed) *Power of Development*. Routledge: London, New York, 1995.

Marglin, S. and Marglin, A. (eds) *Dominating Knowledge*. Oxford University Press, 1990.

Marglin, S. 'Losing Touch: The Cultural Conditions of Worker Accommodation and Resistance' . In S. Marglin and A. Marglin (eds) *Dominating Knowledge*. Oxford University Press, 1990.

Mause, de L. *The History of Childhood*. Souvenir Press: London, 1976.

Mead, M. *'Coming of Age in Samoa'*. Harmondsworth: Penguin, 1928.

Mendelievich, E. *Children at Work*. International Labour Office, 1979.

Metcalf, B.D. *"Traditionalist" Islamic Activism: Deoband, Tablighis, and Talibs*. Essay from Social Science Research Council, USA. Available: www.ssrc.org, 2002.

Mitchell, T. *Colonising Egypt*. Cambridge University Press: Cambridge, 1988.

Mitchell, T. 'The Object of Development: America's Egypt'. In Jonathon Crush (ed) *Power of Development*. Routledge: London, New York, 1995.

Modell, J. 'Changing Adaptations: American Families in the 19th and 20th Centuries'. In Allan J. Lichtman and John R. Challinor (eds) *Kin and Communities*. Smithsonian Institution Press: Washington, 1979.

Mohanty, C. 'Introduction: Cartographies of Struggle'. In C. Mohanty, A. Russo and L. Torres (eds) *Third World Women and the Politics of Feminism*. Bloomington: Indiana University Press, 1991.

Mohanty, C. 'Under Western Eyes: Feminist Scholarship and Colonial Discourses'. *Third World Women and the Politics of Feminism*, 1991.

Montgomery, H. *Anthropology Today*. Volume 16, No.3 June, 2000.

Morrow, V. *Child Labour Force Participation in Developed Countries: Historical Lessons and Current Trends*. Unpublished Working Paper.

_____. *A sociological study of the economic roles of children, with particular reference to Birmingham and Cambridgeshire* Ph.D. Thesis, Faculty of Social and Political Sciences: University of Cambridge, 1992.

Morrow, V. 'Responsible Children? Aspects of Children's Work and Employment Outside School in Contemporary U.K.'. In B. Mayall (ed) *Children's Childhoods: Observed and Experienced*. Falmer Press: London, 1994.

Moser, C. O. *Gender Planning and Development*. Routledge, 1993.

Mosse, D. 'Authority, Gender and Knowledge'. *Development and Change:* Volume 25, Number 3. Blackwell Publishers, July 1994.

Nader, L. 'The Vertical Slice: Hierarchies and Children'. In Ronald Cohen and Gerald M. Britan (eds) *Hierarchy and Society: Anthropological Perspectives on Bureaucracy*. Institute for the Study of Human Issues: Philadelphia, 1980.

Nadvi, K. *Employment creation in Urban Informal Micro Enterprises in the Manufacturing Sector in Pakistan*. ILO-ARTEP: New Delhi, 1990.

_____. 'Shifting Ties: Social Networks in the Surgical Instrument Cluster of Sialkot, Pakistan'. In *Development and Change*. Volume 30. Blackwell Publishers Ltd: Oxford, 1999.

Nandy, A. *The Intimate Enemy*. Oxford University Press: Bombay, 1987.

Nandy, A. 'Colonization of the Mind' In Majid Rahnema with Victoria Bawtree (eds) *'The Post-Development Reader'*. Zed Books, University Press Ltd: London, New Jersey, 1997.

Nardinelli, C. *Child Labour and the Industrial Revolution*. Indiana University Press: Bloomington and Indianapolis, 1990.

Nasr, S.V.R. *The Vanguard of the Islamic Revolution: The Jama'at Islami of Pakistan*. I.B. Tauris: London, 1994.

_____. *Islamic Leviathan: Islam and the Making of State Power*. Oxford University Press: New York, 2001.

Nelson, N. and Wright, S. *Power and Participatory Development*. Intermediate Technology Publications: London, 1997.

Newman-Black, M. *How Can the Convention be Implemented in Developing Countries*. In Report from Radda Barnen, UNICEF Seminar on the UN Draft Convention on the Rights of the Child, Stockholm, 1989.

Nicholson, T. 'Institution building: Examining the fit between bureaucracies and indigenous systems'. In Susan Wright (ed) *Anthropology of Organizations*. Routledge: London, 1994.

Nieuwenhuys, O. *Children's Lifeworlds: Gender, welfare and labour in the developing world*. Routledge, 1994.

_____. 'The Paradox of Child Labour and Anthropology'. *Annual Review of Anthropology*. Volume 25, 1996.

Noman, O. 'The Impact of Migration on Pakistan's Economy and Society'. In H. Donnan and P. Werbner (eds) *Economy & Culture in Pakistan: Migrants and Cities in a Muslim Society*. Macmillan: London, 1991.

Ong, A. *Spirits of resistance and capitalist discipline: Factory women in Malaysia*. State University of New York Press: Albany, 1987.

_____. 'Gender and Labour Politics of postmodernism'. *Annual Review of Anthropology*. Volume 20, 1991.

Parpart, J. 'Post Modernism, Gender and Development'. In Jonathon Crush (ed) *Power of Development*. Routledge: London, New York, 1995.

Parry, J. 'Introduction'. In Jonathan P. Parry, Jan Breman and Karin Kapadia (eds) *The Worlds of Indian Industrial Labour*. Sage Publications: New Delhi, 1999.

Parry, J. P., Breman, J. and Kapadia, K. (eds) *The Worlds of Indian Industrial Labour*. Sage Publications: New Delhi, 1999.

Peters, P. 'Who's local here? The politics of participation in development'. *Cultural Survival Quarterly* 20:3, 1996.

Pollock, L.A. *Forgotten Children: Parent-Child Relations from 1500 to 1900*. Cambridge University Press: Cambridge, 1983.

Pottier, J. 'Introduction: development in practice: assessing social science perspectives'. In Johan Pottier (ed) *Practicing Development: The Social Sciences Perspective*. Routledge: New York, 1993.

_____. 'The role of ethnography in project appraisal'. *Practicing Development: The Social Sciences Perspective*, 1993.

Quigley, D. *The Interpretation of Caste*. Clarendon Press, 1993.

Rahnema, M. and Bawtree, V. (eds) *The Post-Development Reader*. Zed Books: London, New Jersey; University Press Ltd: Dhaka; Fernwood Publishing: Nova Scotia, 1997.

Radda Barnen report, UNICEF Seminar on the UN Draft Convention on the Rights of the Child. Stockholm, October 1988.

Ramonet, I. 'The One and Only Way of Thinking'. In Majid Rahnema and Victoria Bawtree (eds) *The Post-Development Reader*. Zed Books: London, New Jersey; University Press Ltd: Dhaka; Fernwood Publishing: Nova Scotia, 1997.

Rauf, A. Rural Women and the Family: A Study of a Punjabi Village in Pakistan. *Journal of Comparative Family Studies* XVIII (3): 403-15, 1987.

Razavi, S. 'Fieldwork in a familiar setting: the role of politics at the national, community and household levels'. In Stephen Devereux and John Hoddinott (eds) *Fieldwork in Developing Countries*. Harvester Wheatsheaf: UK, 1992.

Rew, A. 'The Donor's Discourse: Official Social Development Knowledge in the 1980s' in Development Discourse in Sri Lanka'. In R.D. Grillo and R.L. Stirrat (eds) *Discourses of Development*. Berg: Oxford, 1997.

Reynolds, P. *Dance Civet Cat: Child Labour in the Zambezi Valley*. Zed Books: London, 1991.

Ridd, R. 'Separate but more than equal'. In Camillia Fawzi El-Solh and Judy Mabro (eds) *Constraints in Muslim Women's Choices*. Berg Publishers, 1994.

Rodgers, G. and Standing, G. (eds) *Child Work, Poverty and Underdevelopment*. International Labour Office: Geneva, 1981.

Roy, Olivier, *The Failure of Political Islam*, Harvard University Press Cambridge, Mass., 1994.

Sahlins, M. *Stone Age Economics*. Routledge, 1988.

Sahoo, U. C. *Child Labour in Agrarian Society*. Rawat: Delhi, 1995.

Said, E. *Orientalism*. Pantheon: New York, 1978.

_____. *The World, the Text, the Critic*. Harvard University Press: Cambridge, Mass., 1983.

_____. *Culture and Imperialism*. Vintage Books: New York, 1994.

Saito, O. 'Children's work and the family economy in Japan, 1872-192'. In H. Cunningham and P. Viazzo (eds) *Child Labour in Historical Perspective*. UNICEF, 1996.

Save the Children *Child Labour Project Sialkot: Social Monitoring Reports, 1998– 2000*.

_____. *Stitching Footballs : Voices of Children*, 1997.

Schanberg, S. H. *Six Cents an Hour*. Life Magazine: The Time Inc. Magazine Company: USA, 1996.

Scheper-Hughes, N. *Child Survival*. D. Reidel Publishing Company, 1987.

Scheper-Hughes, N. (ed) *Small Wars: The cultural politics of childhood*. University of California Press: Berkley, 1998.

Schildkrout, E. 'Women's Work and Children's Work. In Sandra Wallman (ed) *The social anthropology of work*. Academic Press, 1979.

Schildkrout, E. 'Children's work reconsidered'. *International Social Science Journal*, Vol. 32, 3:479:89, 1980.

Schildkrout, E. 'The employment of Children in Kano'. In Gerry Rodgers and Guy Standing (eds) *Child Work, Poverty and Underdevelopment*. International Labour Office: Geneva, 1981.

Scoones, I. and Thompson J. *'Challenging the Populist Perspective: Rural Peoples' Knowledge, Agricultural Research and Extension Practice'*. Institute of Development Studies Discussion Paper 332. Institute of Development Studies: Sussex, 1993.

Scott, J. C. *The Infrapolitics of Subordinate Groups*. Zed Books: London, New Jersey. University Press Ltd: Dhaka. Fernwood Publishing: Nova Scotia, 1997.

Scott, J. *Domination and the Arts of Resistance: Hidden Transcripts*. Yale University Press, 1990.

Seidel, G. 'Political Discourse Analysis'. In Teun Van Dijk (ed) *Handbook of Discourse Analysis: Volume Four*. Academic: London, 1985.

Sen, S. 'At the Margins: Women workers in the Bengal Jute Industry'. In Jonathan P. Parry, Jan Breman and Karin Kapadia (eds) *The Worlds of Indian Industrial Labour*. Sage Publications: New Delhi, 1999.

Seymour-Smith, C. *Macmillan Dictionary of Anthropology*. Macmillan Press, 1986.

Shahid-ul-Alam. *Thank You Mr. Harkin*. The New Internationalist (July 1997): New Internationalist Publications Ltd, 1997.

Shaw, A. *A Pakistani Community in Britain*. Basil Blackwell: Oxford, 1988.

Shaw, A. 'Women, the Household and Family Ties: Pakistani Migrants in Britain'. In Hastings Donnan and Frits Selier (eds) *Family and Gender in Pakistan*. Hindustan Publishing Corporation: New Delhi, 1997.

Sherani, S.R. 'Ulema and Pir in the Politics of Pakistan'. In H. Donnan and P. Werbner (eds) *Economy & Culture in Pakistan: Migrants and Cities in a Muslim Society*. Macmillan: London, 1991.

Siddiqi, Faraz and Patrinos, Harry Anthony *Child Labour: Issues, Causes and Interventions*. Human Resources Development and Operations Policy Working Papers, World Bank, Washington, 1995.

Silvers, J., 'Child Labour in Pakistan'. *The Atlantic Monthly*, February 1996.

Simmons, P. 'Women in Development: A Threat to Liberation'. In Majid Rahnema and Victoria Bawtree (eds) *The Post-Development Reader.* Zed Books: London, New Jersey; University Press Ltd: Dhaka; Fernwood Publishing: Nova Scotia, 1997.

Solberg, A. 'Negotiating Childhood: Changing Conceptions of Age from Norwegian Children'. In Alison James and Alan Prout (eds) *Constructing and Reconstructing Childhood*. Falmer Press, 1997.

Spradley, J. P. *The Ethnographic Interview*. Holt, Rinehart and Winston: USA, 1979.

Stephens, S. (ed) *Children and the Politics of Culture*. Princeton University Press: New Jersey, 1995.

Szanton, BC. et al. *Urban Child in Distress: Global Predicaments and Innovative Strategies*. Florence, Gordon and Breach Scientific Publications: New York; in association with UNICEF International Child Development Centre, 1994.

Talbot, I. *Pakistan: A Modern History*. Hurst & Company: London, 1998.

The News International. Special Report on Child Labour. The Jang Group of Newspapers: Rawalpindi, Pakistan, July 1999.

Thompson, E.P. *The Making of the English Working Class*. Pelican Books, 1968.

Toren, C. 'Making History: The Significance of Childhood Cognition for a Comparative Anthropology of Mind'. *Man*. 28,3. Royal Anthropological Institute, 1993.

Tripathy, S. K. *Child Labour in India*. Discovery Publishing House: New Delhi, 1989.

Turton, D. 'Anthropology and development'. In P.F. Leeson and M.M. Minogue (eds) *Perspectives on Development: Cross-disciplinary themes in development*. Manchester University Press: Manchester, New York, 1988.

UNICEF, *The State of the World's Children*. Oxford University Press: Oxford, 1997.

UNICEF, *The State of the World's Children*. Oxford University Press: Oxford, 2000.

Van Ufford, P. Q. 'Knowledge and Ignorance in the practice of development policy'. In M. Hobart (ed) *An Anthropological Critique of Development*. Routledge: London, 1993.

Wadel, C. 'The Hidden Work of Everyday Life'. In Sandra Wallman (ed) *The Social Anthropology of Work*. Academic Press, 1979.

Wallerstein, I. *Historical Capitalism*. Cambridge University Press: Cambridge, 1983.

Wallman, S. *The Social Anthropology of Work*. Academic Press, 1979.

Washbrook, D. 'South Asia, the World System and World Capitalism', *Journal of Asian Studies*. Vol. 49, 3. Association for Asian Studies, 1990.

Watts, M. 'A new deal in emotions: Theory and practice and the crisis of development'. In Jonathon Crush (ed) *Power of Development: Imagining Development*. Routledge: London, New York, 1995.

Weber, M. *The Theory of Social and Economic Organisation*. The Free Press: New York, 1947.

Weber, M. *Economy and Society*. Bedminster Press: New York, 1968.

Weiner, M. *The Child and the State in India: Child Labour and Education Policy in Comparative Perspective*. Princeton University Press: New Jersey, 1991.

Weiner, M. and Noman, O. *The Child and the State in India and Pakistan*. Oxford University Press, 1997.

Weiss, A. M. *Culture, Class and Development in Pakistan*. Westview Press, 1991.

Werbner, P. 'The Ranking of Brotherhoods: The Dialectics of Muslim Caste Among Overseas Pakistanis'. *Contributions to Indian Sociology*. Vol. 23, 2. Sage Publications: New Delhi, 1989.

Werbner, R. 'The Reach of the Postcolonial State: Development, Empowerment/ Disempowerment and Technocracy'. In Angela Cheater (ed) *The Anthropology of Power*. Routledge: London, 1999.

White, B. 'Globalisation and the child labour problem'. In *Journal of International Development*. Vol. 8, 6: 139-161, 1996.

White, B. and Tjandraningsih, I. *Rural Children in Industrialisation Process: Child and Youth Labour in Traditional and Modern Industries in West Java, Indonesia*. Institute of Social Studies: The Hague, 1992.

Wolf, E. R. *Peasants*. Prentice Hall Inc.: New Jersey, 1966.

Woost, M.D. 'Alternative Vocabularies of Development: 'Community' and 'Participation' in Development Discourse in Sri Lanka'. In R.D. Grillo and R.L. Stirrat (eds) *Discourses of Development*. Berg: Oxford, 1997.

World Bank- Multi-Donor Support Unit *Determinants of Primary Students' Achievement: National Survey Results*. Islamabad, 1995.

World Bank *World Development Report: Attacking Poverty*. Oxford University Press, 2000/01.

Wright, S. and Shore, C. (eds) *The Anthropology of Policy*. Routledge: London, 1997.

Wright, S. (ed) *Anthropology of Organizations*. Routledge: London, 1994.

Zaidi, A. S. *Issues in Pakistan's Economy*. Oxford University Press, 1999.

Zaman, M.Q. 'Religious Education and the Rhetoric of Reform: The Madrasa in British India and Pakistan'. *Comparative Studies in Society and History*. 41,2. Cambridge University Press: Cambridge, 1999.

Zelizer V.A. *Pricing the Priceless Child*. Basic Books: USA, 1985.

INDEX